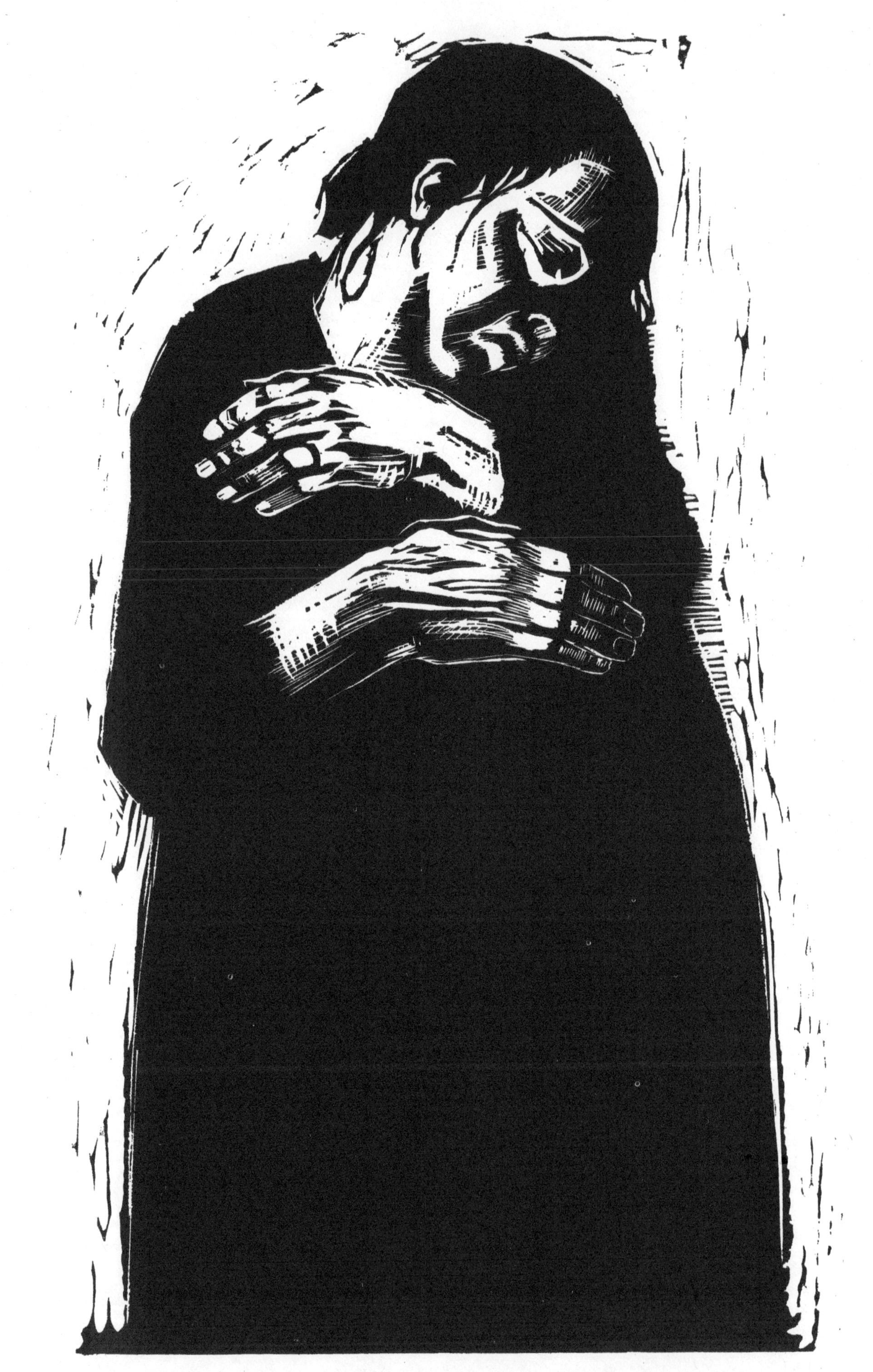

GERMAN EXPRESSIONIST WOODCUTS

Edited by

Shane Weller

DOVER PUBLICATIONS, INC.
New York

Copyright

Bibliographical Note

German Expressionist Woodcuts is a new work, first published by Dover Publications, Inc., in 1994.

Library of Congress Cataloging-in-Publication Data

German expressionist woodcuts / edited by Shane Weller.
p. cm.
ISBN-13: 978-0-486-28069-1
ISBN-10: 0-486-28069-1
1. Wood-engraving, German. 2. Wood-engraving—20th century—Germany. 3. Expressionism (Art)—Germany. I. Weller, Shane.
NE1150.35.E9G46 1994
769.943'09'041—dc20 94-22083
CIP

Printed in Canada
28069112 2025
www.doverpublications.com

CONTENTS

INTRODUCTION

THE USE OF the term Expressionism to describe the artistic movement that flourished in Germany in the early years of the twentieth century seems to date from around 1911, although the movement was active earlier: Die Brücke (the bridge), an association of artists espousing the Expressionist ideal, was established in 1905 and held annual exhibitions until 1913.

Expressionism was in part a reaction against Impressionism's emphasis on atmospherics and surface appearances, and against academic painting's rigid technique, stressing instead the emotional state of the artist and subject (both in portraiture and landscape, the latter depicted through the technique of pathetic fallacy). To this the viewer was to add his own emotions, creating an experience rich in drama that conveyed the inner reality of the subject matter.

The Expressionists found their inspiration in ancient and modern sources: the work of such late Gothic artists as Dürer, Baldung, Cranach, Altdorfer and Grünewald and the work of van Gogh, Gauguin and the Pont-Aven School, Cézanne and Ensor and the appreciation of African and Oceanic art.

The movement was marked by a bewildering profusion of associations and publications. Along with Die Brücke there was Der Blaue Reiter (the blue rider), formed 1911, a close association of artists with little in the way of a specific program other than the desire to show together and a tendency toward abstraction. Other groups included the Berlin and Munich Secessions, the Red Group, the November Group and the New Artists' Association. Among the publications were *Der Sturm* (the storm), 1910–32, and *Die Aktion*. Many of these groups and publications had socialist or communist goals.

While the Expressionists produced canvases and sculptures of note, they are perhaps most famous for their graphics, especially their woodcuts. Germany had a brilliant heritage in the medium, which involves cutting a wooden plank on a plane parallel to the grain (as opposed to wood engraving, in which the design is cut across the grain). Modern woodcuts by Gauguin and Munch (who had turned to the medium in the 1890s) served as examples to the Expressionists of the raw, almost brutal effect that can be obtained from gouging the wood, providing a means of expression that suited their purposes perfectly.

A change occurred in Expressionism with World War I. The horror of the war left an indelible mark, and the chaotic years of the Weimar Republic (1919–33) introduced a sharply satirical tone in the work of many of the artists. New movements such as Neue Sachlichkeit (new objectivity) and Dada arose, attracting many of the same artists who had participated in Expressionism. The rise to power of the Nazis, with their repressive artistic programs, put an end to the Expressionists' period of greatest productivity, although many continued their work until well after World War II.

THE ARTISTS

(Unless otherwise noted, the artists are German.)

BARLACH, ERNST (1870–1938; pages 1 & 2). Barlach studied at the academies in Hamburg and Dresden and at the Académie Julian, Paris. His work, especially his wood sculpture and engravings, is strongly influenced by the late German Gothic. Barlach also drew for the famed periodical *Simplicissimus*. At the time of his death, he had fallen into disfavor with the Nazis, who removed his work from public view.

BECKMANN, MAX (1884–1950; pages 3–5). A member of the Berlin Secession, Beckmann was influenced by Lovis Corinth and Edvard Munch. His experiences in the medical corps during World War I contributed a raw power to his work. He fled the Nazis, settling in New York.

CAMPENDONK, HEINRICH (1889–1957; pages 6 & 7). In a style that is a fusion of African/Oceanic art, post-Cubism and Expressionism, Campendonk created a unique approach to rustic scenes. He taught at the School of Fine Arts in Düsseldorf, but fled Germany for Holland, where he continued to teach. In his later years he designed fabrics, stained glass and theatrical sets.

FEININGER, LYONEL (American, 1871–1956; pages 8–14). Having left the United States in 1887 to study music in Europe, Feininger redirected his studies to fine art. He became a popular cartoonist, but returned to painting, developing a prismatic style in part influenced by Robert Delaunay. A figure central to the Bauhaus and Der Blaue Reiter, he returned to the United States after the Nazis came to power.

FELIXMÜLLER, CONRAD [Felix Müller prior to 1918] (1897–1977; pages 15–21). Early in his career he moved in Expressionist circles, illustrating Schoenberg's *Pierrot Lunaire* and contributing to the periodicals *Der Sturm* and *Die Aktion*. Like Beckmann, his work was affected by his experiences in the medical corps during World War I.

GOLDBLUM, ERICH (page 22). Contributor to *Die Aktion*.

HECKEL, ERICH (1883–1970; pages 23–35). Along with Kirchner and Schmidt-Rottluff a founder of Die Brücke. He produced his first woodcuts while a student at vocational high school. Heckel's work was denounced as degenerate by the Nazis and his studio was destroyed in 1944, with the loss of many of his works.

HEINRICH-SALZE, KARL-LUIS [Katharina Heise] (1891–1964; page 36). A sculptor, graphic artist and painter, she worked in Paris and Berlin.

HIRSCH, KARL JAKOB (1892–1952; pages 37 & 38). Having studied art history and painting in Munich, Berlin and Paris, Hirsch engaged in painting, writing, graphics and stage design. He left Germany, first for Switzerland in 1933, then for the United States in 1936, but returned to Munich after the war.

HULEWICZ, JERZY (Polish, 1886–1941; pages 39–41). After study in Paris and Cracow, he founded the avant-garde periodical *Zdrój* (the spring) and the artists' group Bunt (revolt). A contributor to *Die Aktion*, he conducted a private art school in Warsaw.

JANSEN, FRANZ M. (1885– ; page 42). His earlier work was inspired by van Gogh. In 1912 he began several series of etchings and woodcuts, some satirical in tone. He showed at the Berlin Secession in 1911 and 1920.

KIRCHNER, ERNST LUDWIG (1880–1938; pages 43–60). A central figure in German Expressionism, Kirchner was one of the founders of Die Brücke. His style reflects his study of van Gogh, Munch, German Gothic and African/Oceanic art. Discharged from the army after a mental and physical breakdown, Kirchner stayed in various sanatoriums, becoming dependent on drugs and alcohol. Depressed by Nazi attacks on his work, he committed suicide.

KLEIN, CÉSAR (1876–1954; page 61). One of the founders of the Berlin Secession and the November

Group, Klein had studied in Düsseldorf and Berlin. He was noted for his paintings, graphics and stage designs.

KOLLWITZ, KÄTHE (1867–1945; pages 62–71). As the wife of a doctor practicing in a working-class area in Berlin, Kollwitz developed a profound sympathy for the oppressed poor that she expressed in prints and sculpture. The impact of the death of her son Peter during World War I can be seen in her depictions of mothers, children and the figure of Death. Kollwitz was the first woman elected to the Prussian Academy of Arts, a post of which she was deprived by the Nazis. In 1943 much of her work was destroyed when her studio was bombed.

MARC, FRANZ (1880–1916; pages 72–76). Originally painting as an academic, he altered his style after exposure to van Gogh, the Impressionists, Jugendstil and Jean Boé Niestlé, a Swiss animalier who inspired Marc's lifelong fascination with animals. Marc evolved a vocabulary of symbolic shapes and colors that reflected his belief in an underlying, unifying spirit in nature. He was killed at Verdun.

MARCKS, GERHARD (1889–1981; pages 77–80). Known primarily as a sculptor, Marcks taught at the Bauhaus between 1919 and 1925.

MATHÉY, GEORG ALEXANDER (1884–1968; pages 81 & 82). A painter and graphic artist, Mathéy was noted for his landscapes. He edited the art review *Wieland* and had a distinguished teaching career.

MUNCH, EDVARD (Norwegian, 1863–1944; pages 83–87). One of the great modern masters, Munch was influenced by Art Nouveau, Gauguin and Toulouse-Lautrec. A brief, controversial exhibition of his work in Berlin in 1892 made him known to the German public. Munch lived in Berlin and Paris. In 1894 he began a prolific production of graphics that influenced the artists who were to become Expressionists.

NOLDE [HANSEN], EMIL (1867–1956; pages 88–91). Of peasant stock, Nolde early revealed a strong affinity for the woodcut, in which he worked with great power. He was associated with Die Brücke for a year and a half, but withdrew, preferring to work alone. His graphics, oils and watercolors feature religious themes, landscapes and flower studies.

PECHSTEIN, MAX (1881–1955; pages 92–99). A member of Die Brücke and the New Secession, Pechstein shows the influence of the Fauves and Matisse. His interest in African/Oceanic art led him to travel to the South Seas in 1913.

ROHLFS, CHRISTIAN (1849–1938; page 100). One of the older Expressionists, Rohlfs had a career that reflected the major movements of his lifetime from academic painting to Impressionism, Divisionism, Expressionism, Cubism and Abstractionism.

RUDOLPH, WILHELM (1889– ; page 101). Influenced by Impressionism, he painted a wide variety of subjects, from landscapes and animal studies to portraits. Rudolph found in Expressionism the style that provided the emotional approach he wanted for his woodblocks.

SCHMIDT-ROTTLUFF, KARL (1884–1976; pages 102–127). As an architecture student in Dresden, he made the acquaintance of Heckel, Kirchner and Fritz Bleyl, with whom he founded Die Brücke. He also showed with Der Blaue Reiter and contributed to *Die Aktion*. One of the most prolific of the Expressionists, Schmidt-Rottluff made over 300 woodcuts, many revealing his interest in Cubism and African/Oceanic art. Fifty-one of his works were shown by the Nazis in the infamous show of "Degenerate Art."

SEGAL, ARTHUR (Romanian, 1875–1944; page 128). Initially an Expressionist, Segal spent World War I in Zurich, where he associated with the Dadaists.

SŁODKI, MARCEL (Polish, 1892–1943; page 129). Having studied in Munich and traveled to Italy, Słodki spent World War I in Zurich where, like Segal, he worked with the Dadaists. He died at Auschwitz.

STEINHARDT, JAKOB (Polish, 1887–1968; page 130). A pupil of Lovis Corinth, he illustrated scenes from the Bible and Jewish history, becoming a leading artist in Israel.

TAPPERT, GEORG (1880–1957; pages 131–136). One of the founders of the art school at the Worpswede colony, Tappert was a regular contributor to *Der Sturm* and *Die Aktion*. He exhibited with Der Blaue Reiter and was a cofounder of the New Secession and the November Group.

WETZEL, INES (1882– ; page 137). She studied in Munich and participated in the November Group and the Red Group.

ZITZEWITZ, AUGUSTE VON (1880–1960; pages 138–142). Having studied in Berlin and Paris, she became a close associate of Franz Pfemfert, publisher of *Die Aktion*, to which she contributed.

GERMAN EXPRESSIONIST WOODCUTS

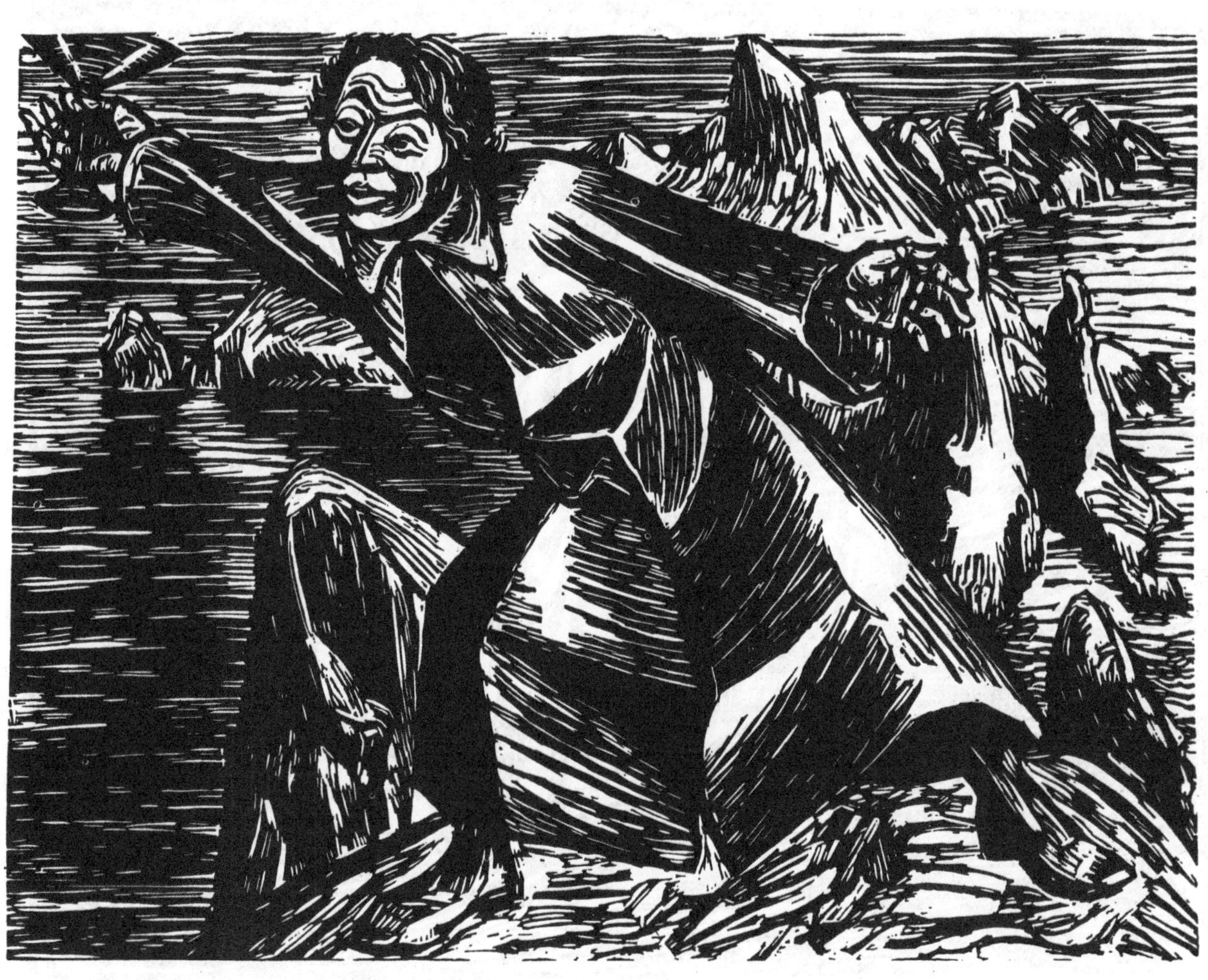

Ernst Barlach. *To Joy*, 1927.

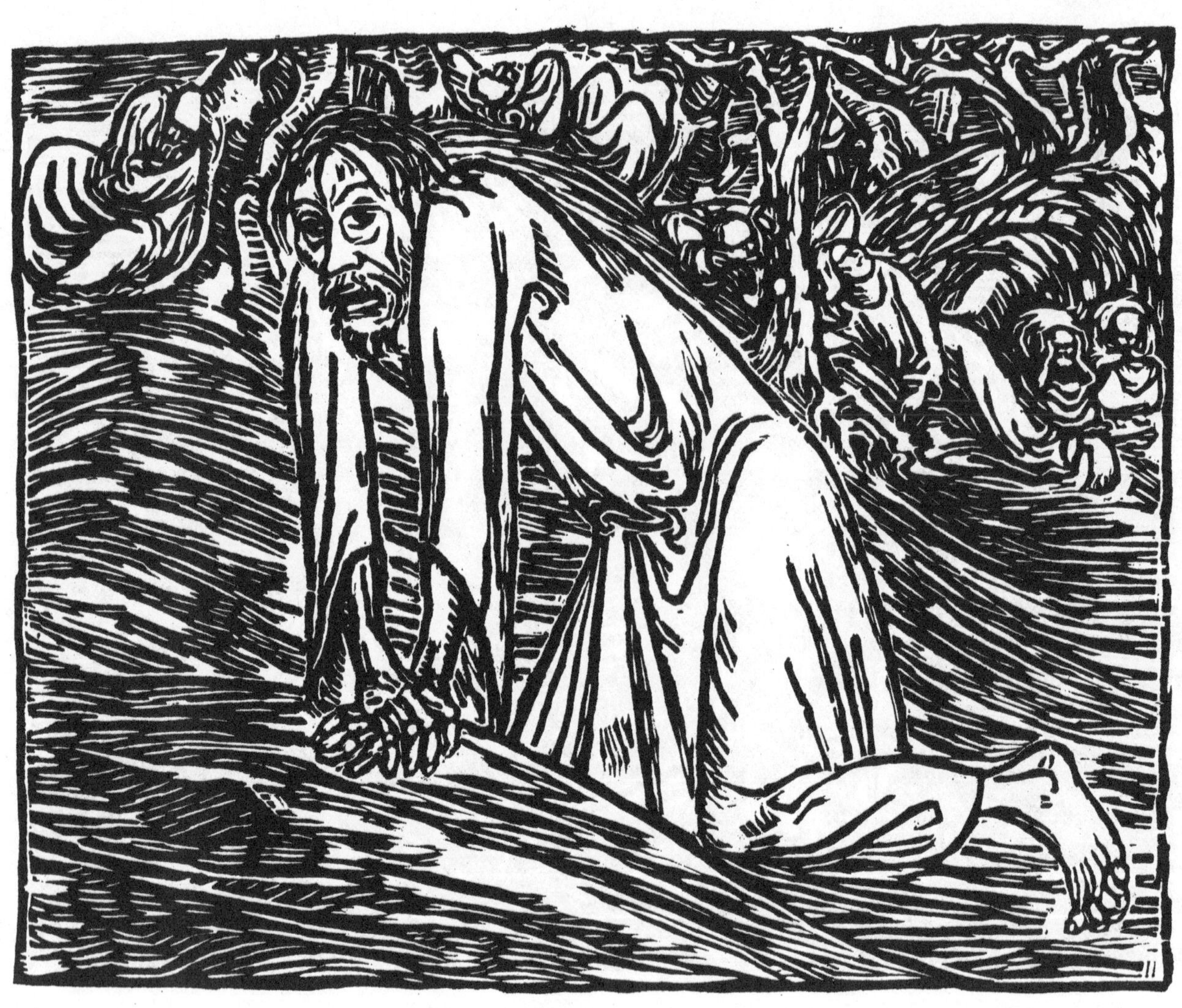

 Ernst Barlach. *Christ on the Mount of Olives*, 1920.

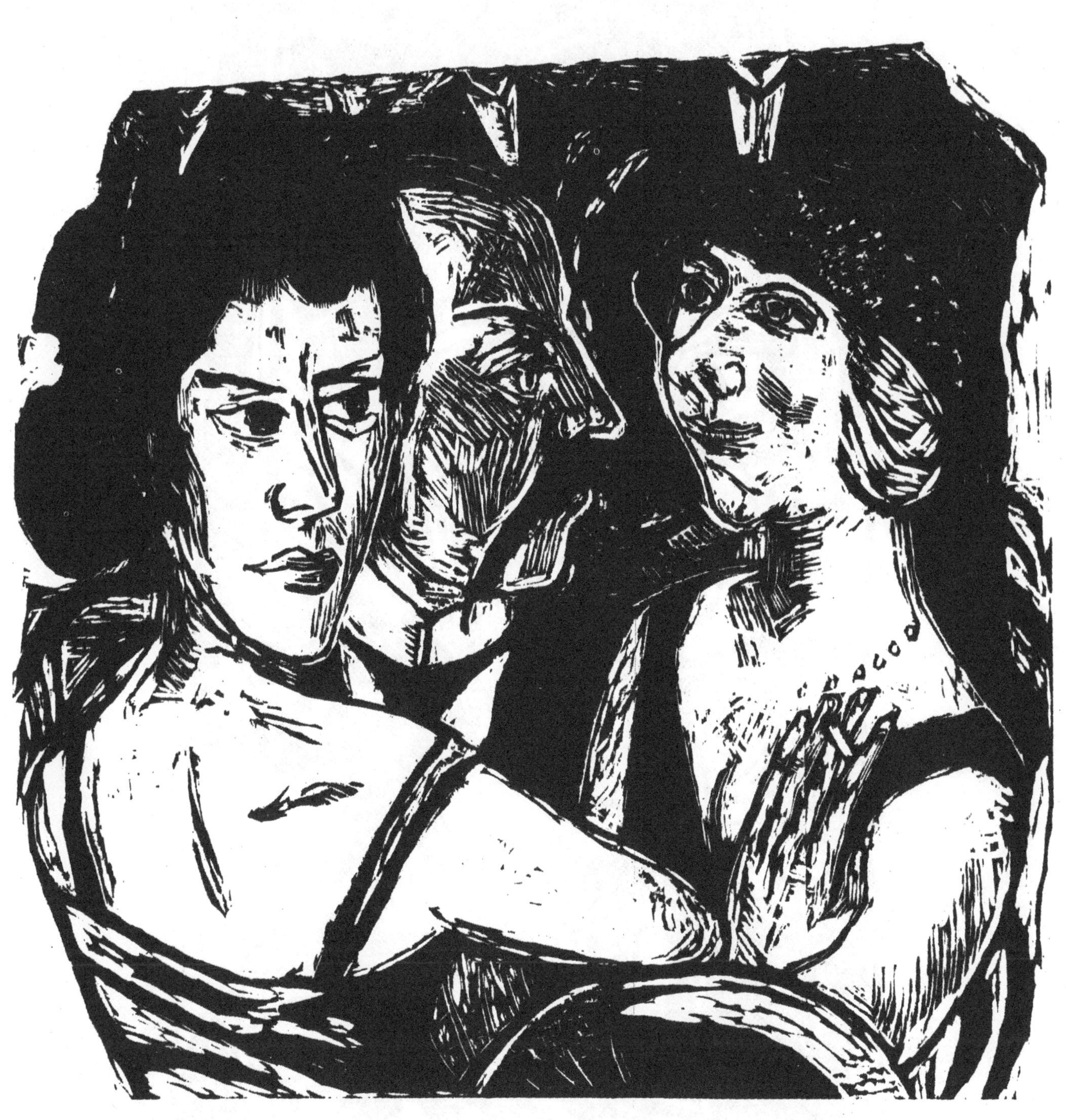

Max Beckmann. *Group Portrait, Eden Bar*, 1923.

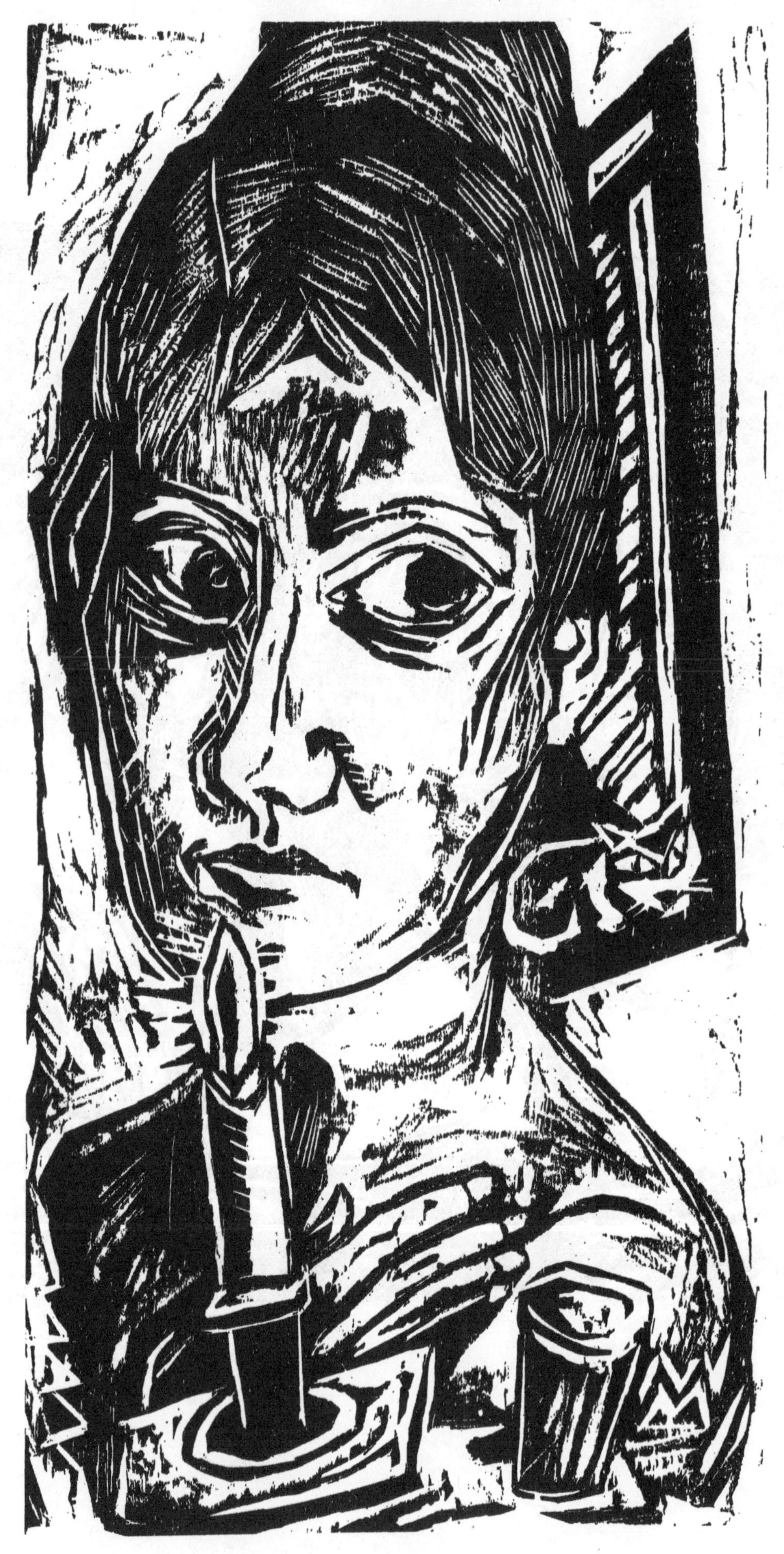

Max Beckmann. *Woman with Candle*, 1920.

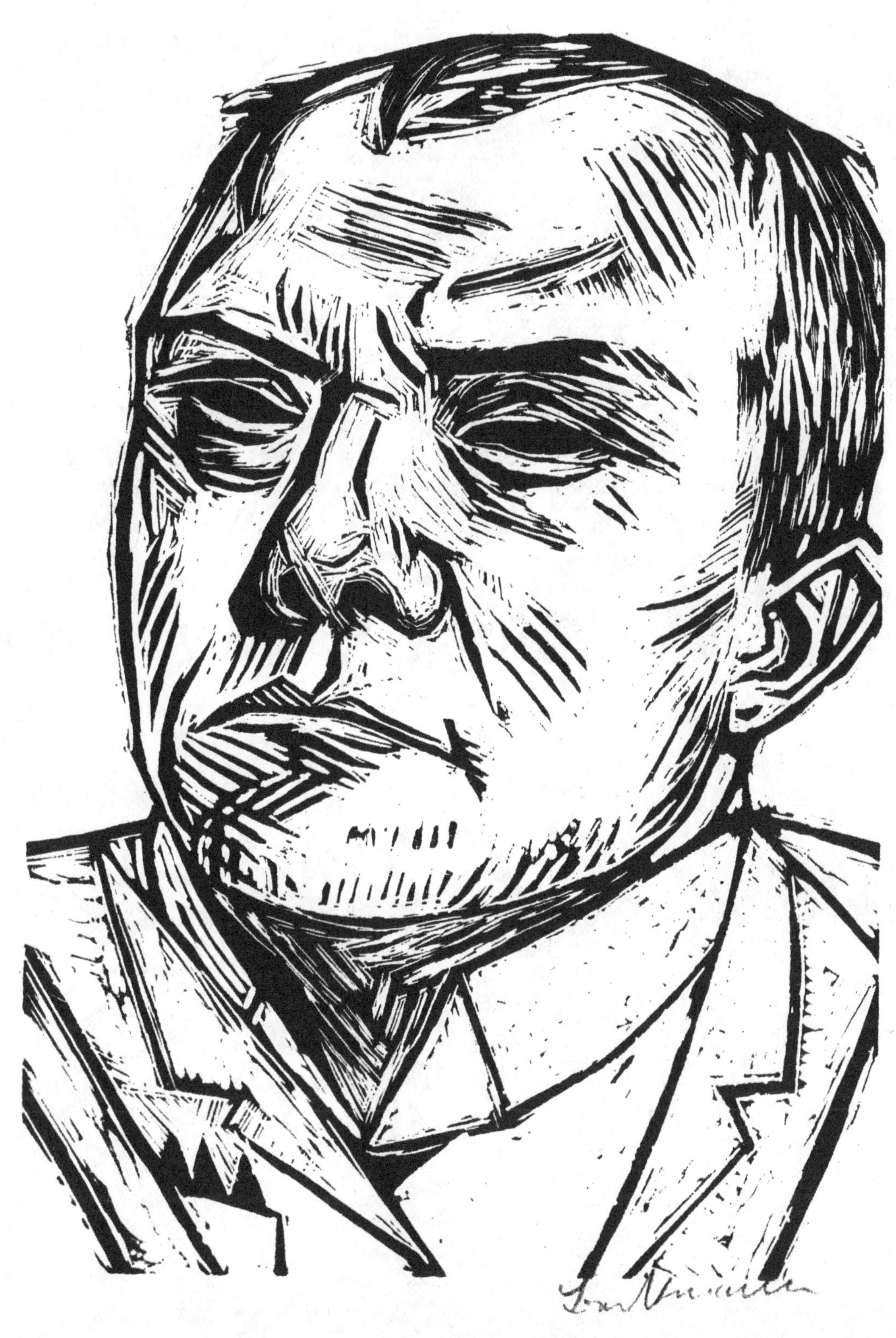

Max Beckmann. *Self-portrait*, 1922.

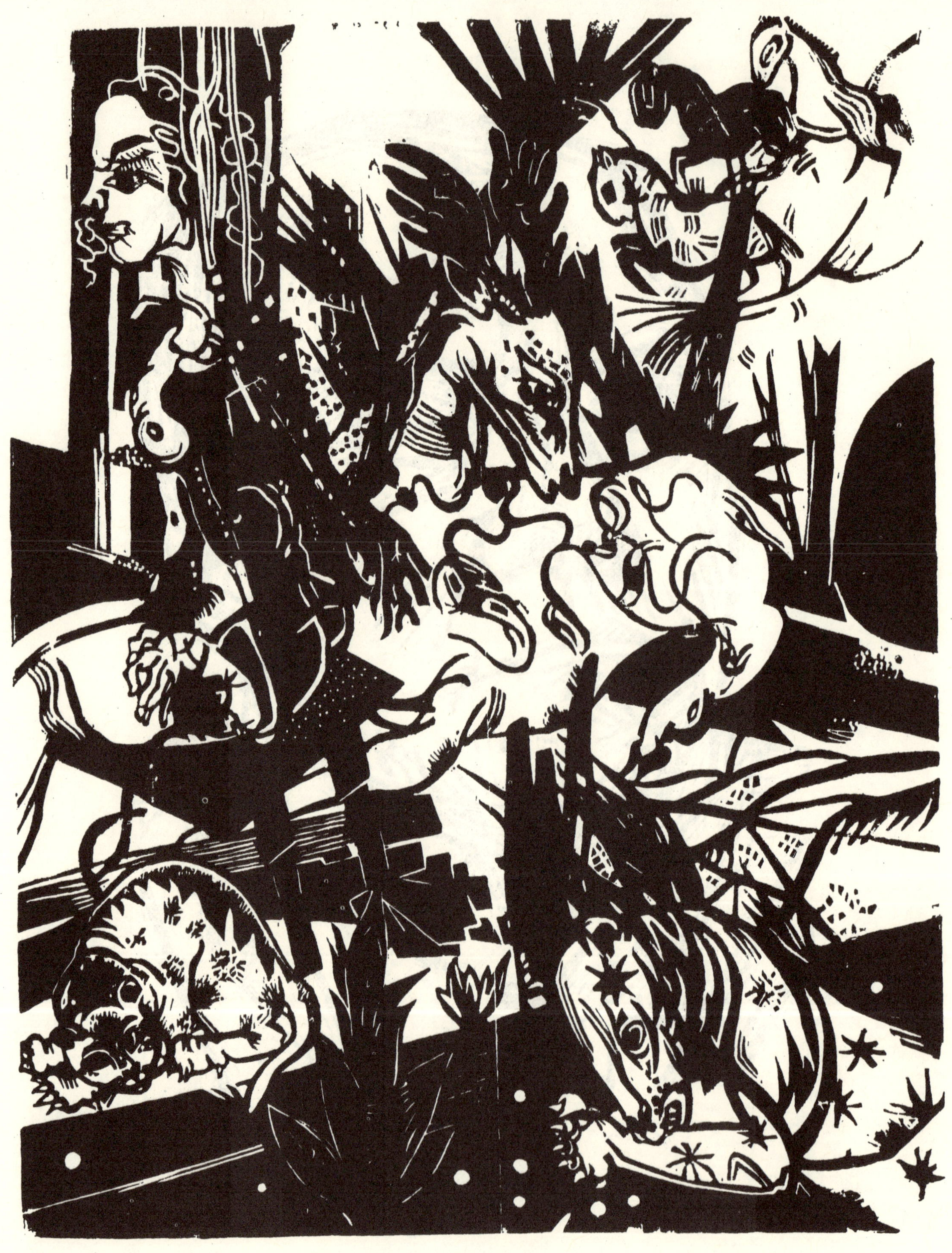

Heinrich Campendonk. *Seated Girl with Stag*, 1916.

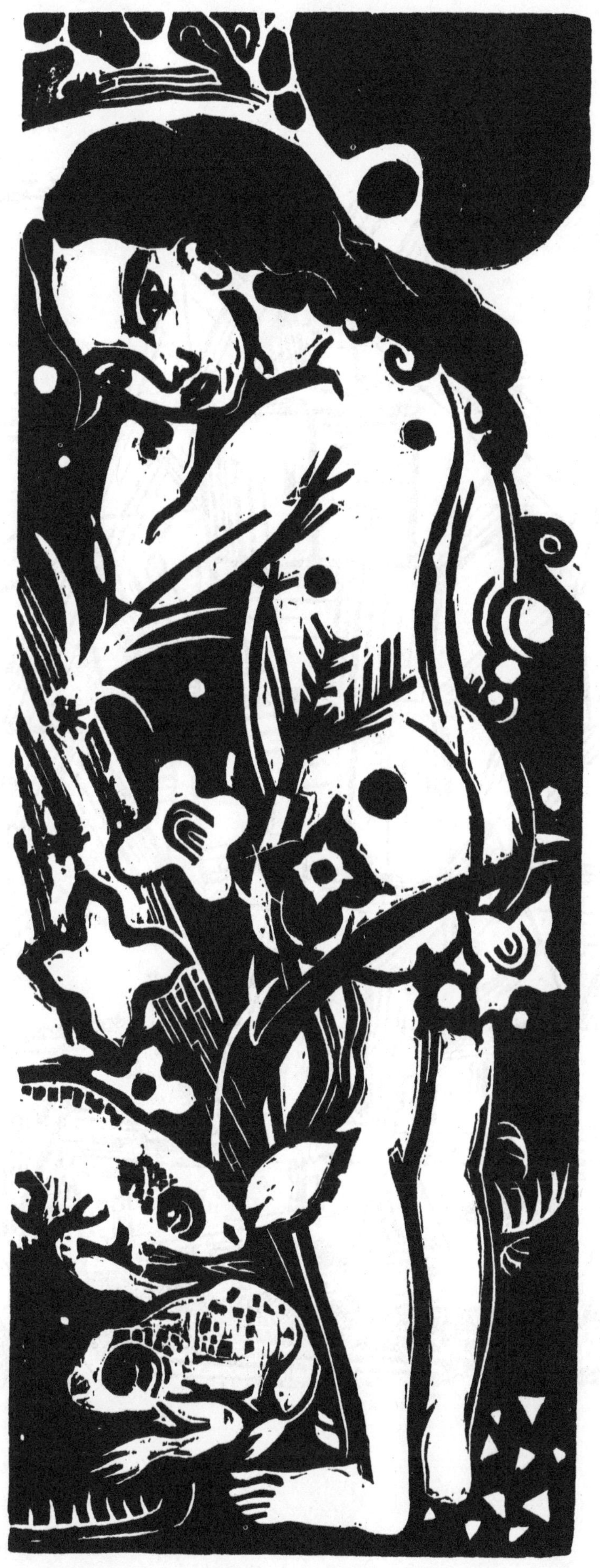

Heinrich Campendonk. *Standing Nude with Flowers and Frogs*, ca. 1914.

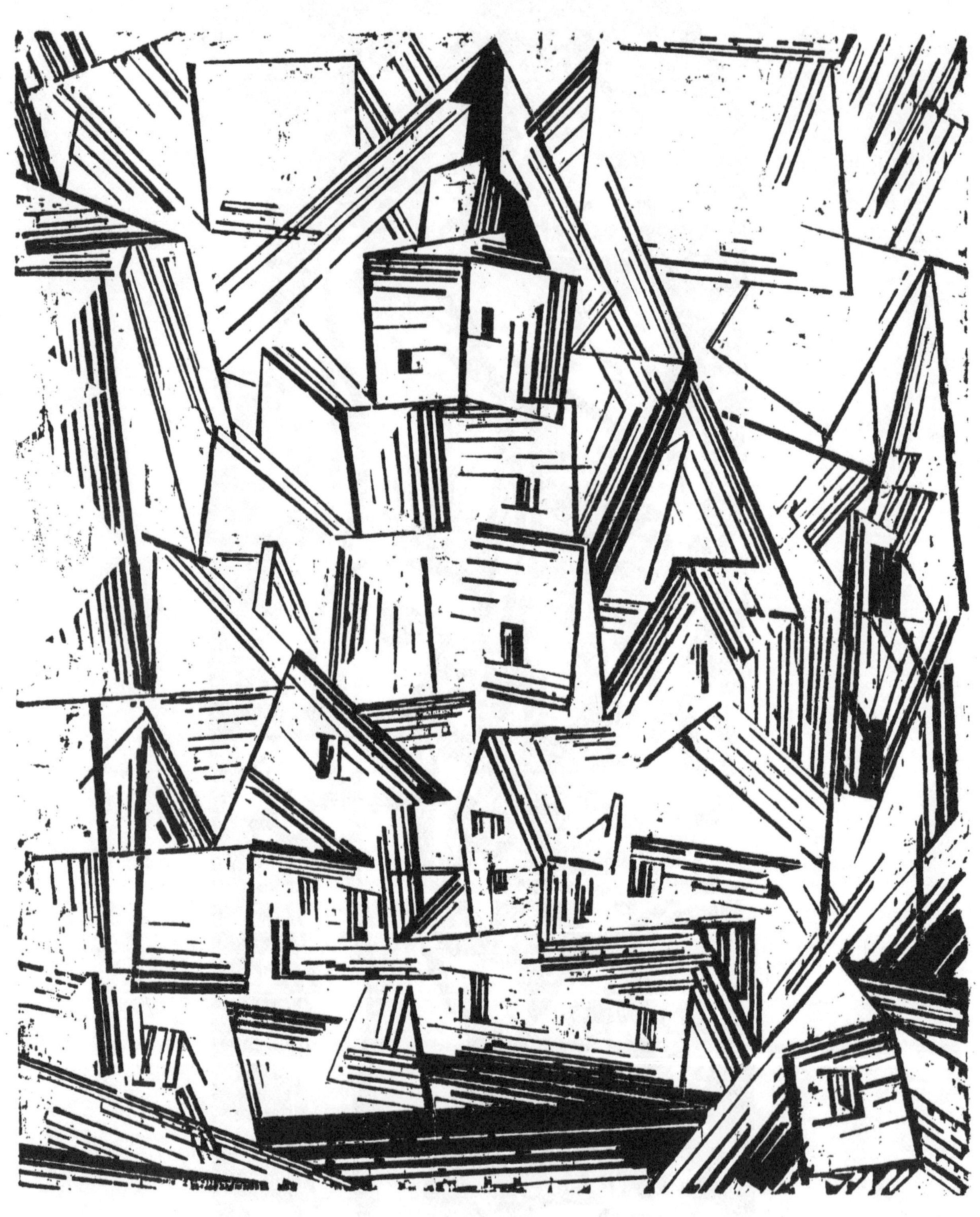

Lyonel Feininger. *Mellingen*, 1919.

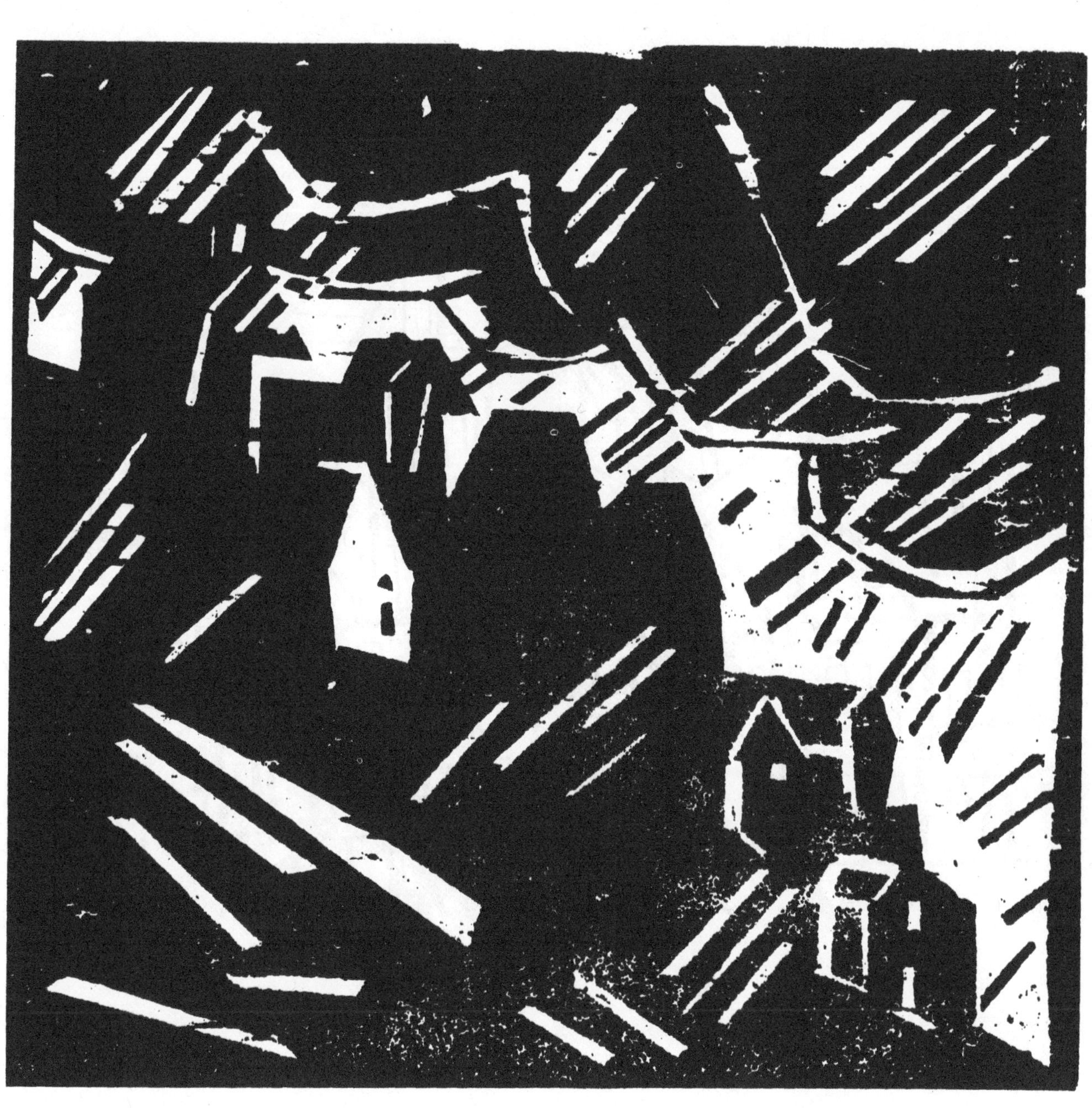

Lyonel Feininger. *Thunderstorm*, 1918.

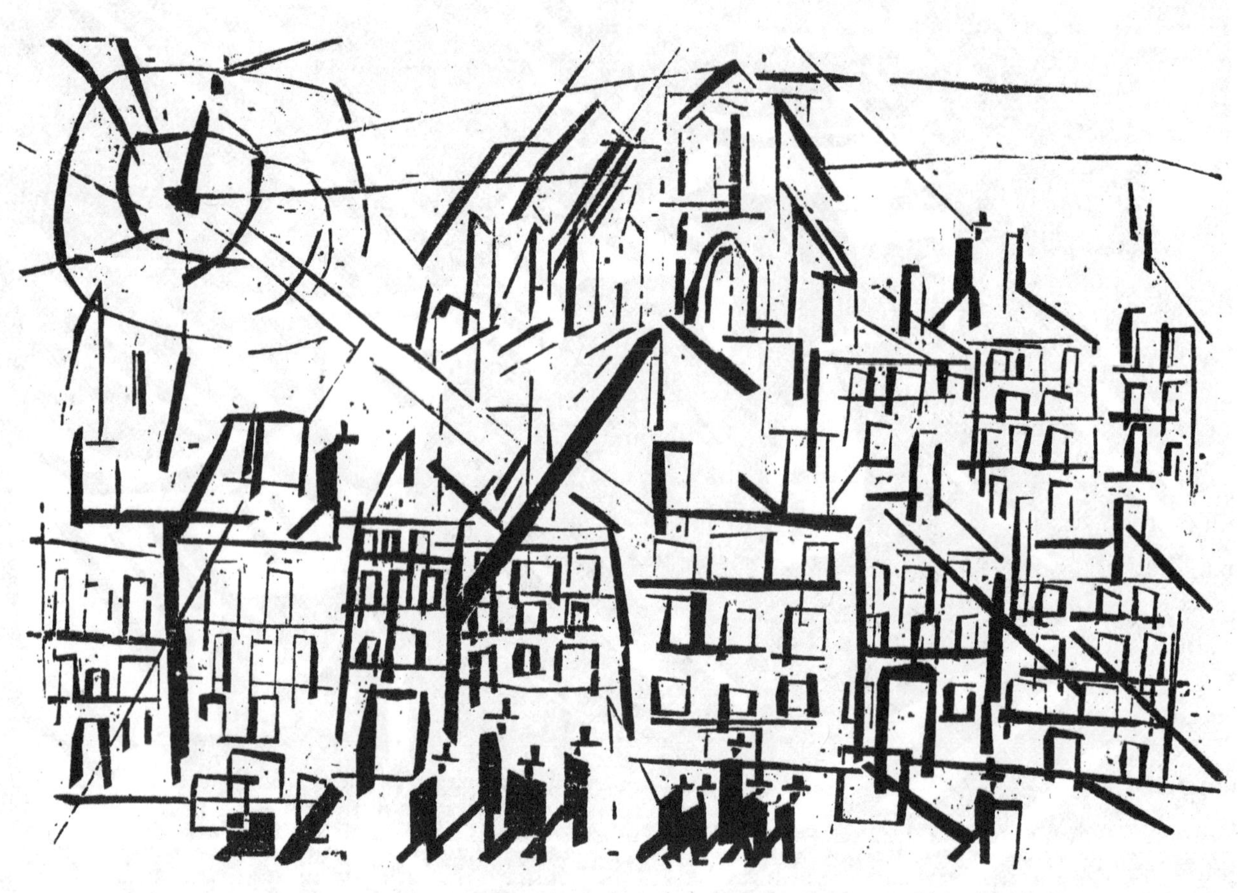

Lyonel Feininger. *The City*, ca. 1920.

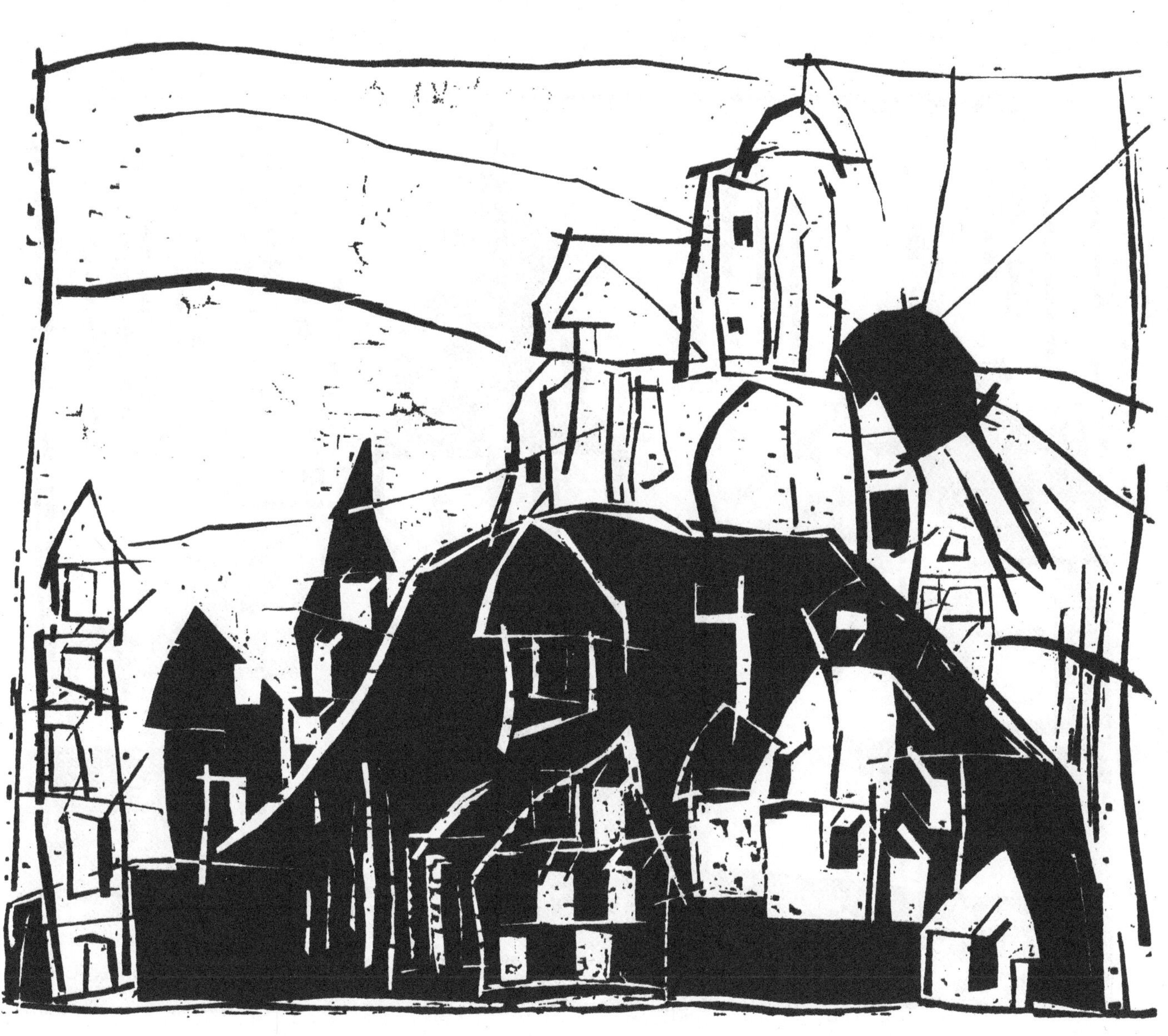

Lyonel Feininger. *Town on the Hill*, 1918.

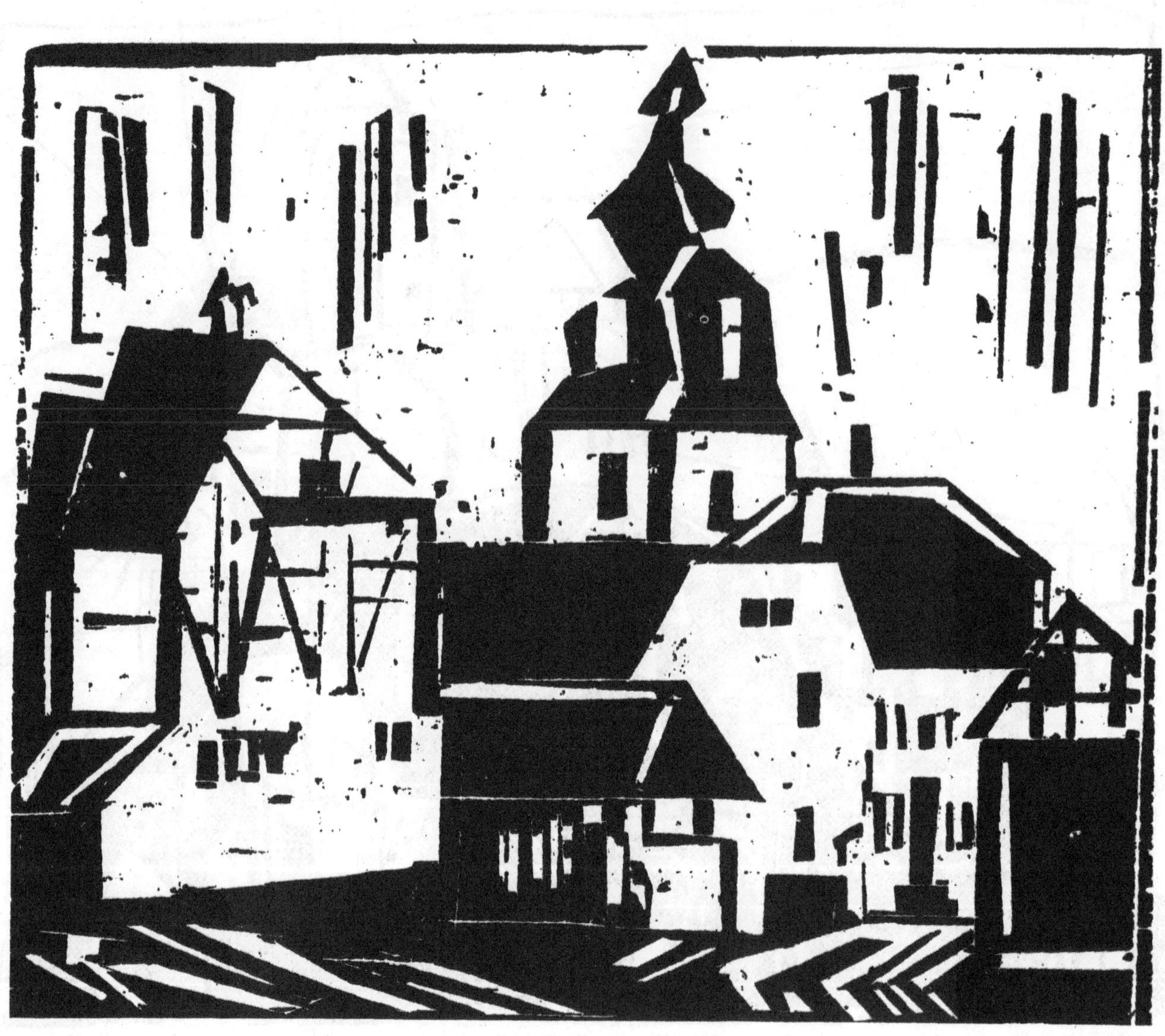

Lyonel Feininger. *Troistedt*, 1919.

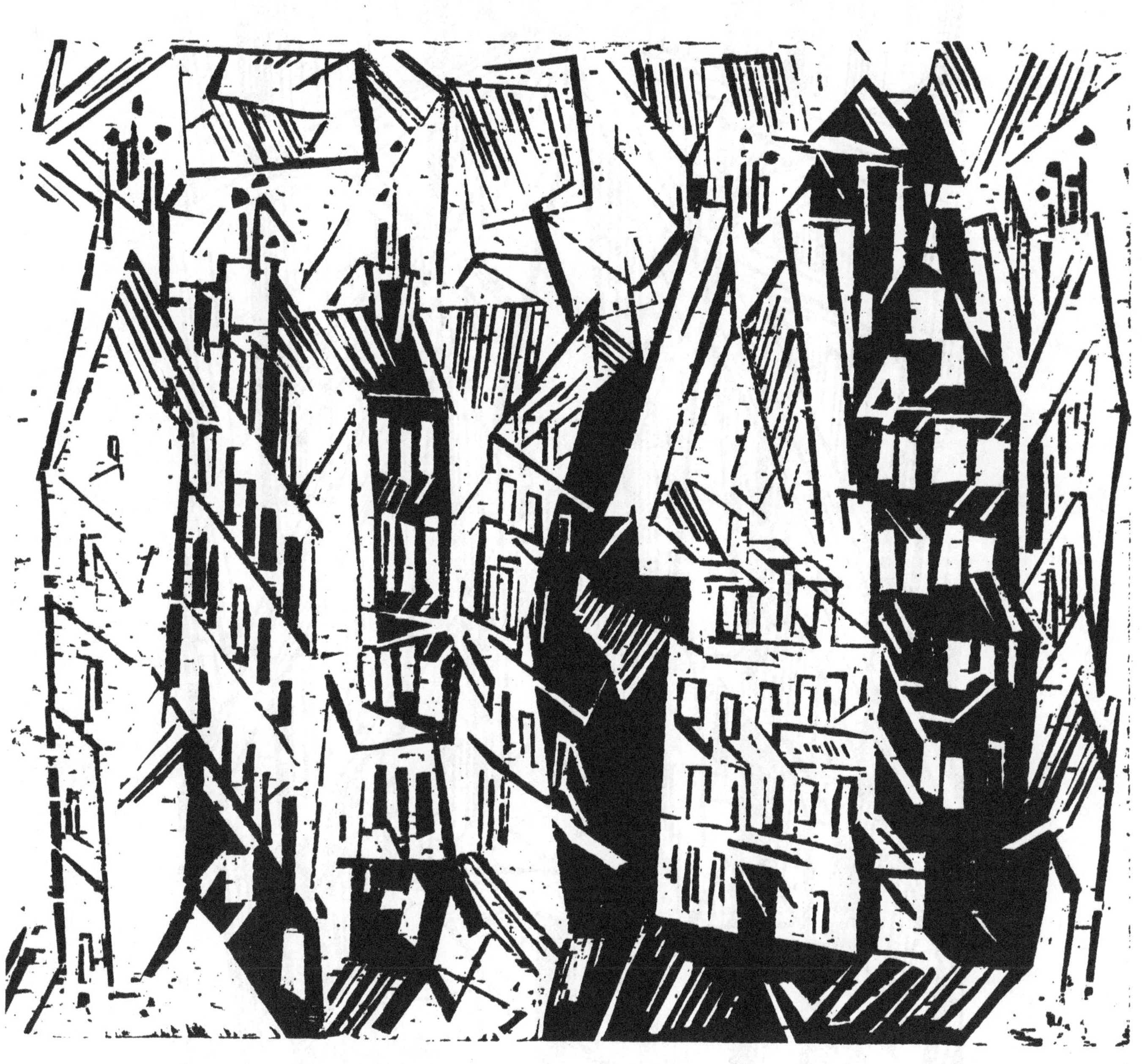

Lyonel Feininger. *Parisian Houses*, 1918.

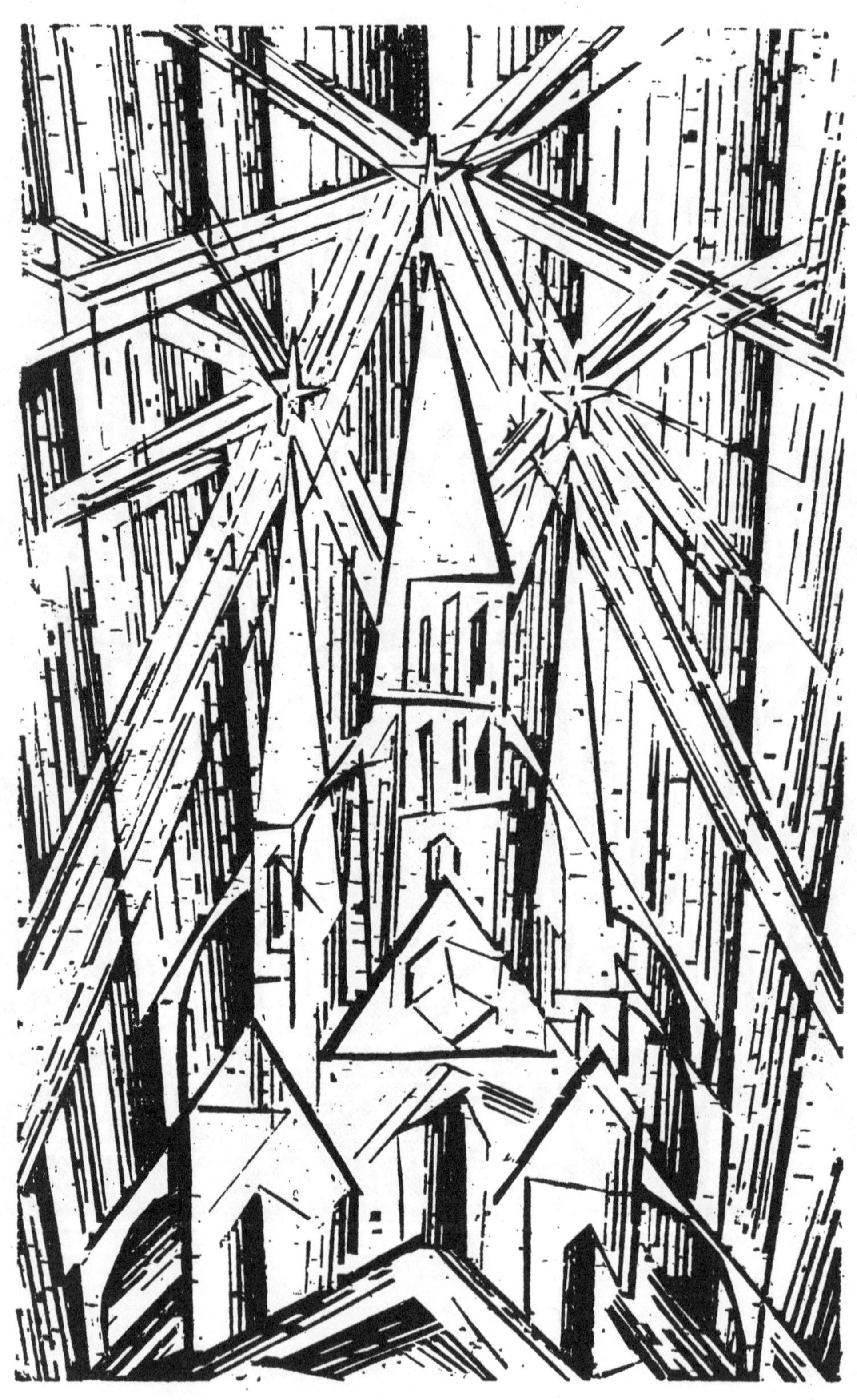

Lyonel Feininger. *Cathedral*, 1919.

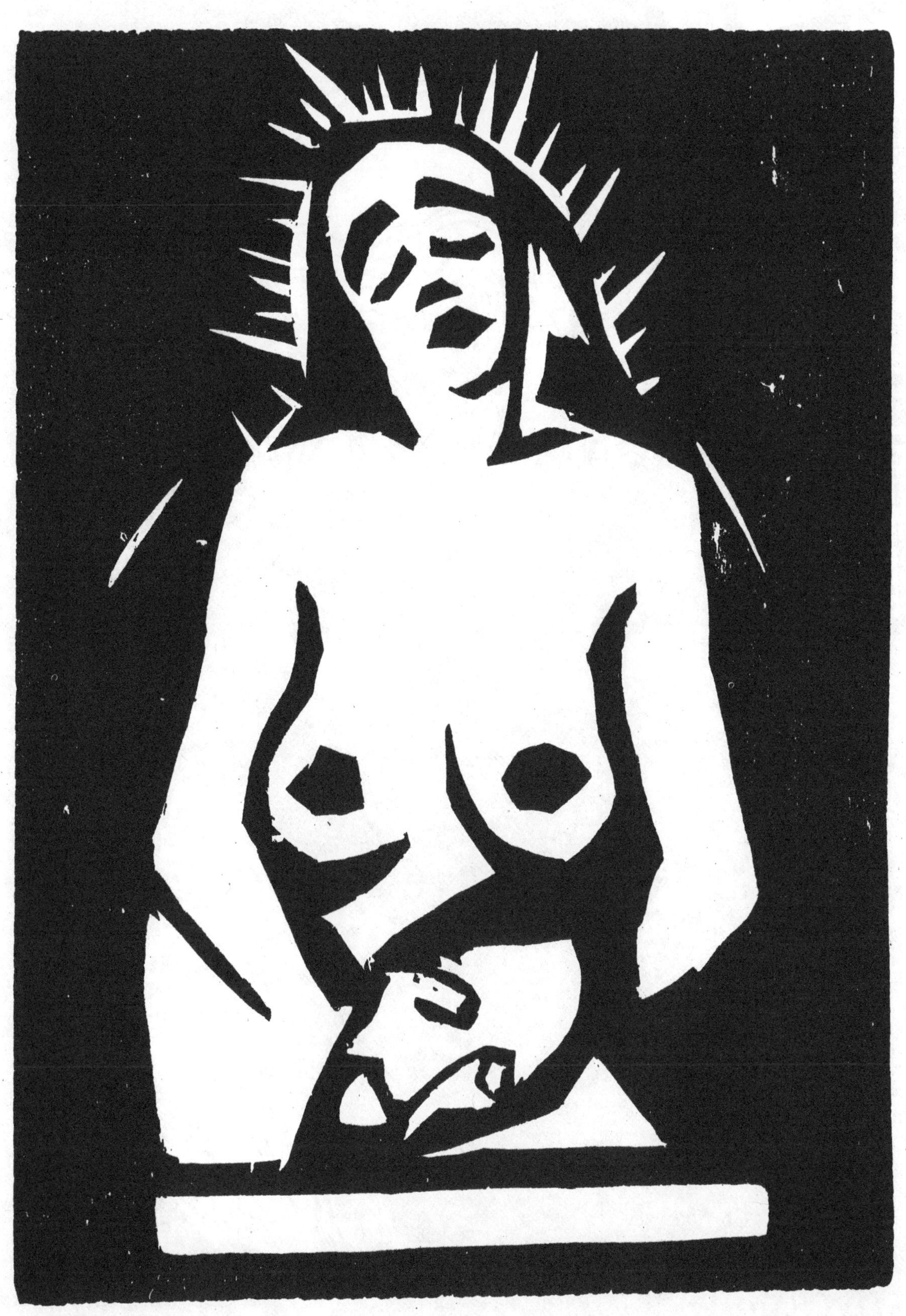

Conrad Felixmüller. Untitled, 1917.

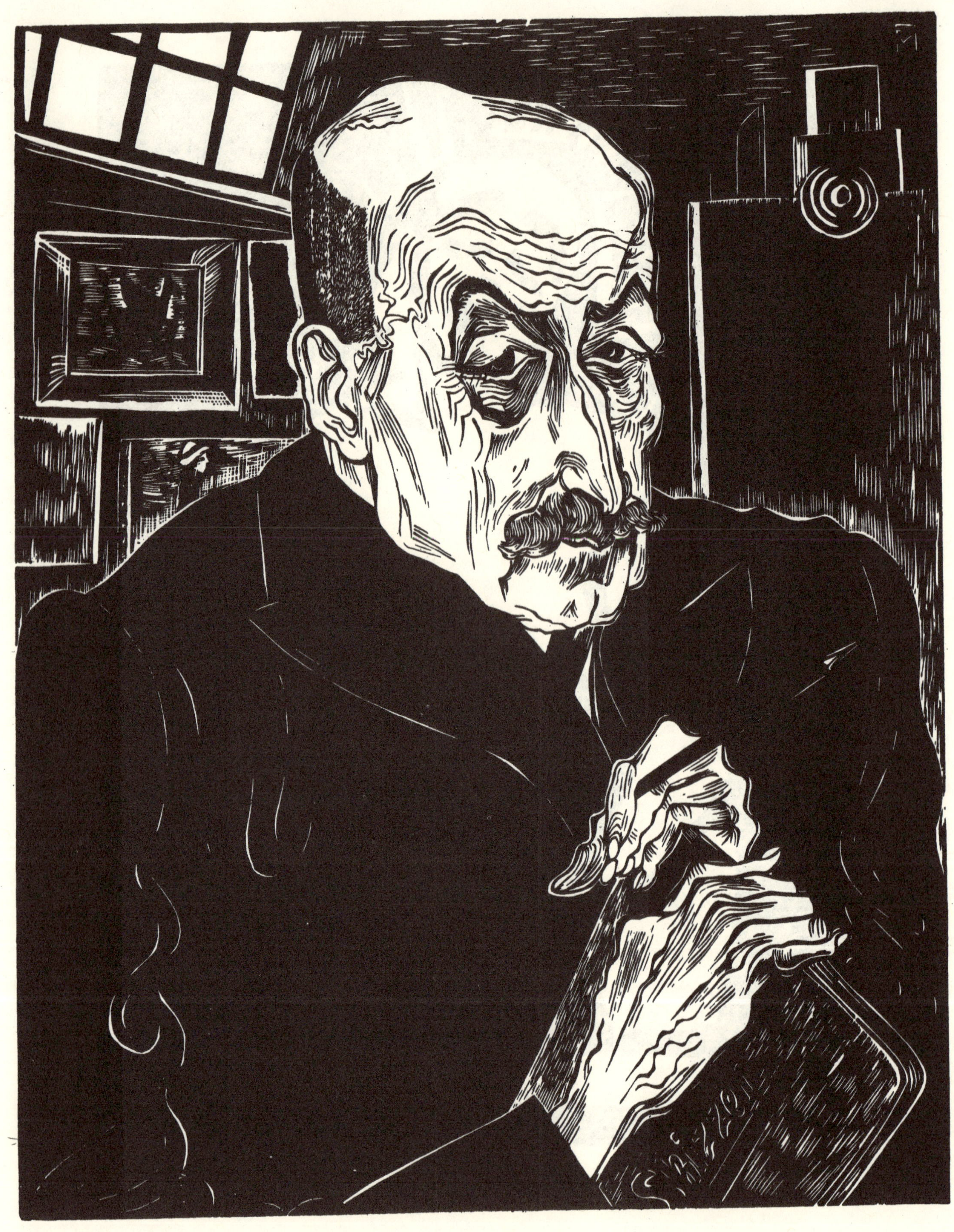

 Conrad Felixmüller. *Max Liebermann* (painter, 1847–1935), 1926.

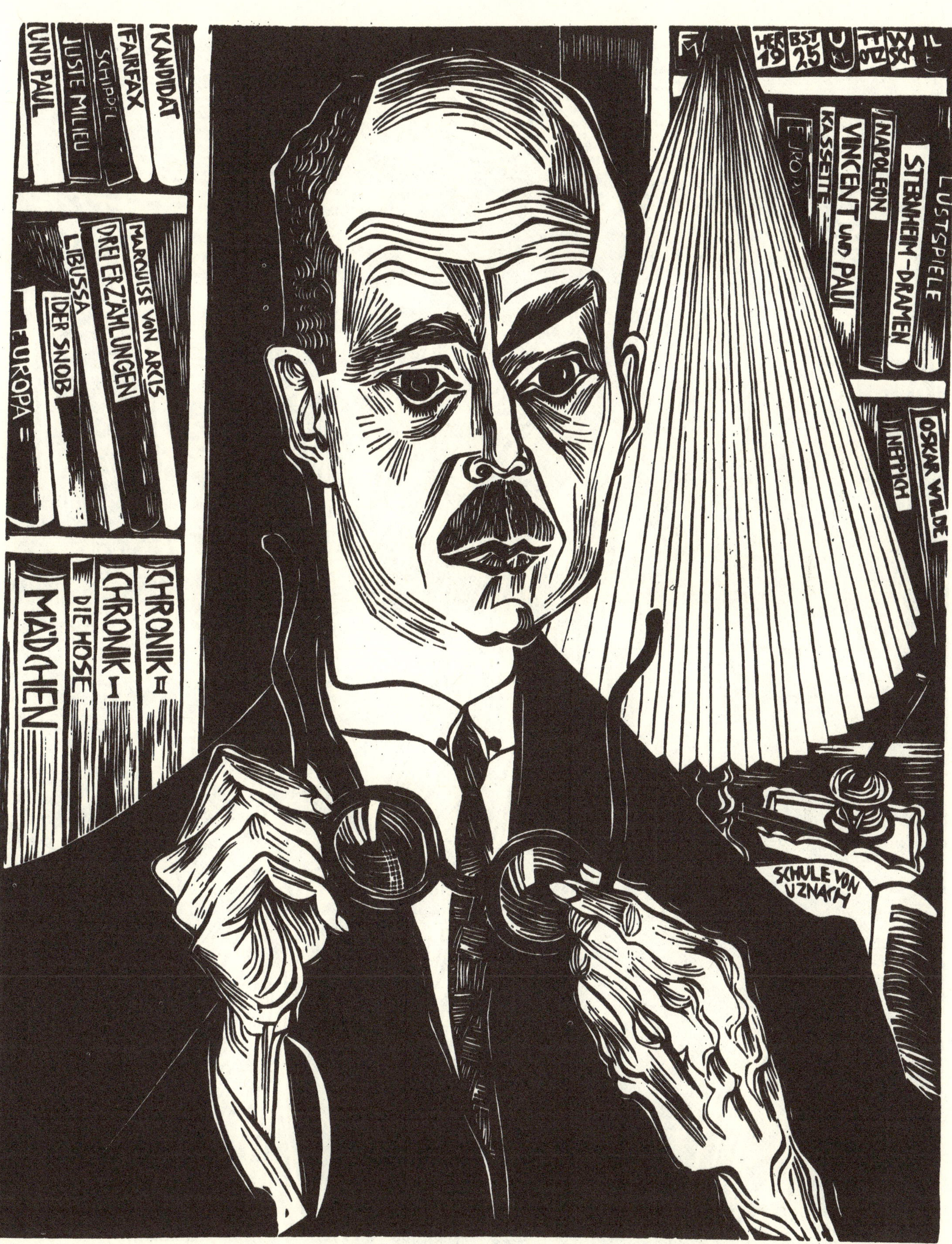

Conrad Felixmüller. *Carl Sternheim* (author, 1878–1942), 1925.

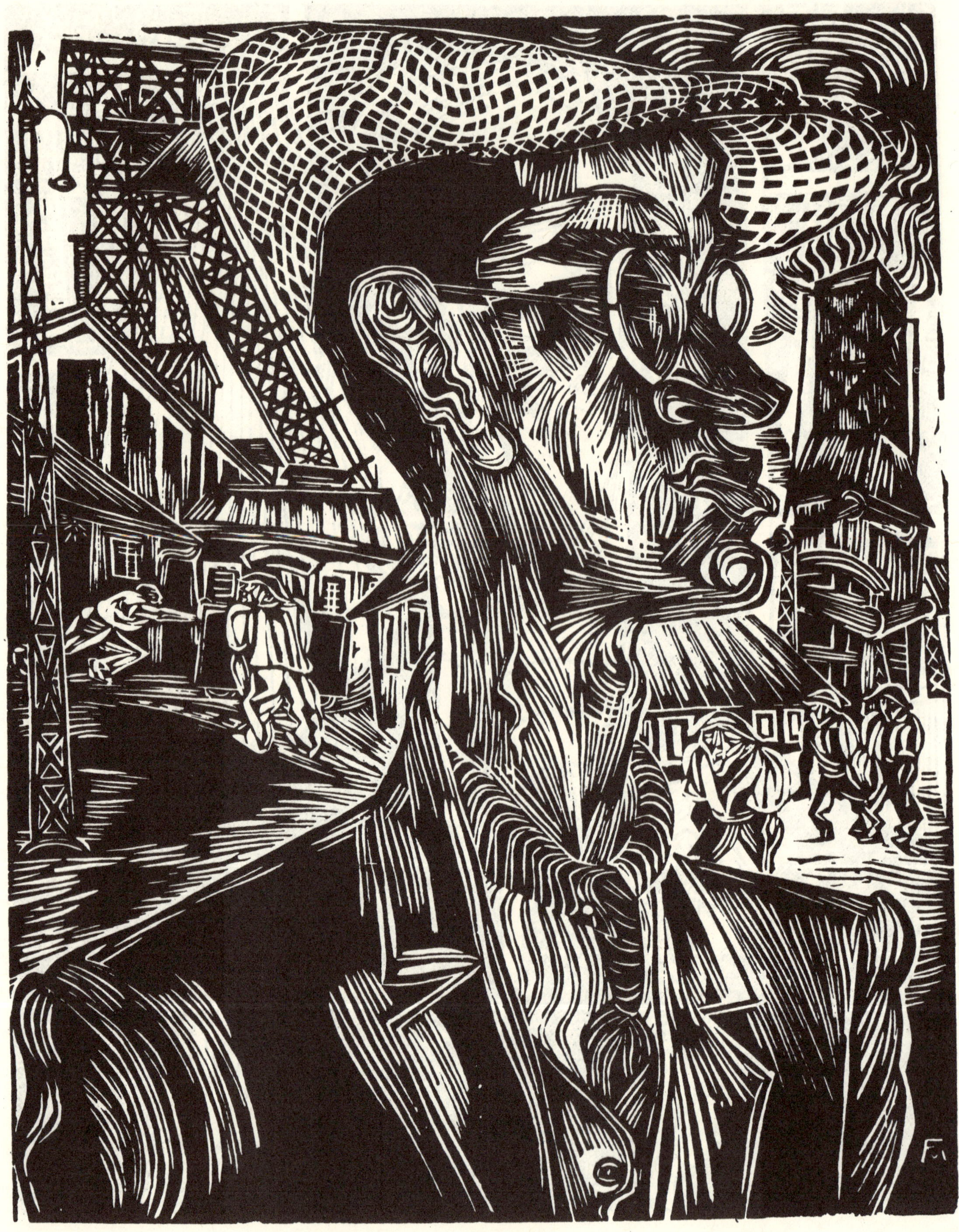

 Conrad Felixmüller. *The Mining Engineer*, 1922.

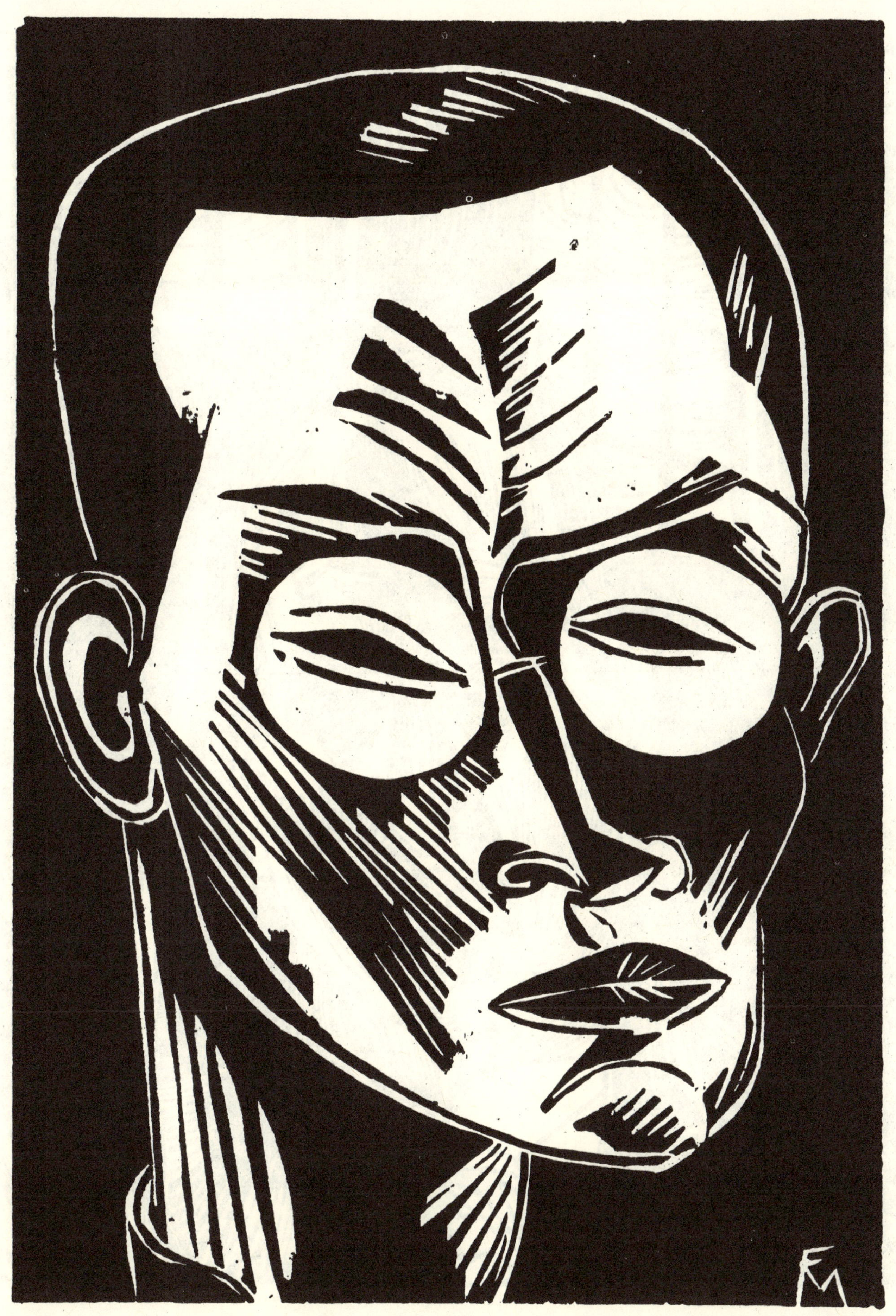

Conrad Felixmüller. *Self-portrait*, 1919.

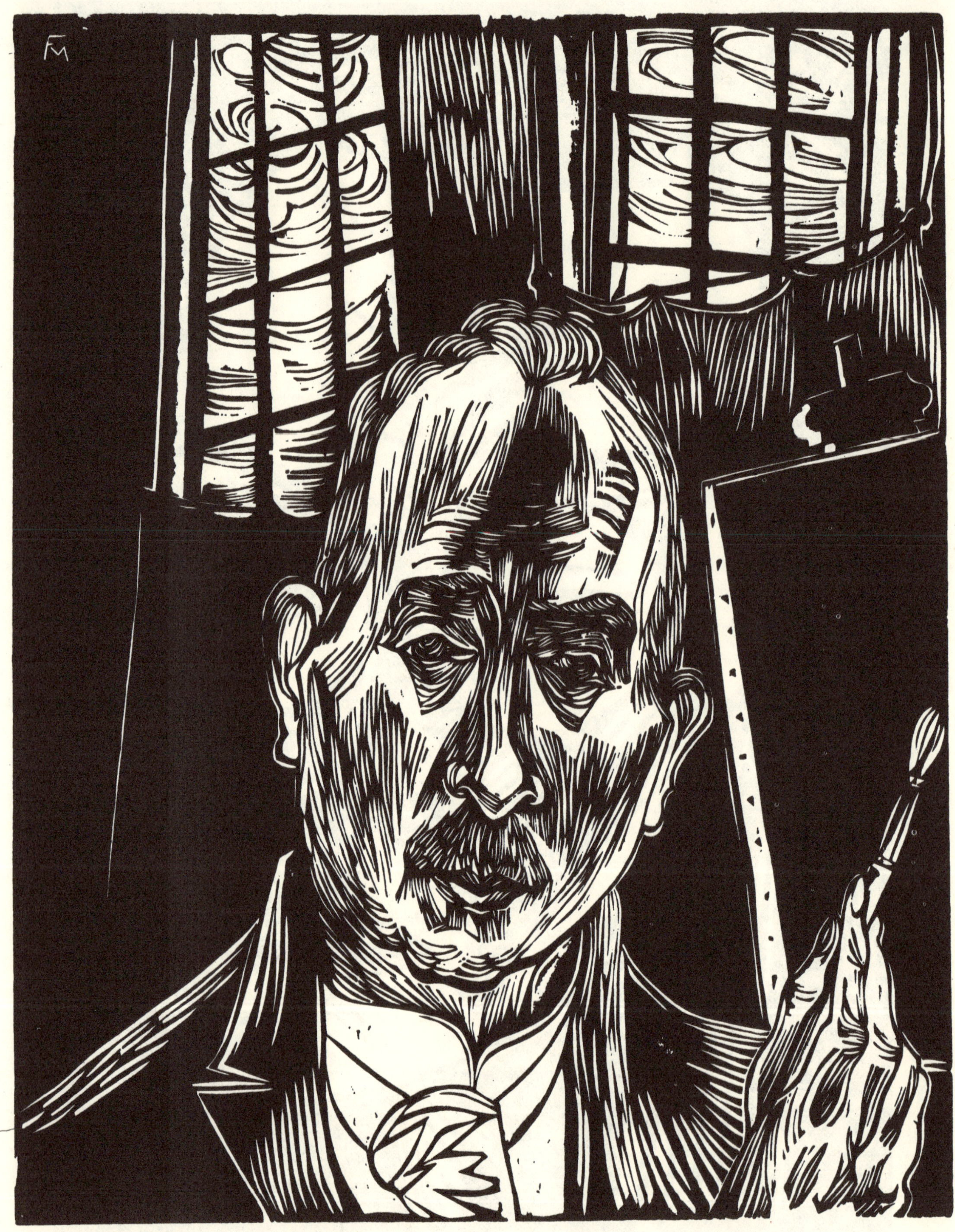

Conrad Felixmüller. *The Painter Christian Rohlfs* (1849–1938), 1927.

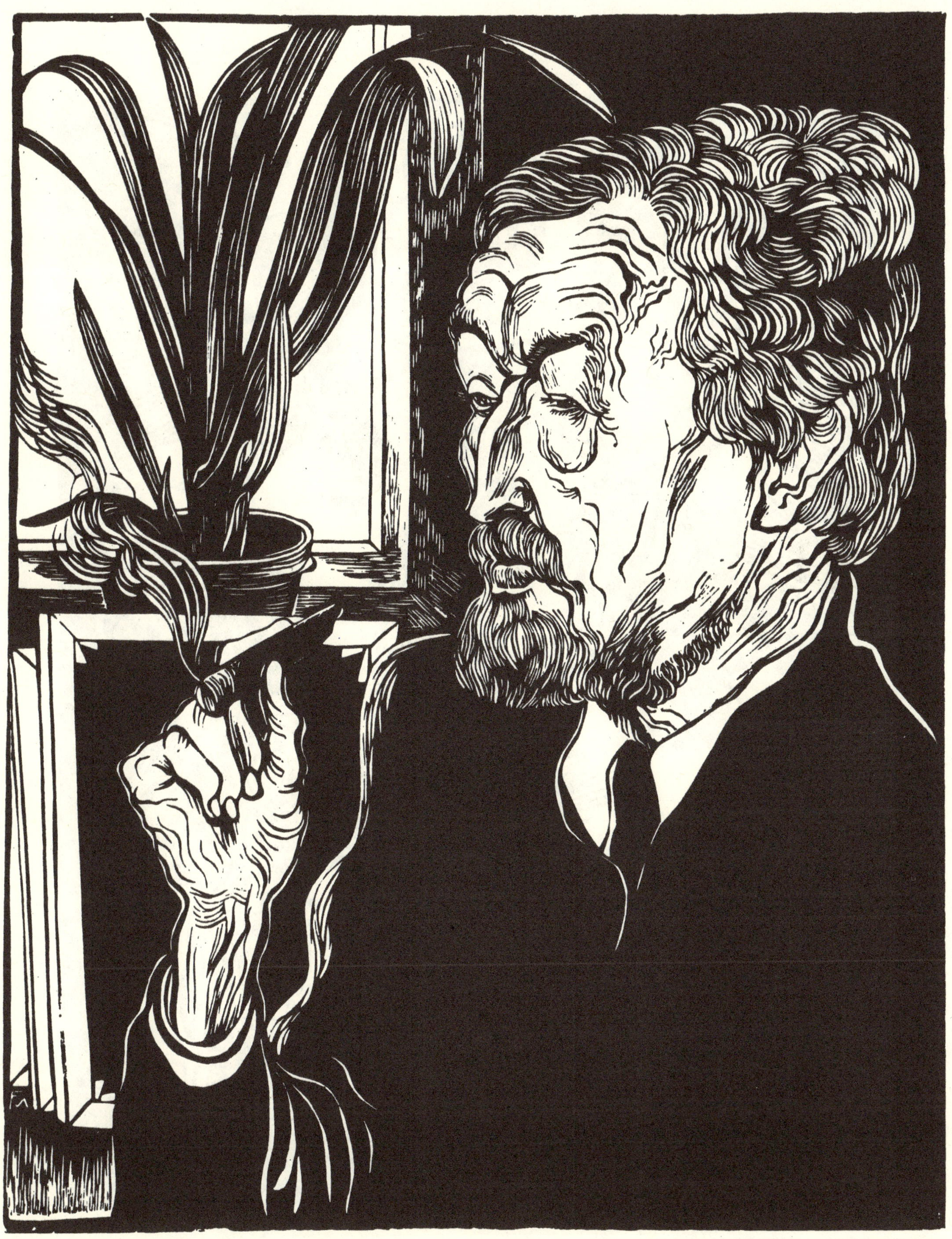

Conrad Felixmüller. *Lovis Corinth* (painter, 1858–1925), 1925.

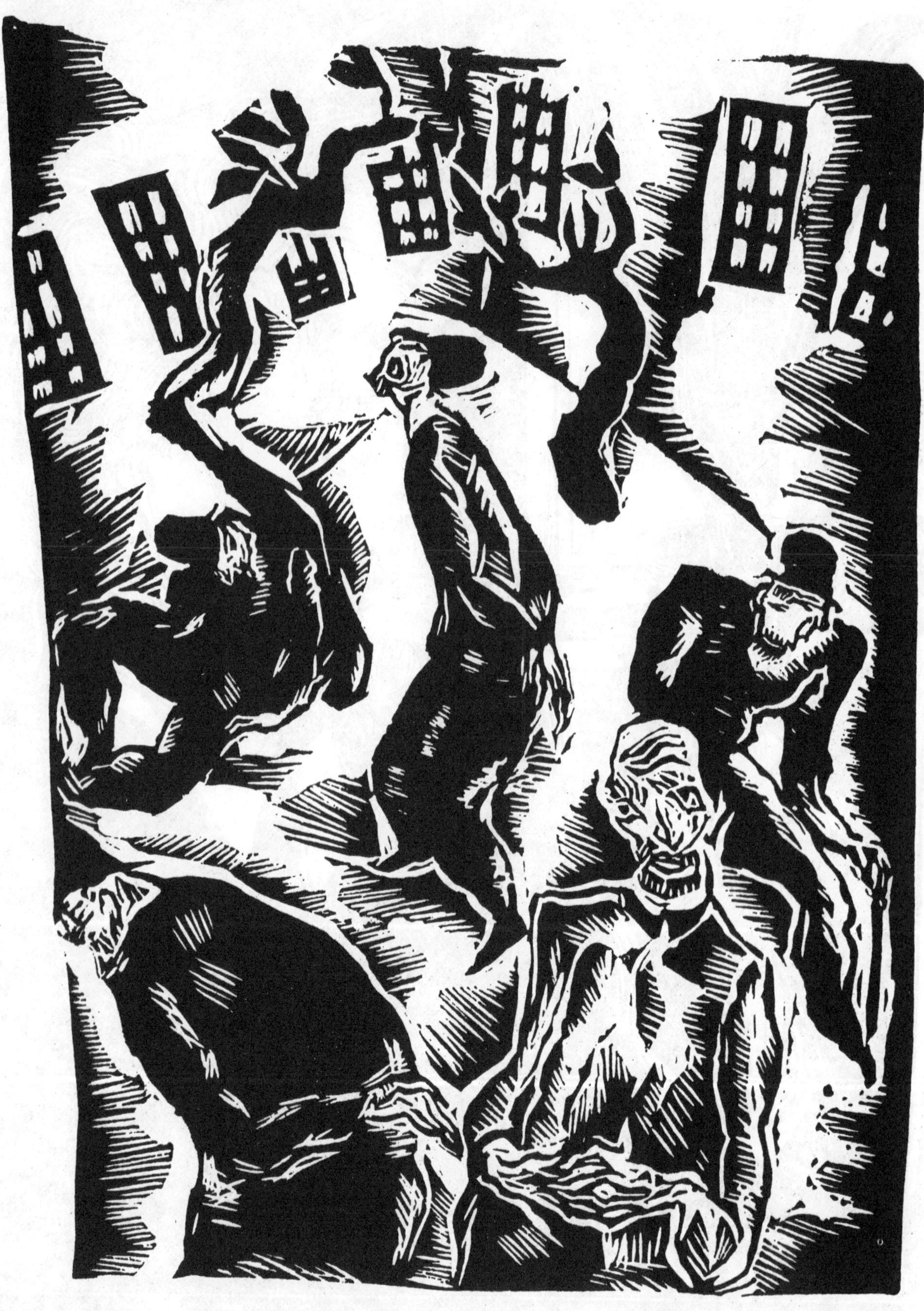

Erich Goldblum. *Lunatics*, 1918.

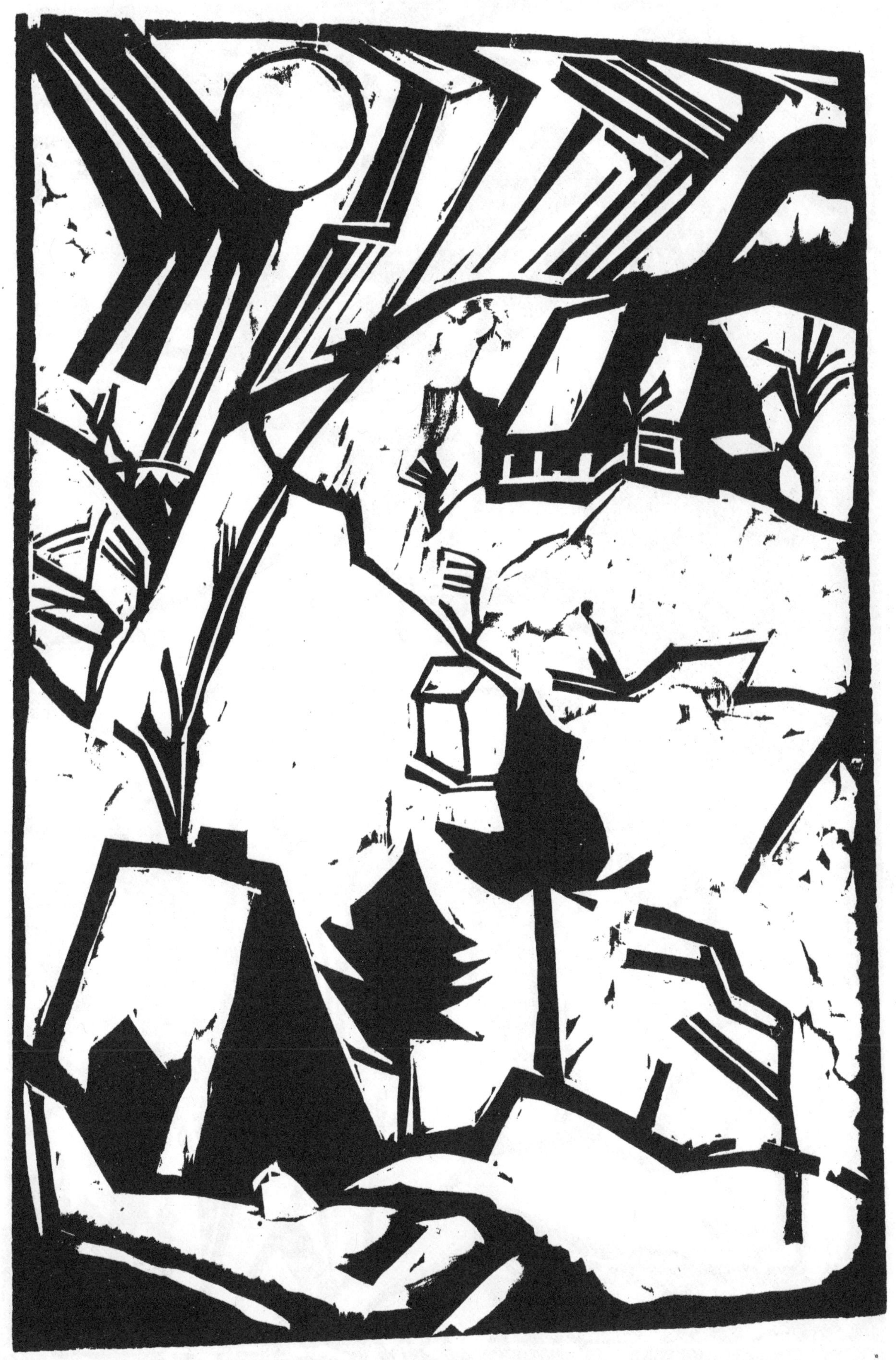

Erich Heckel. *Snowstorm*, 1914.

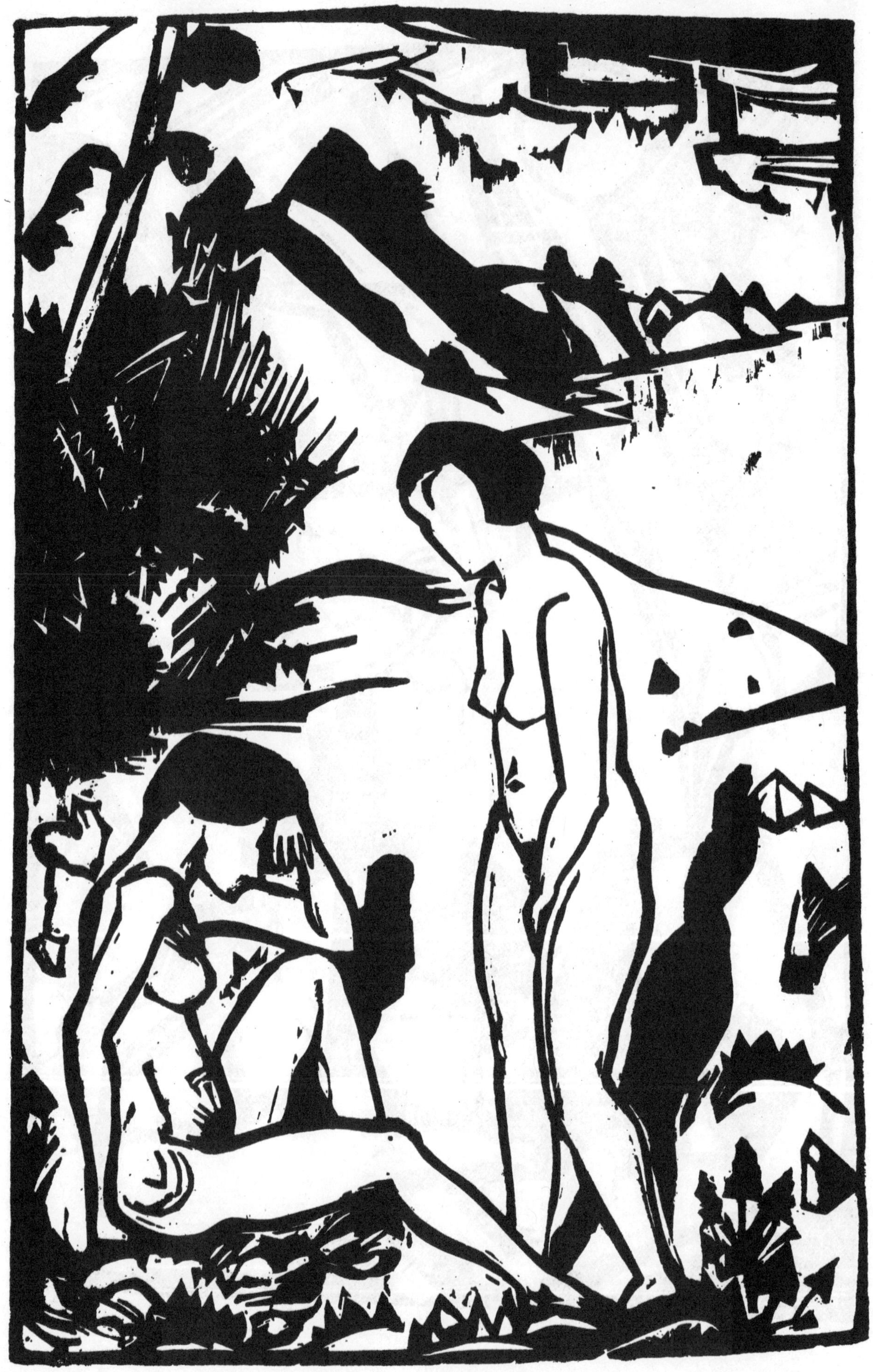

Erich Heckel. *On the Beach*, 1923.

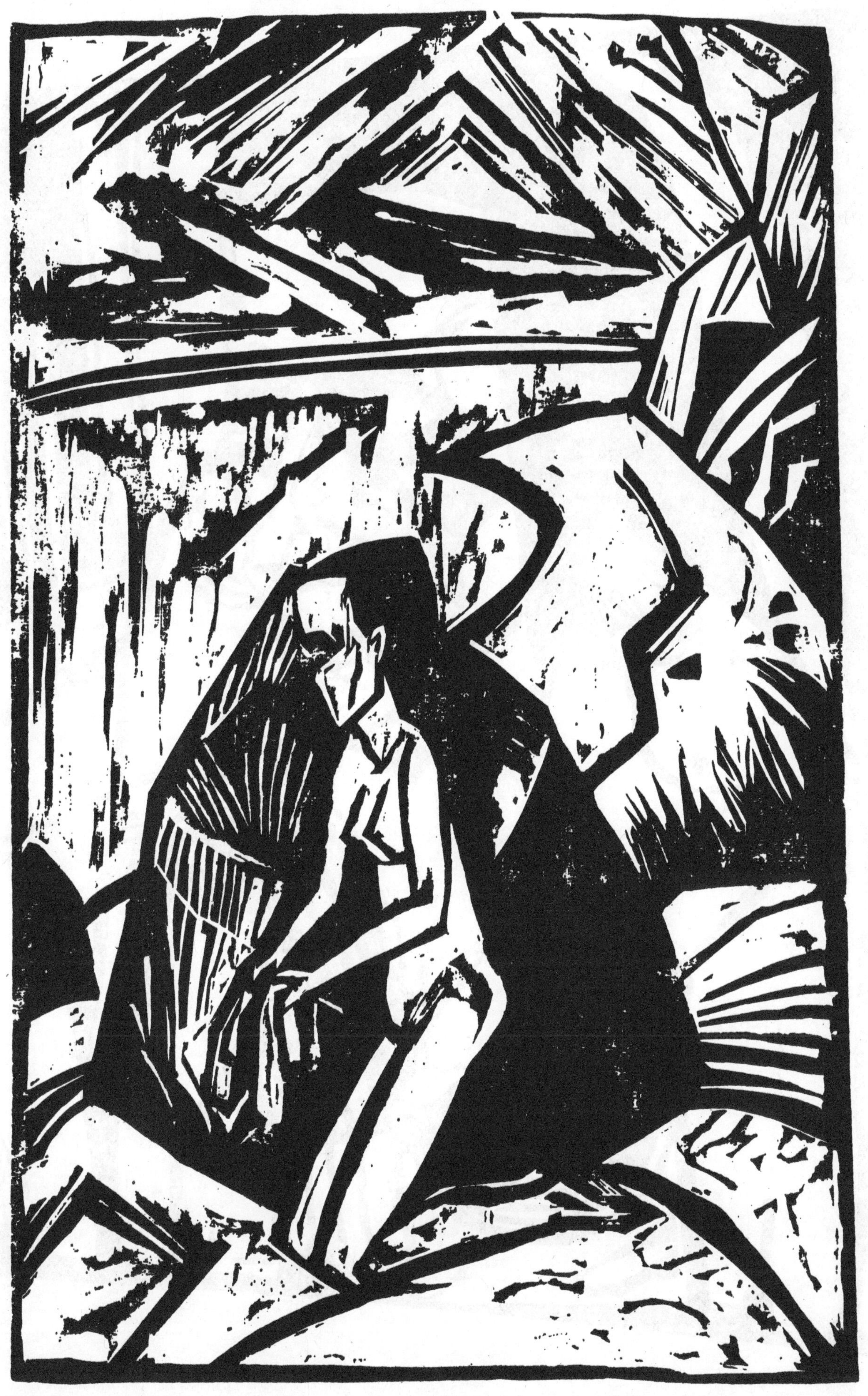

Erich Heckel. *Woman Kneeling by a Rock*, 1913.

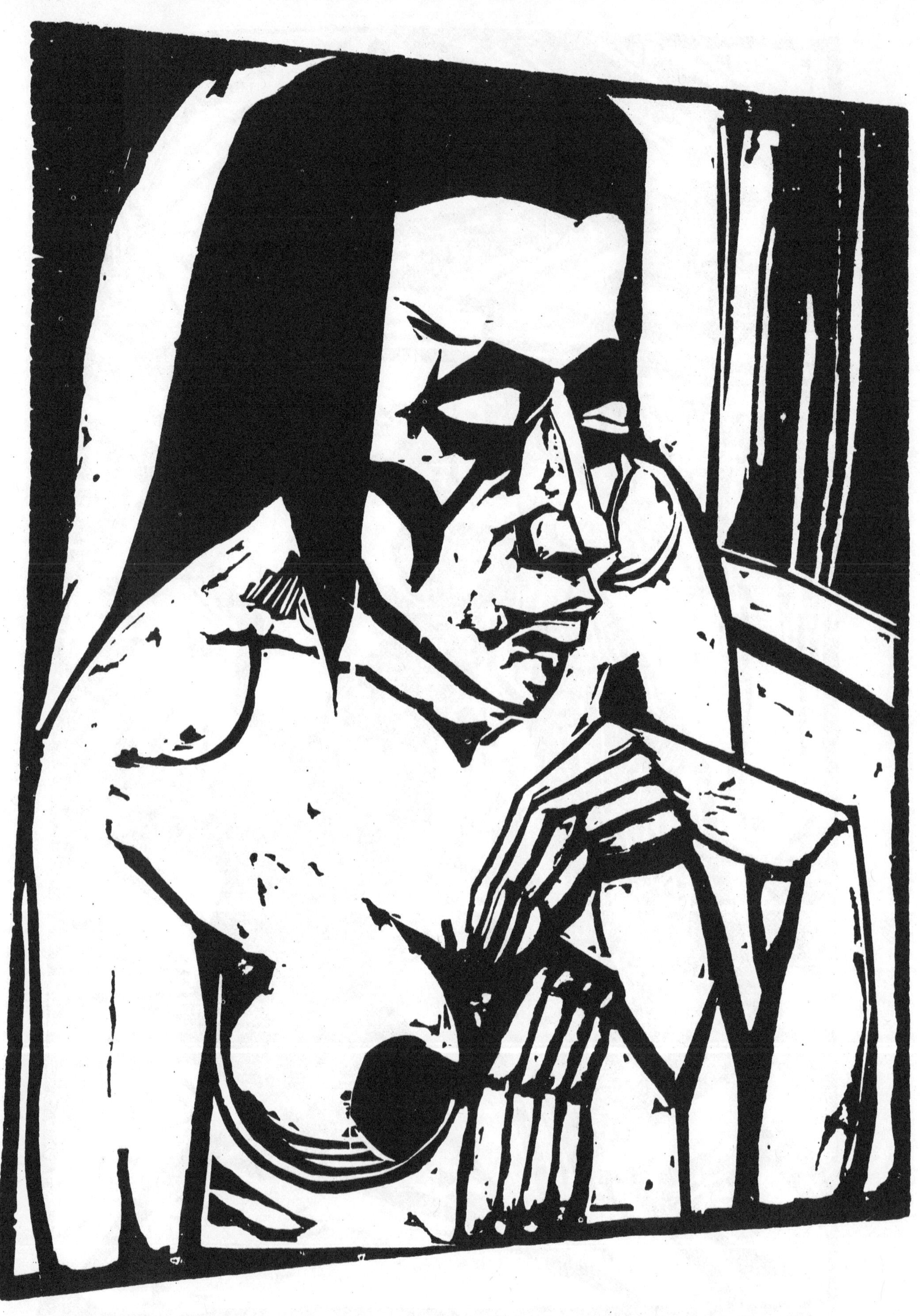

Erich Heckel. *Seated Woman*, 1913.

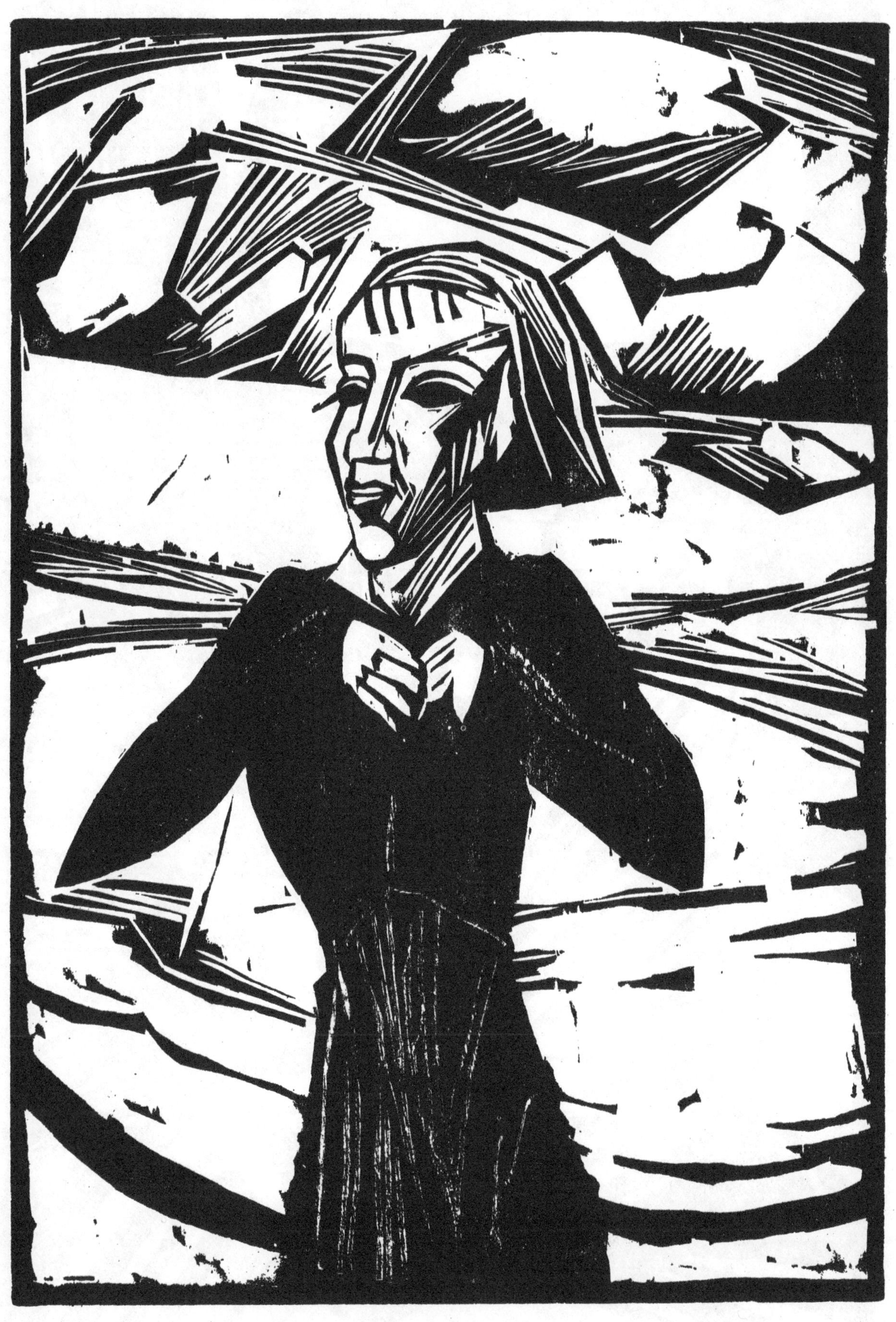

Erich Heckel. *Girl by the Sea*, 1918.

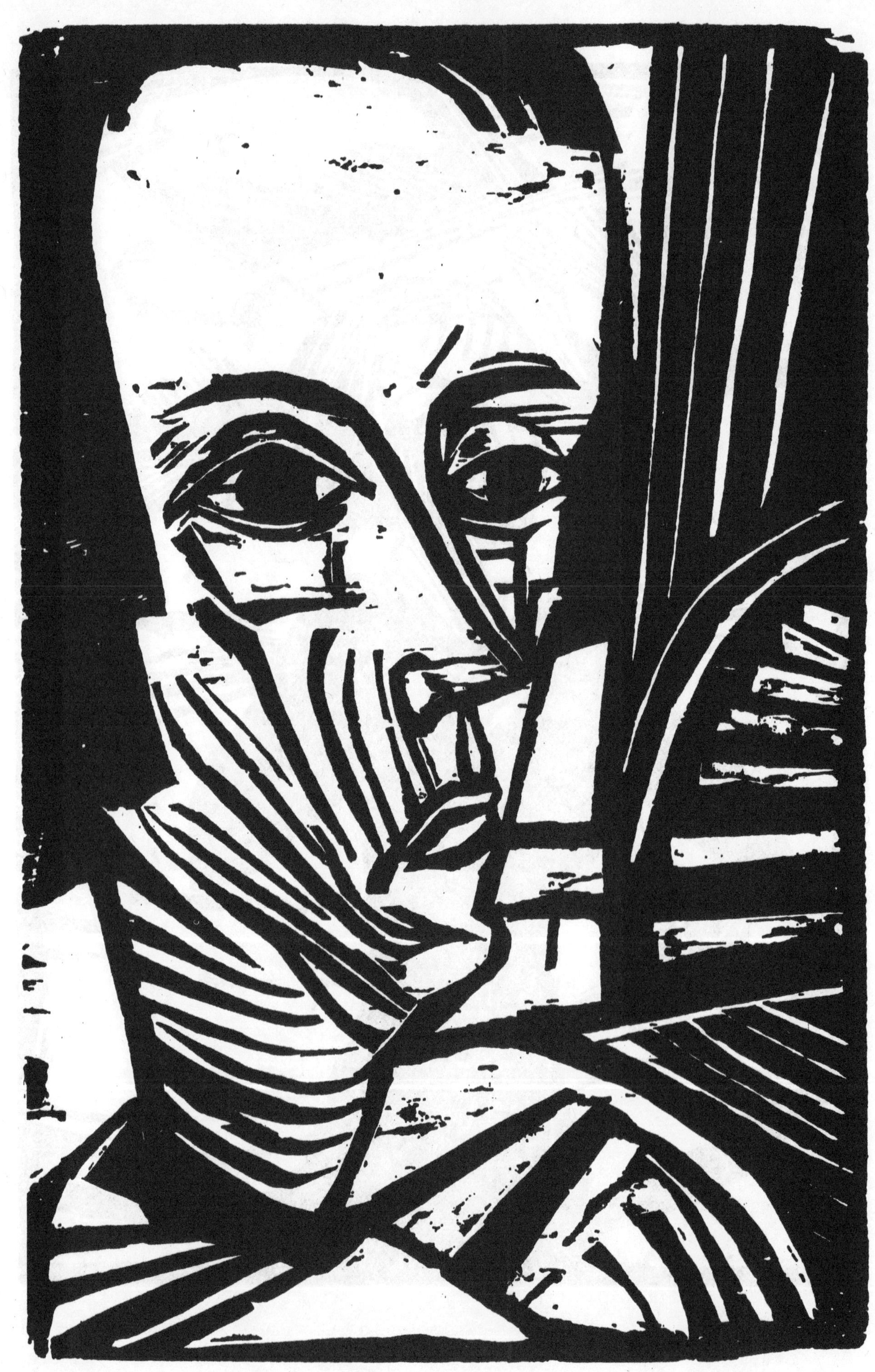

Erich Heckel. *Asta Nielsen* (film star, 1881–1972), 1919.

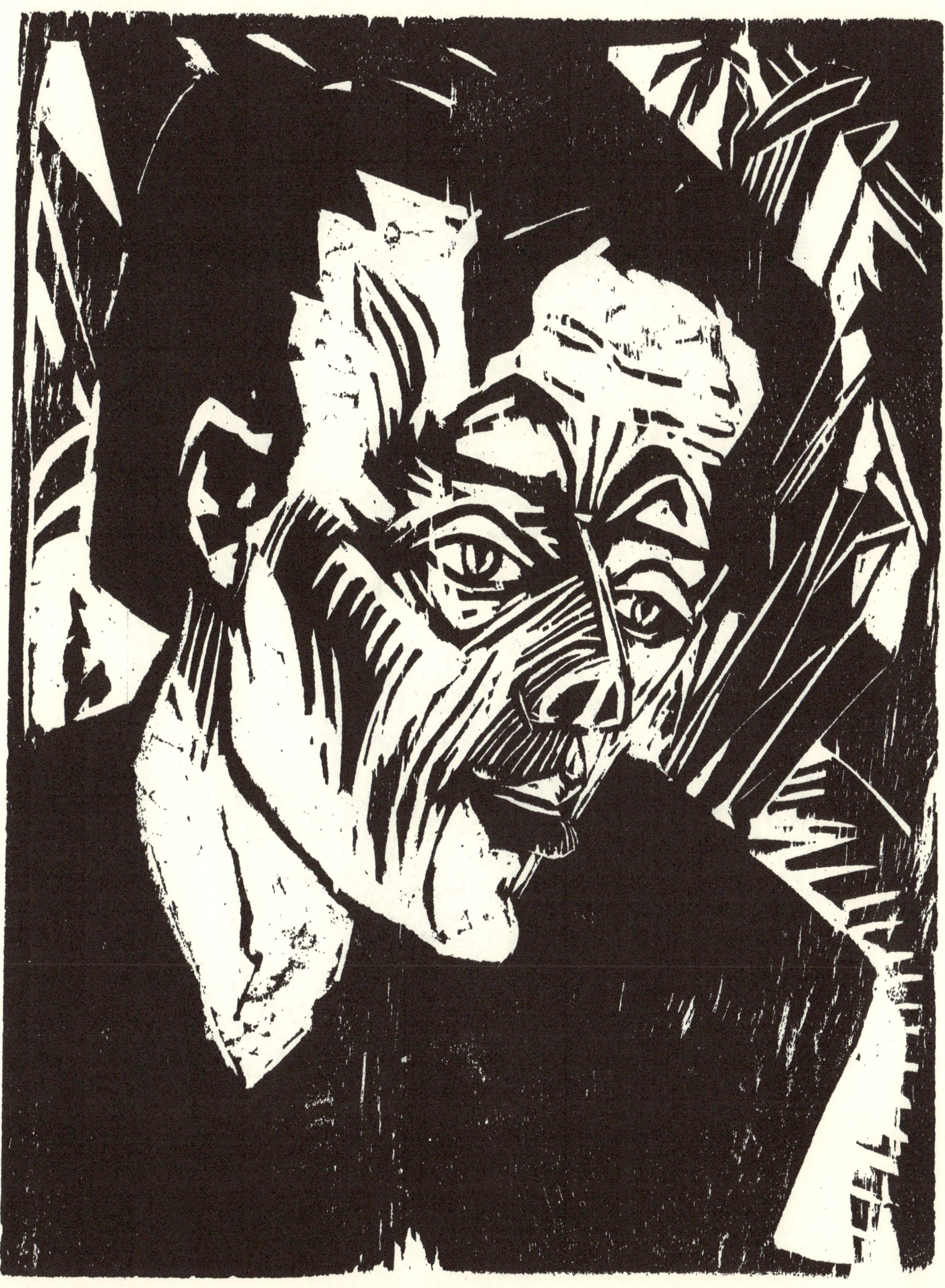

Erich Heckel. *Roquairol* (character in Jean Paul's novel *Titan*), 1917.

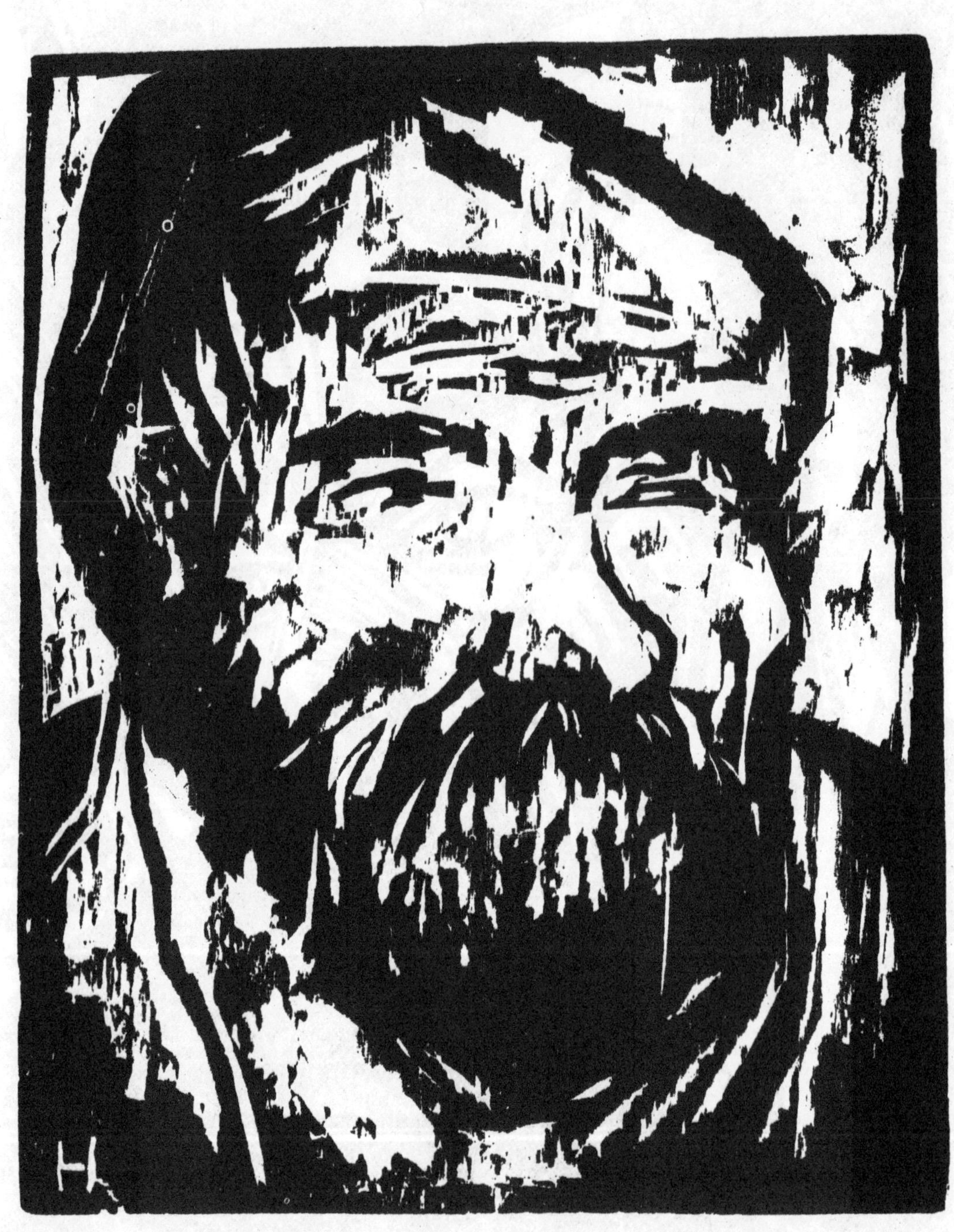

Erich Heckel. *Bearded Man*, 1908.

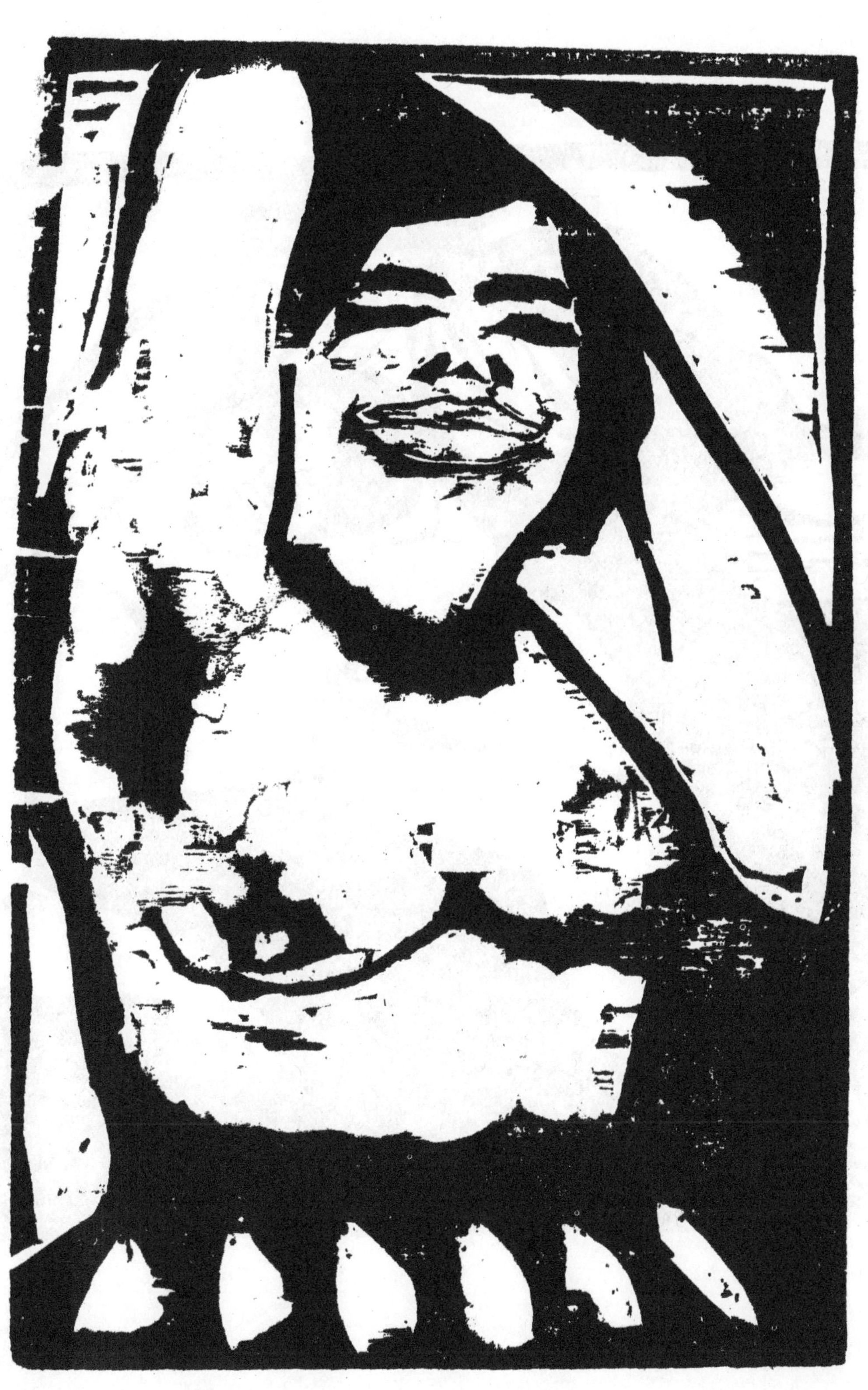

Erich Heckel. *Woman with Raised Arms*, 1910.

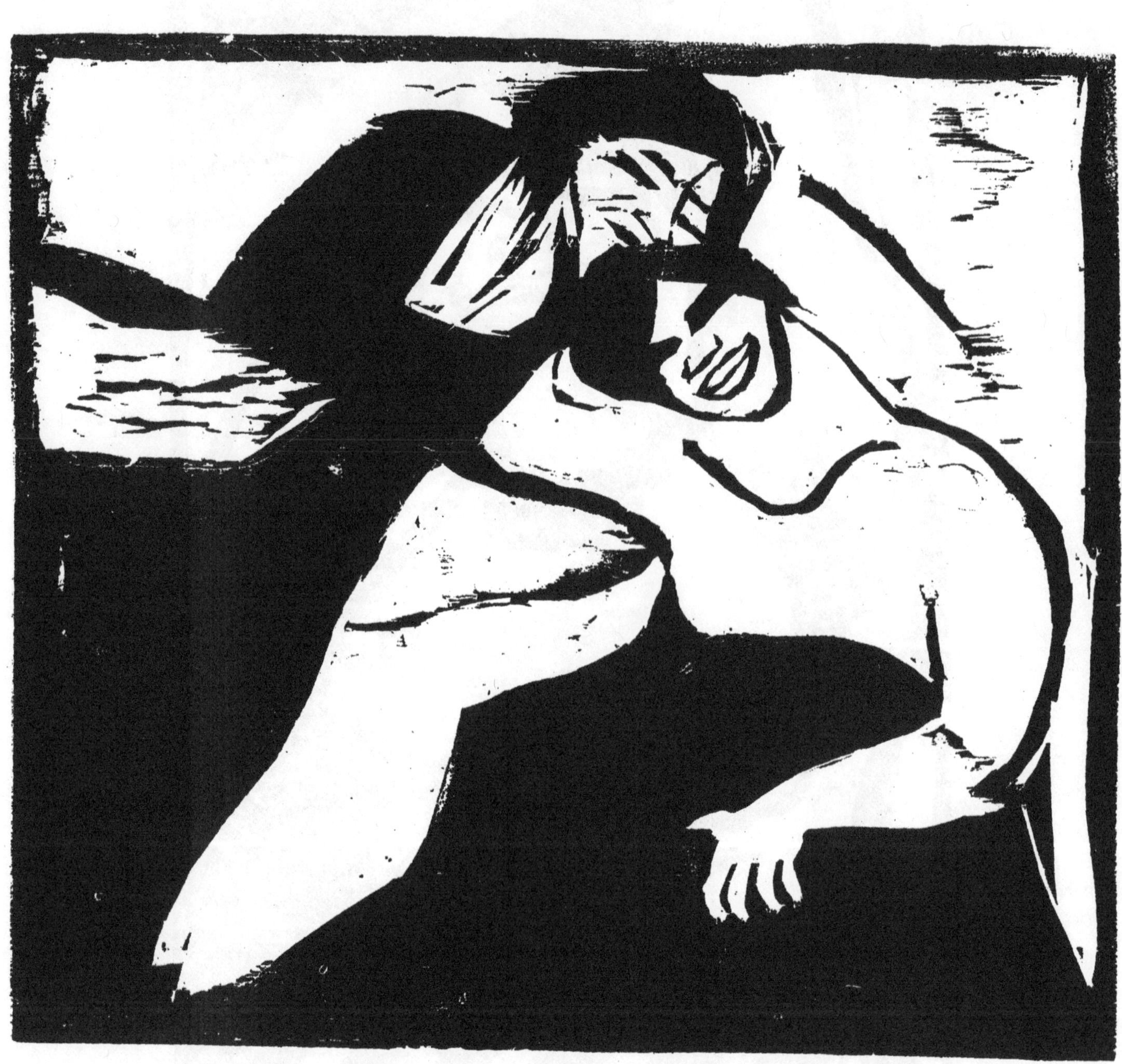

Erich Heckel. *Two Women Resting*, 1909.

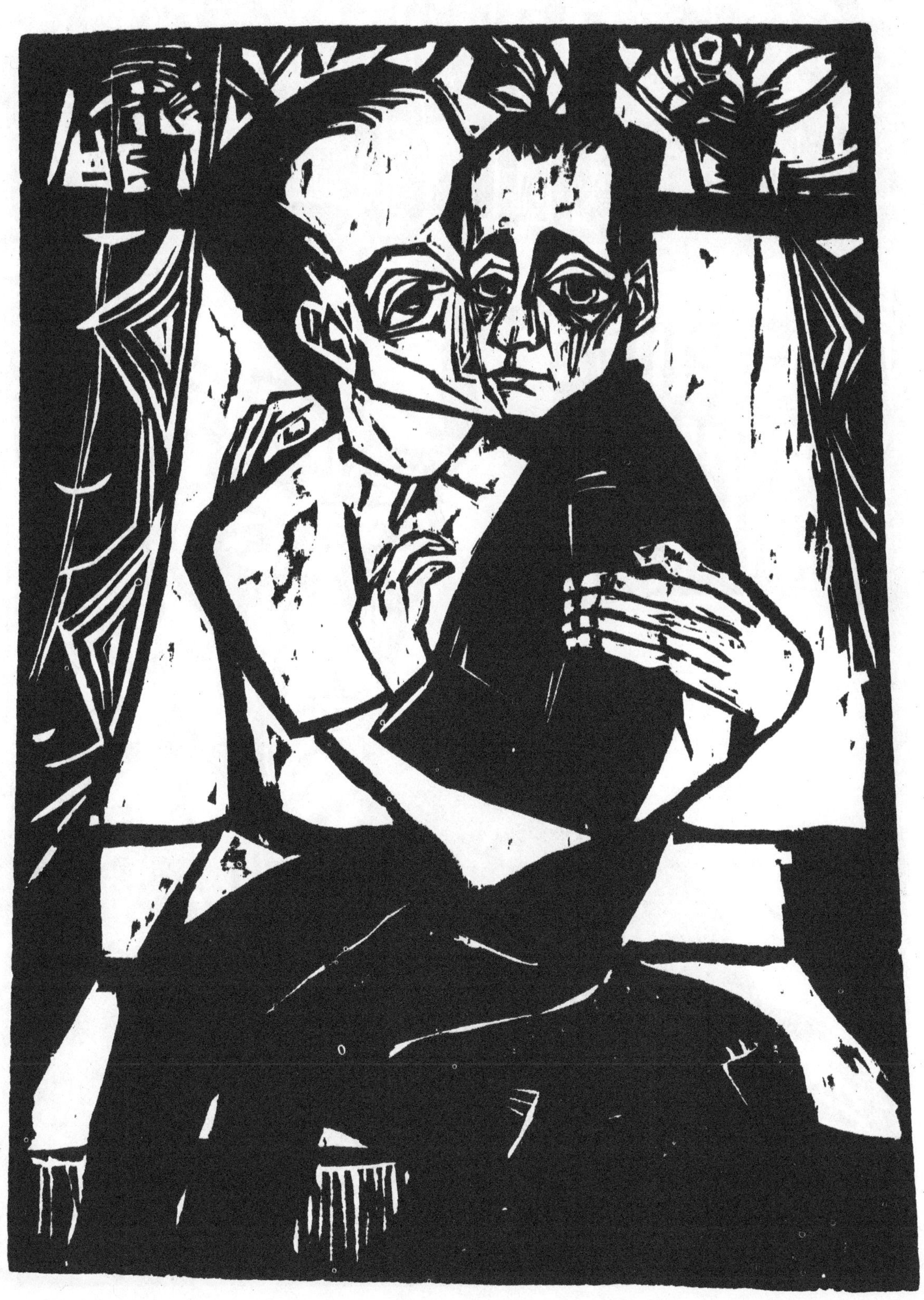

Erich Heckel. *Siblings*, 1913.

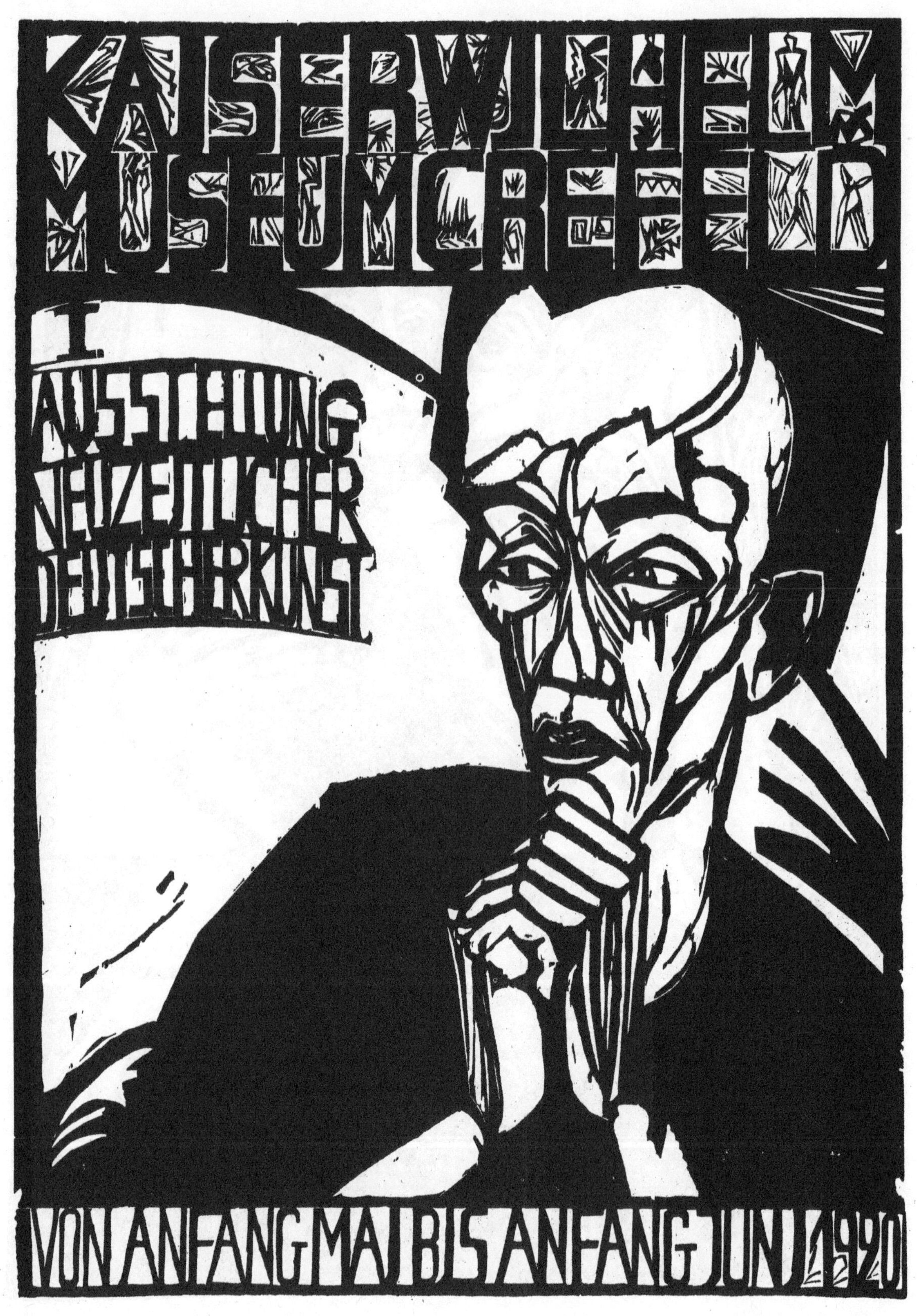

Erich Heckel. Poster. ["Kaiser Wilhelm Museum, Crefeld / First Exhibition of Modern German Art / From the Beginning of May to the Beginning of June 1920." The self-portrait is based on a work of 1919.]

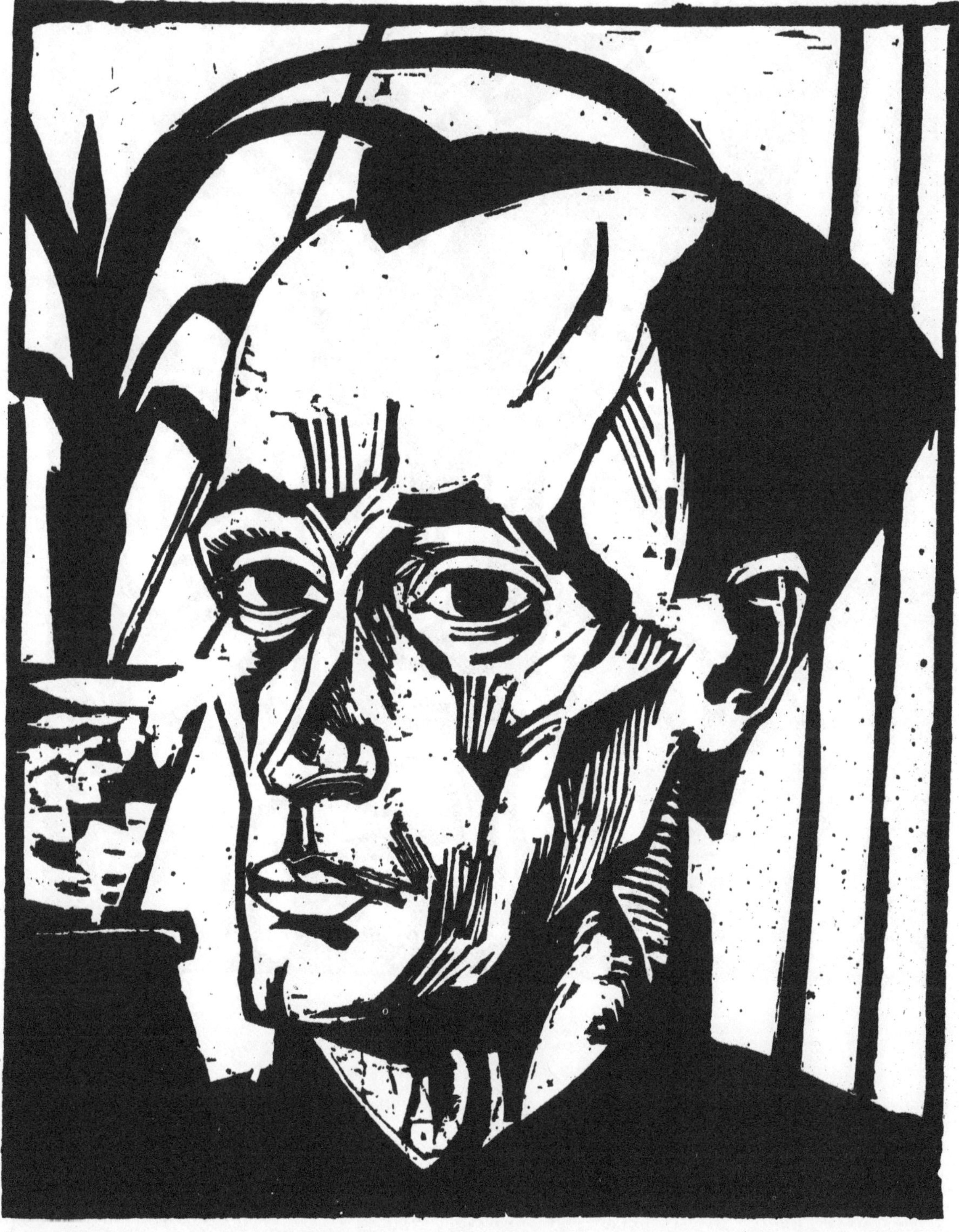

Erich Heckel. Cover for *Der Anbruch* (the beginning), 1919.

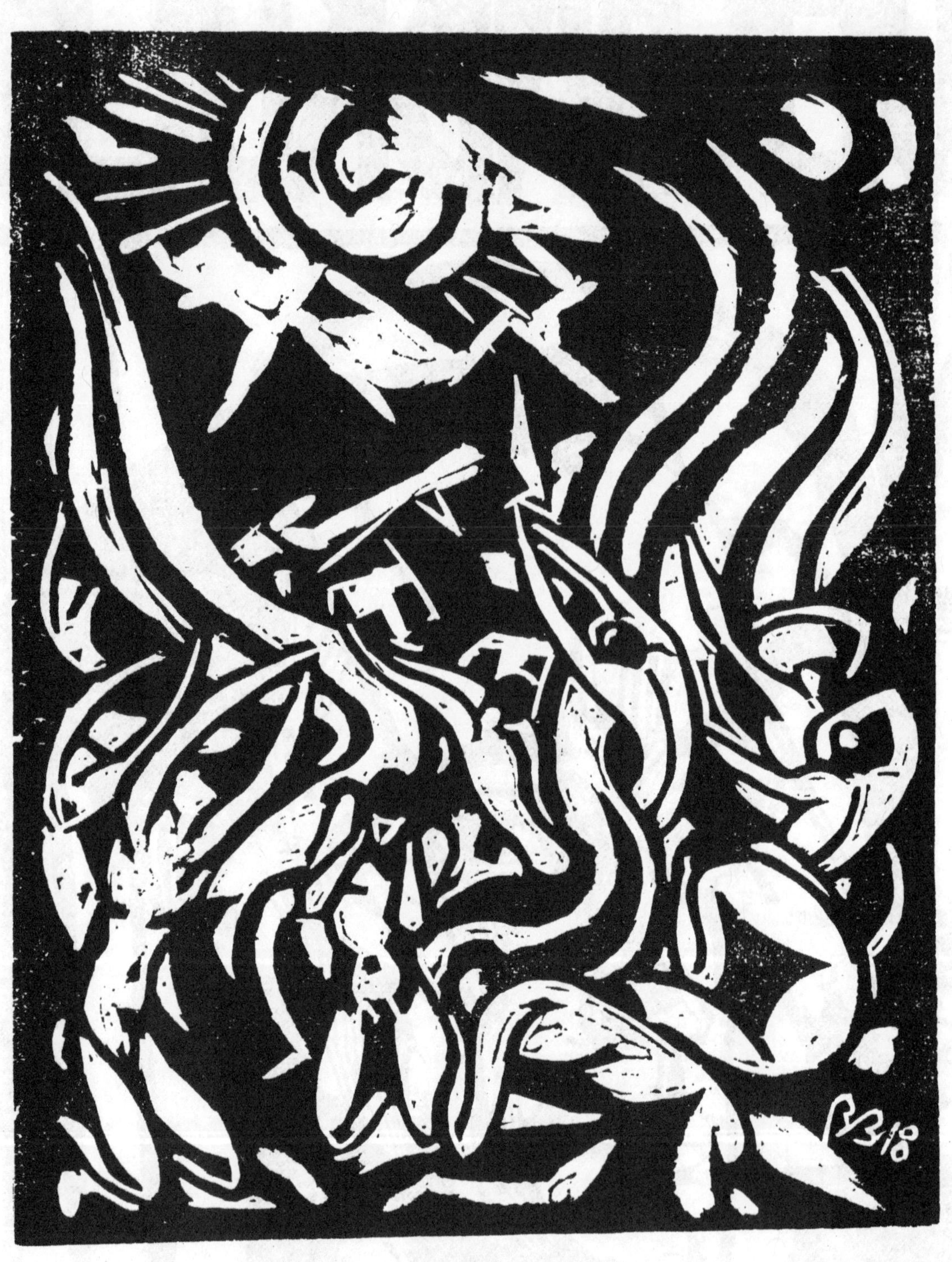

 Karl-Luis Heinrich-Salze. *Nudes in a Forest*, 1918.

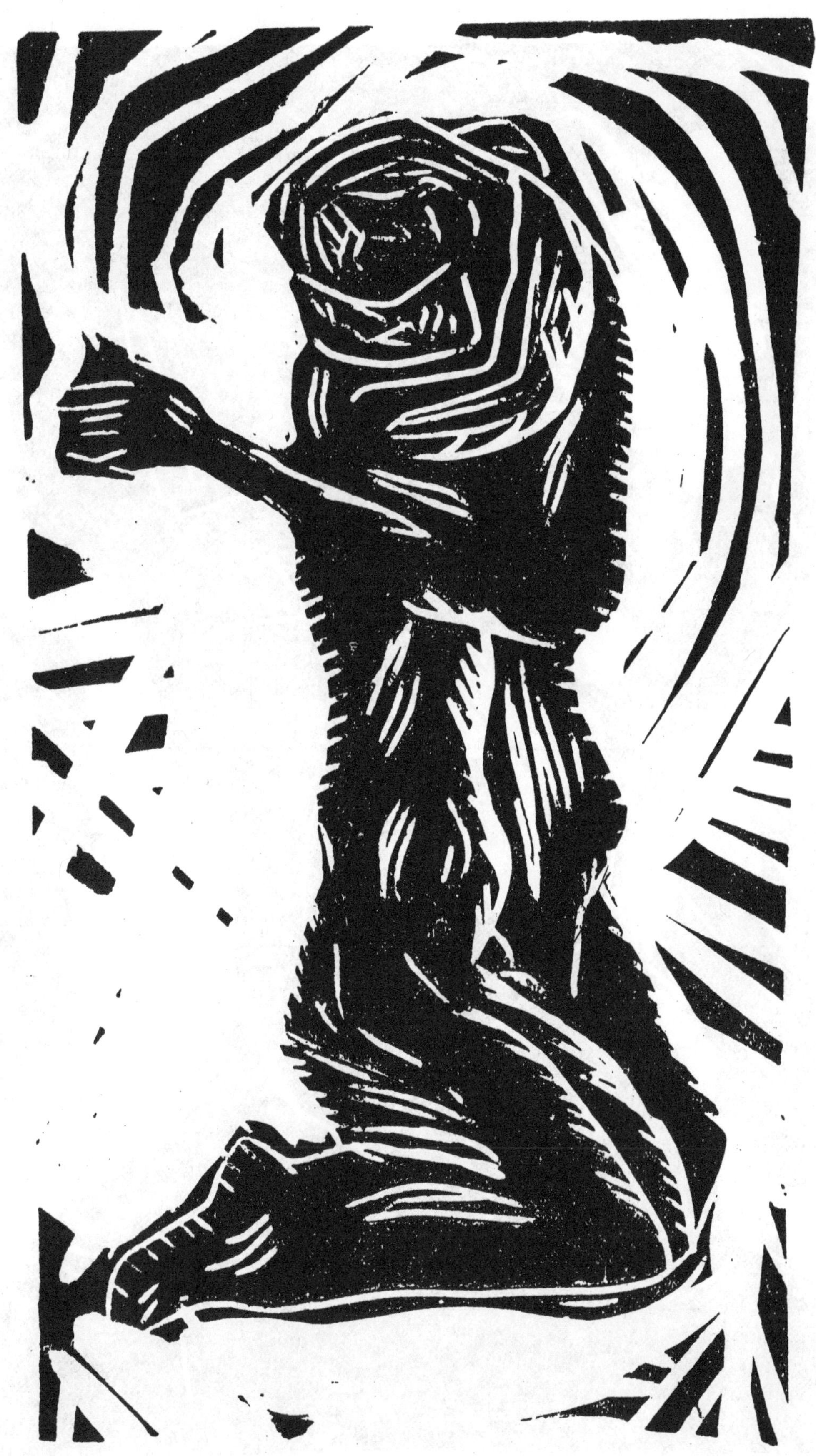

Karl Jakob Hirsch. Untitled, 1916.

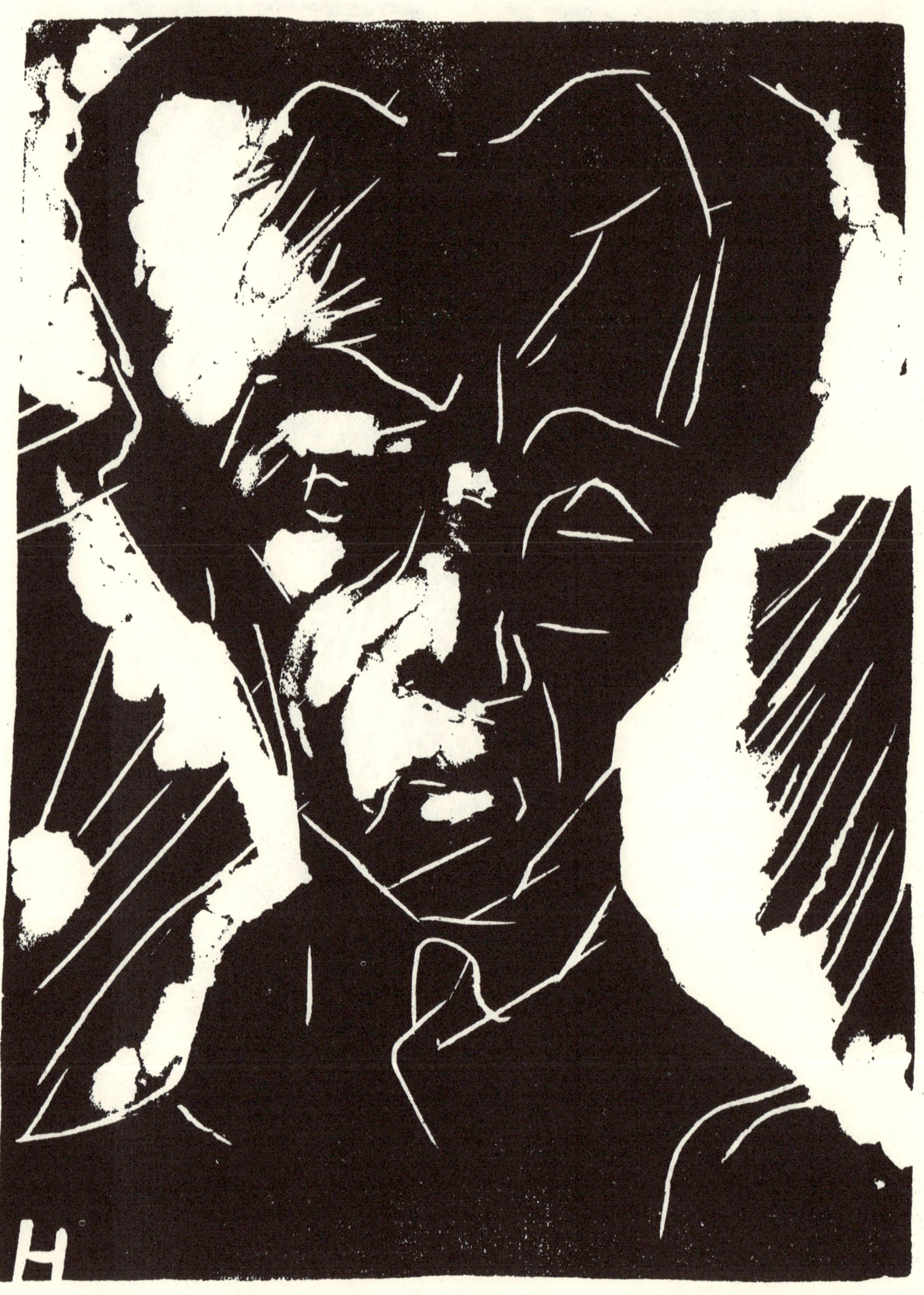

Karl Jakob Hirsch. *Self-portrait*, 1915.

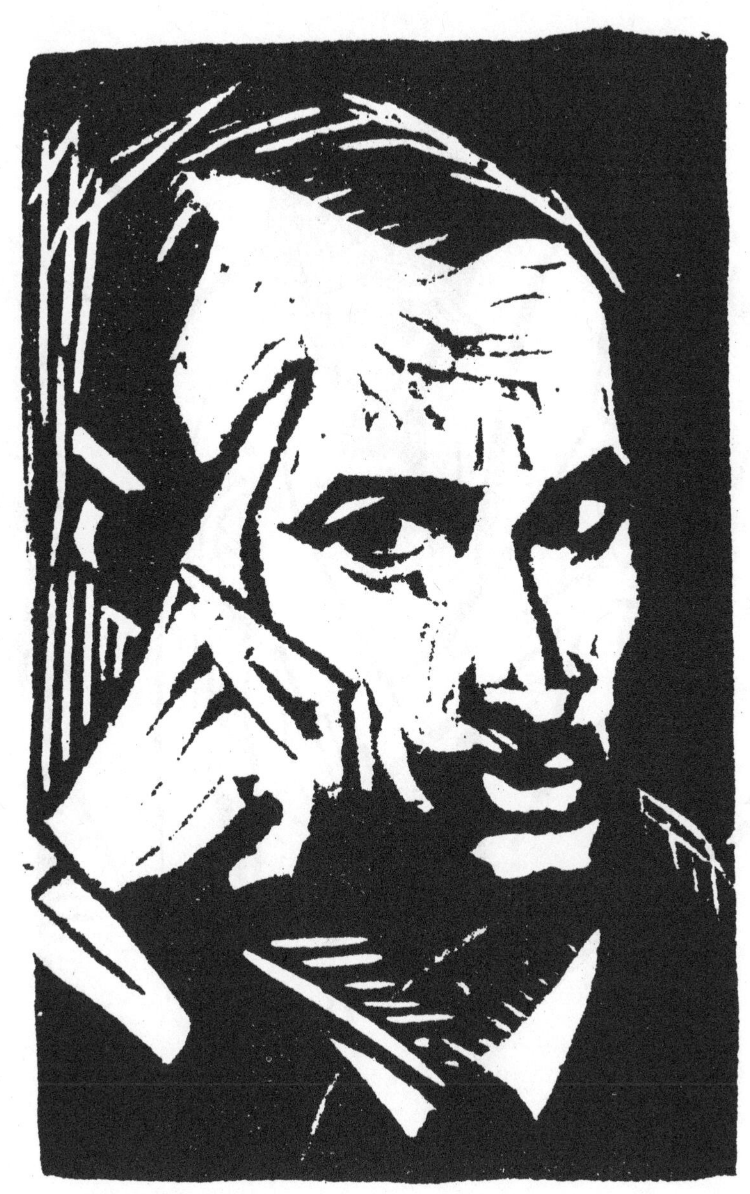

Jerzy Hulewicz. *Portrait*, 1918.

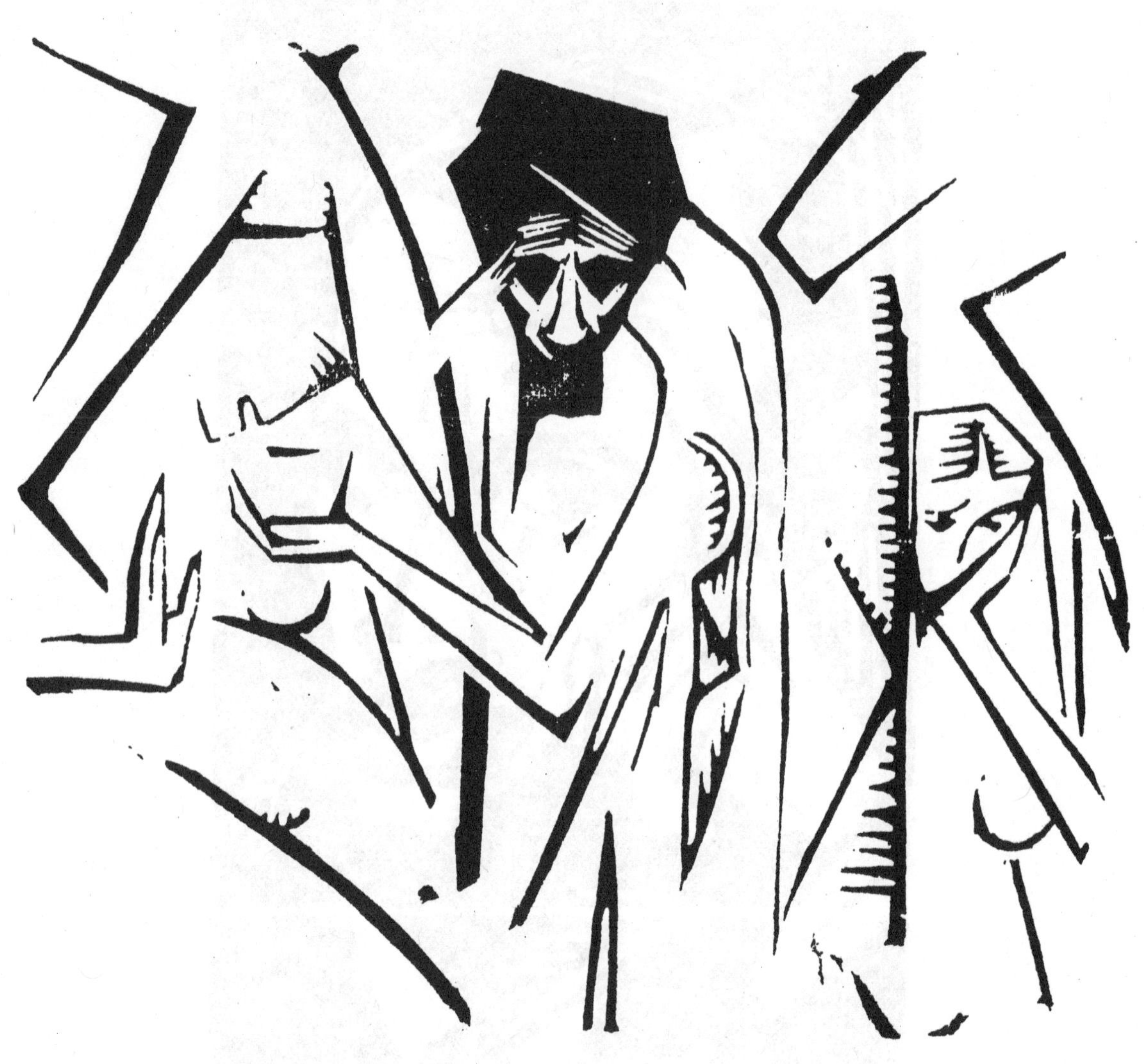

Jerzy Hulewicz. *Self-portrait*, 1918.

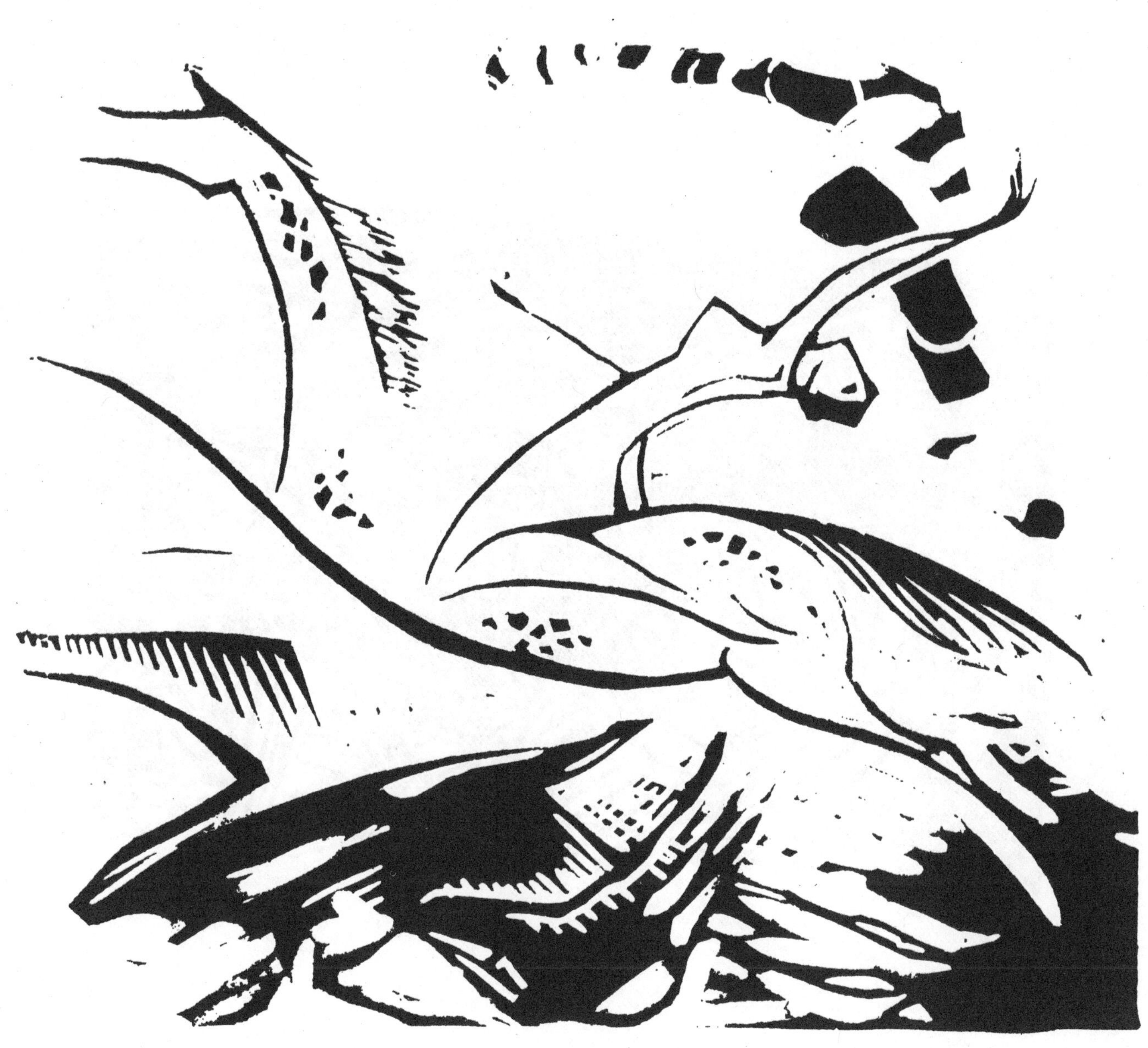

Jerzy Hulewicz. *Amazon*, 1918.

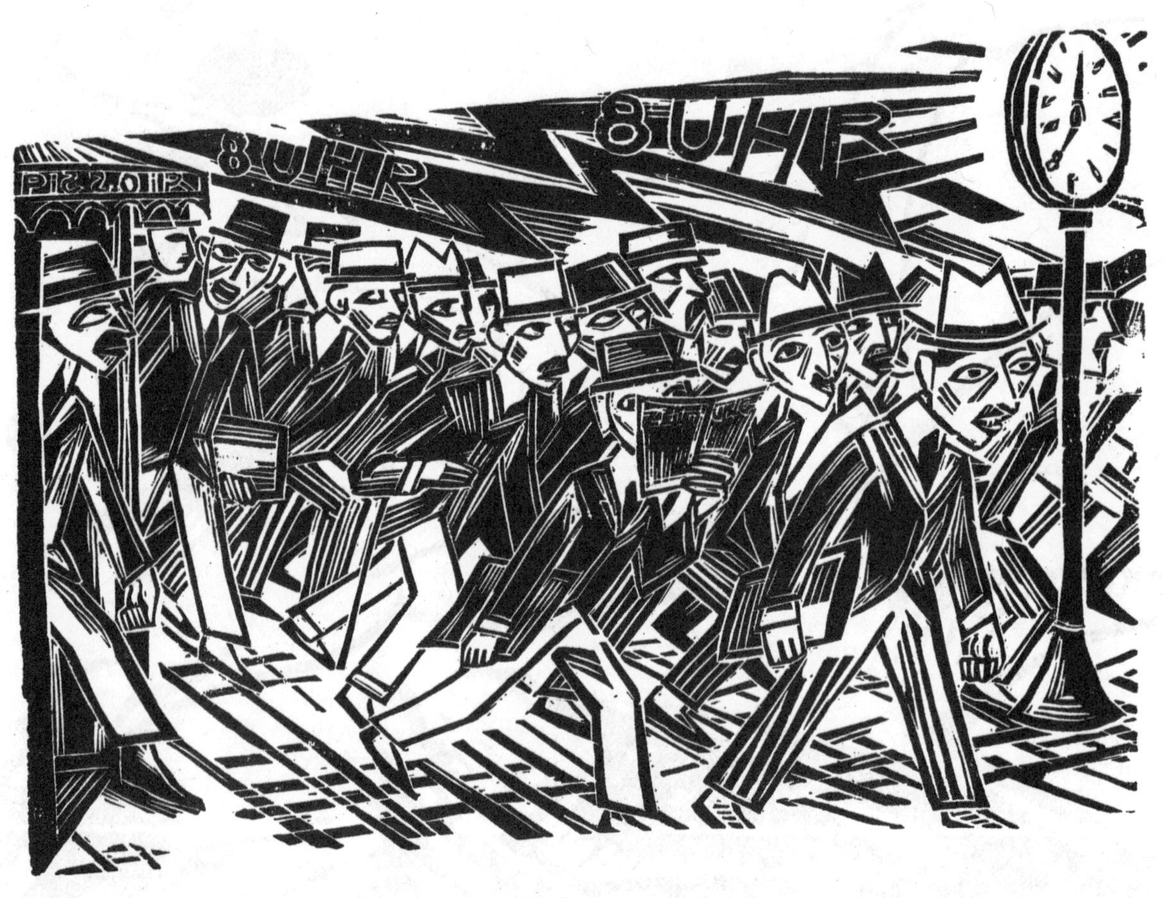

Franz M. Jansen. *8 O'Clock*, 1920.

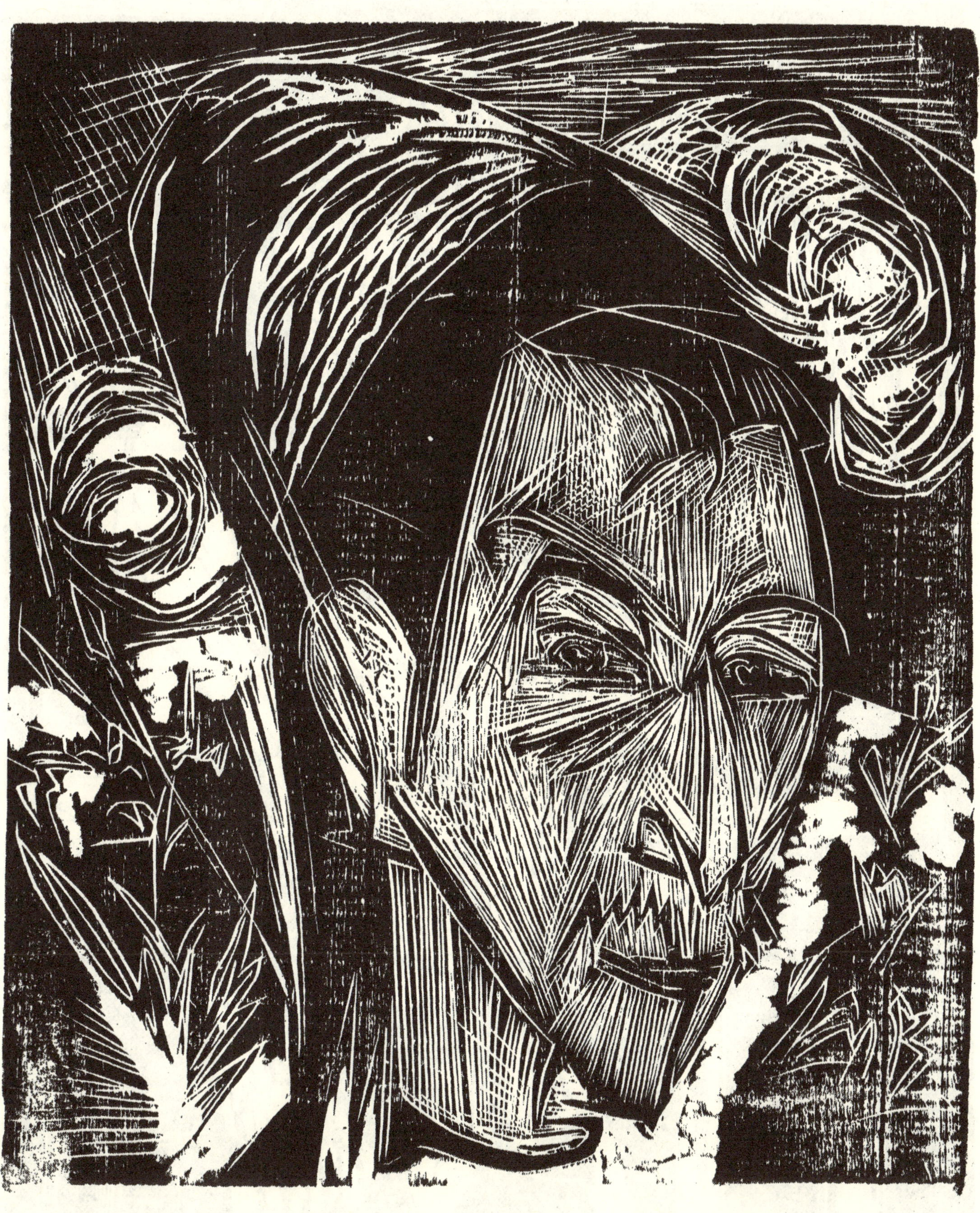

Ernst Ludwig Kirchner. *Head of David Müller*, 1919.

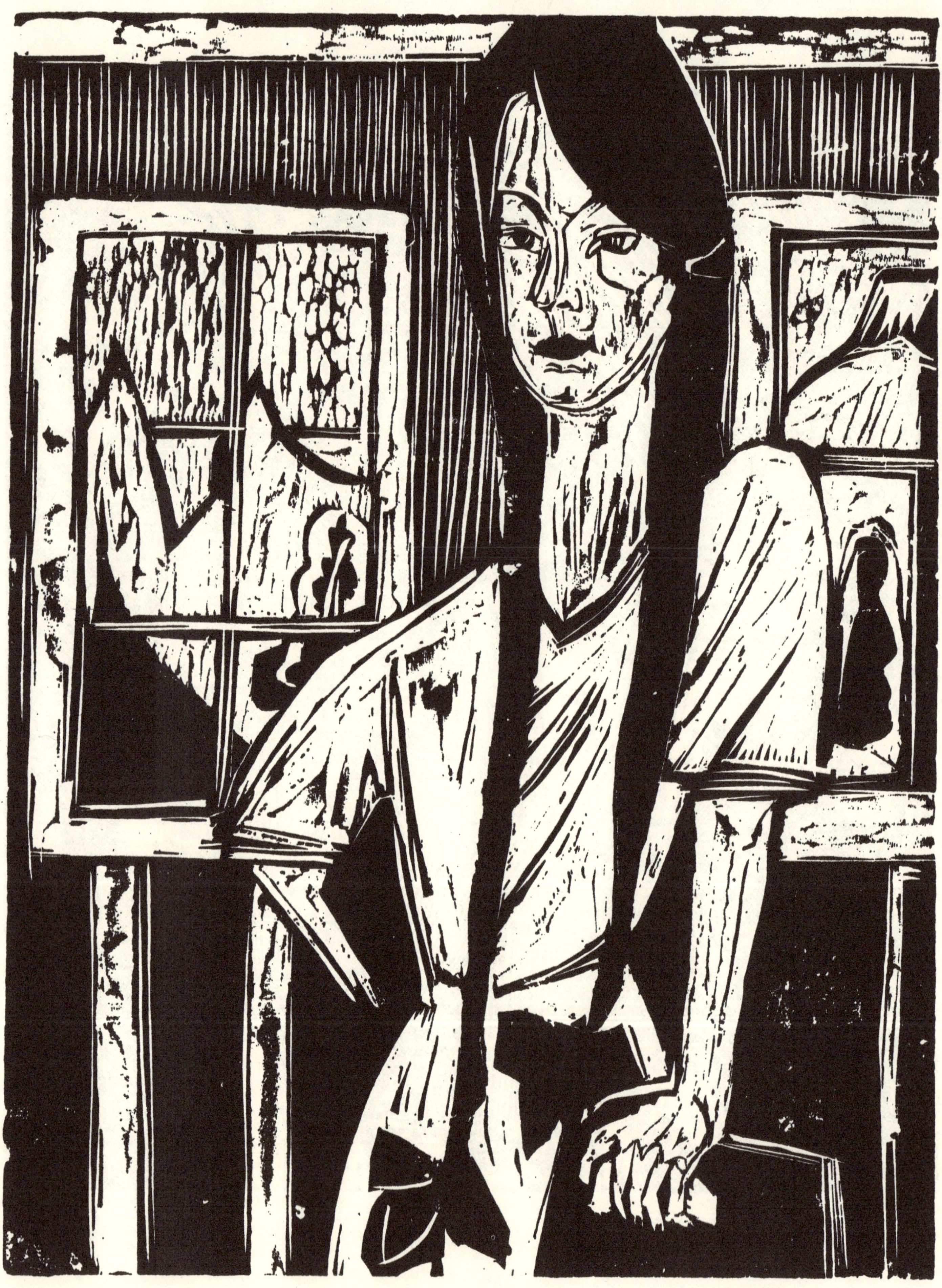

 Ernst Ludwig Kirchner. *Young Girl*, 1919.

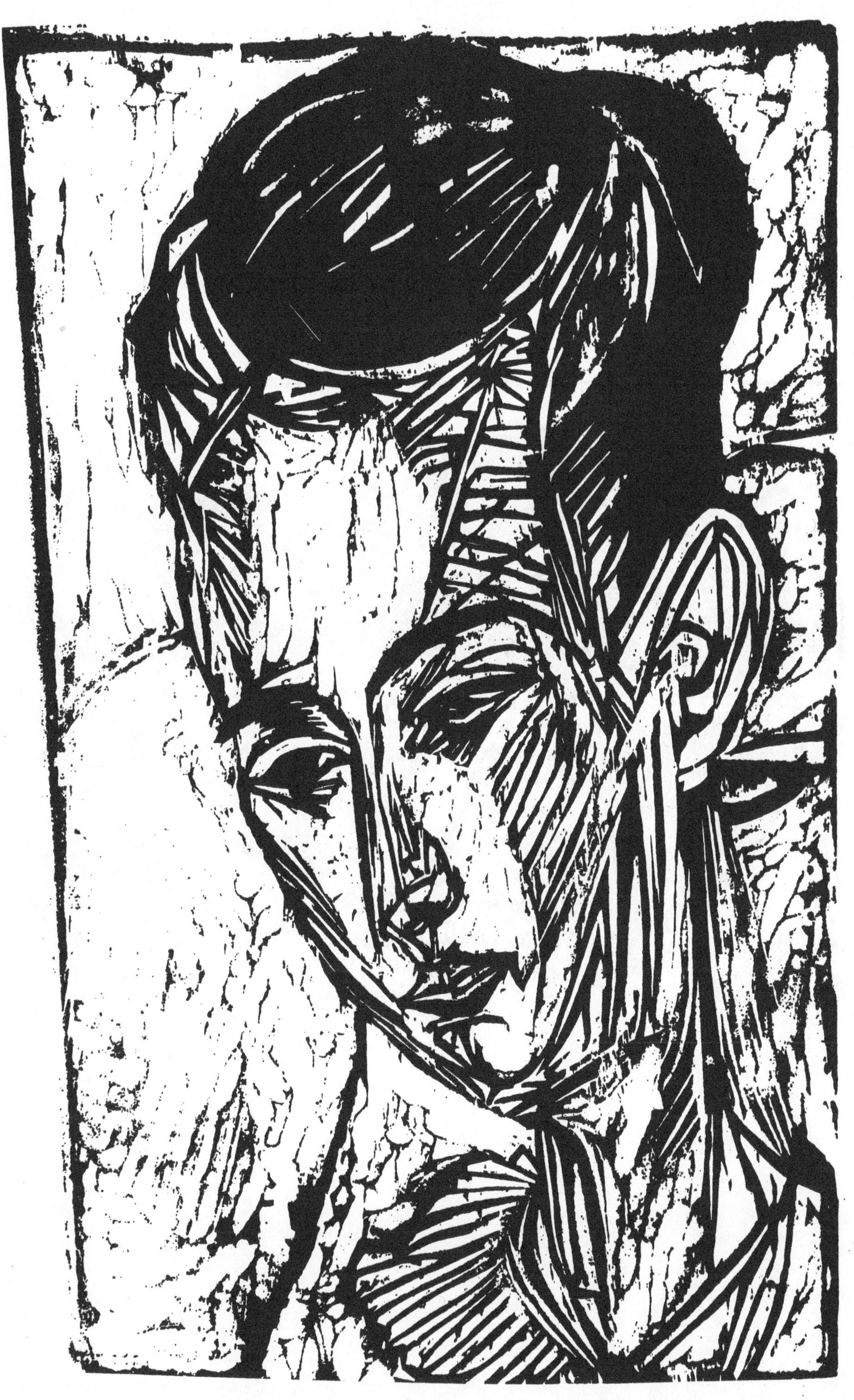

Ernst Ludwig Kirchner. *Head of Miss Hardt*, 1914.

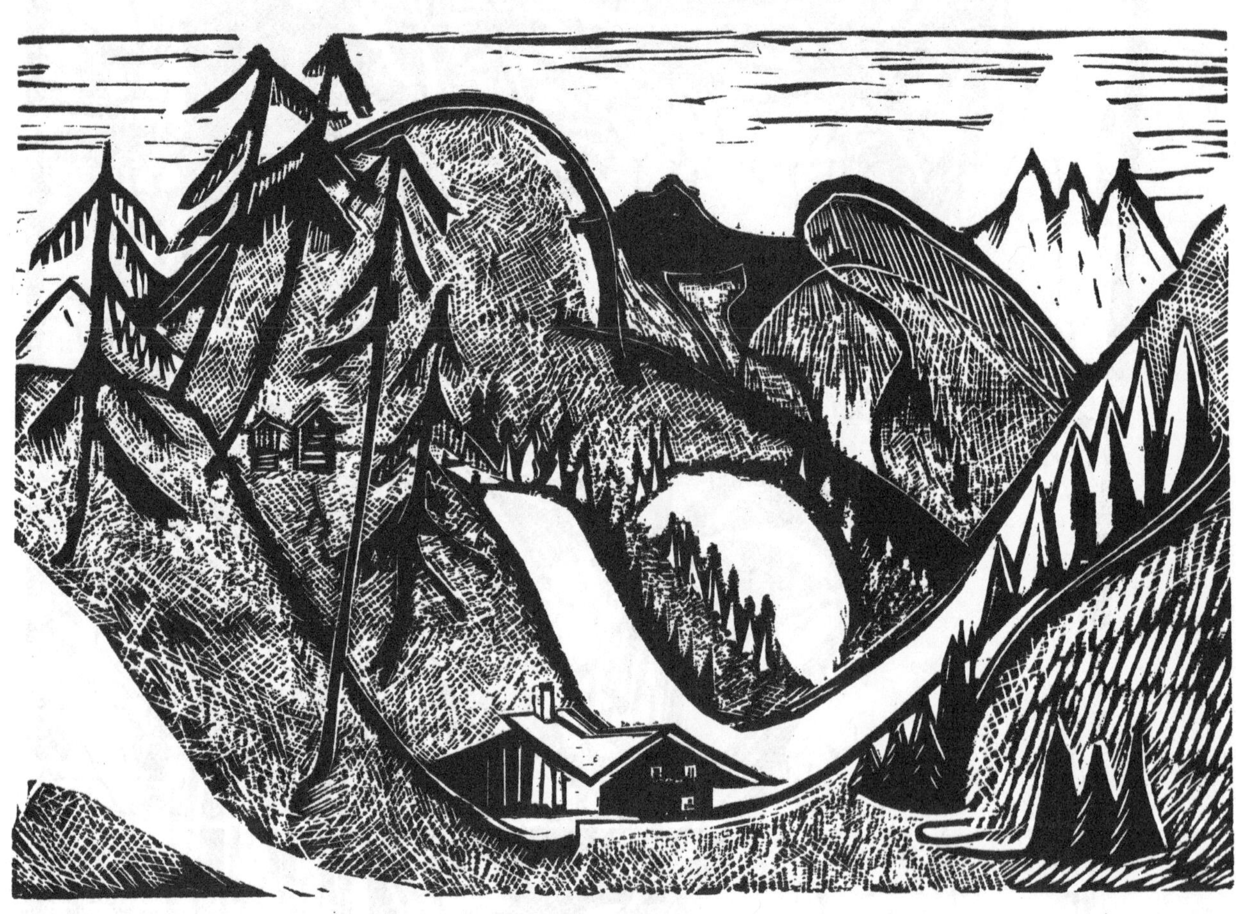

Ernst Ludwig Kirchner. *Mountain Landscape near Glarus* [Switzerland], 1933.

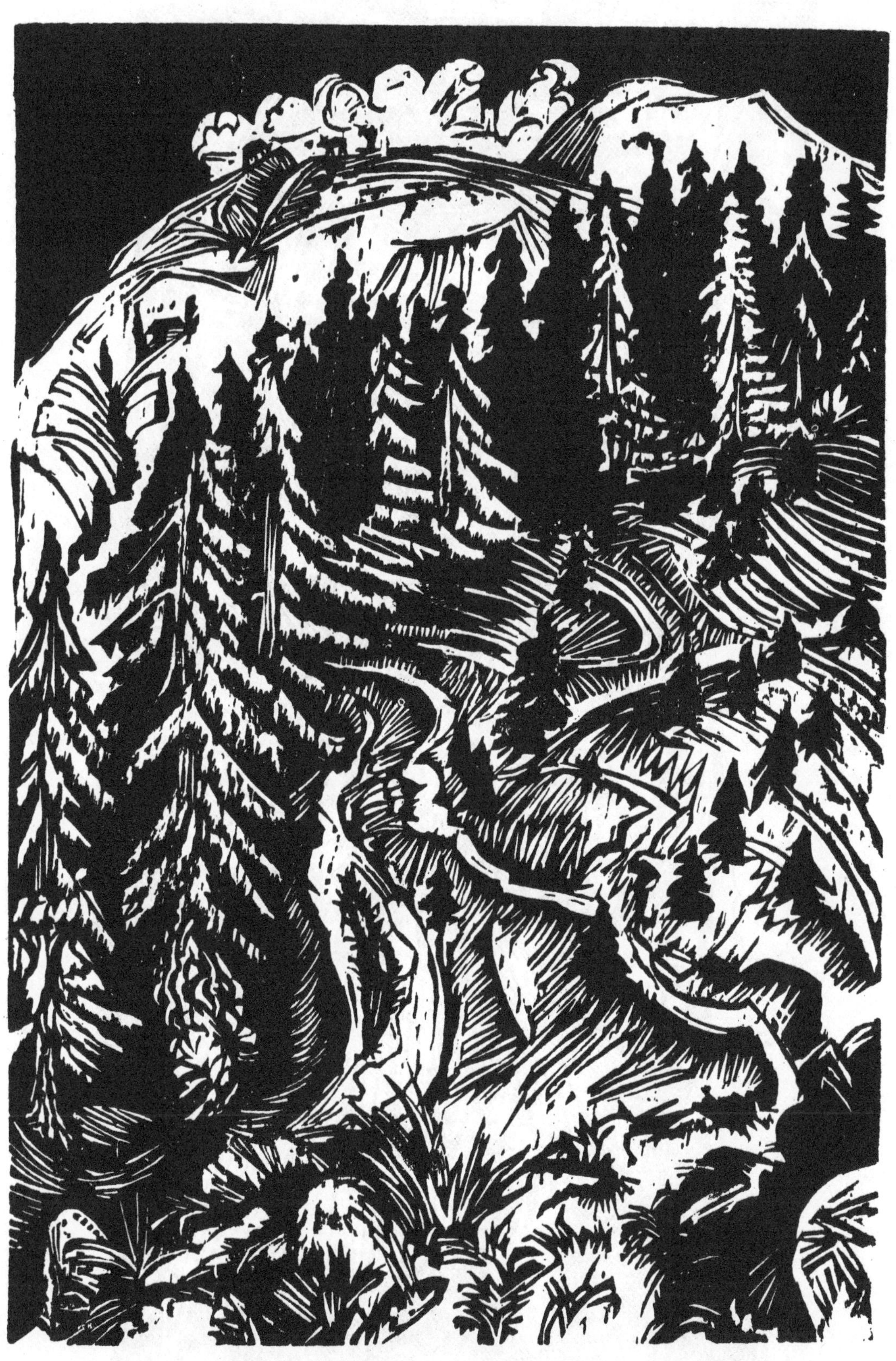

Ernst Ludwig Kirchner. *Three Paths*, 1917.

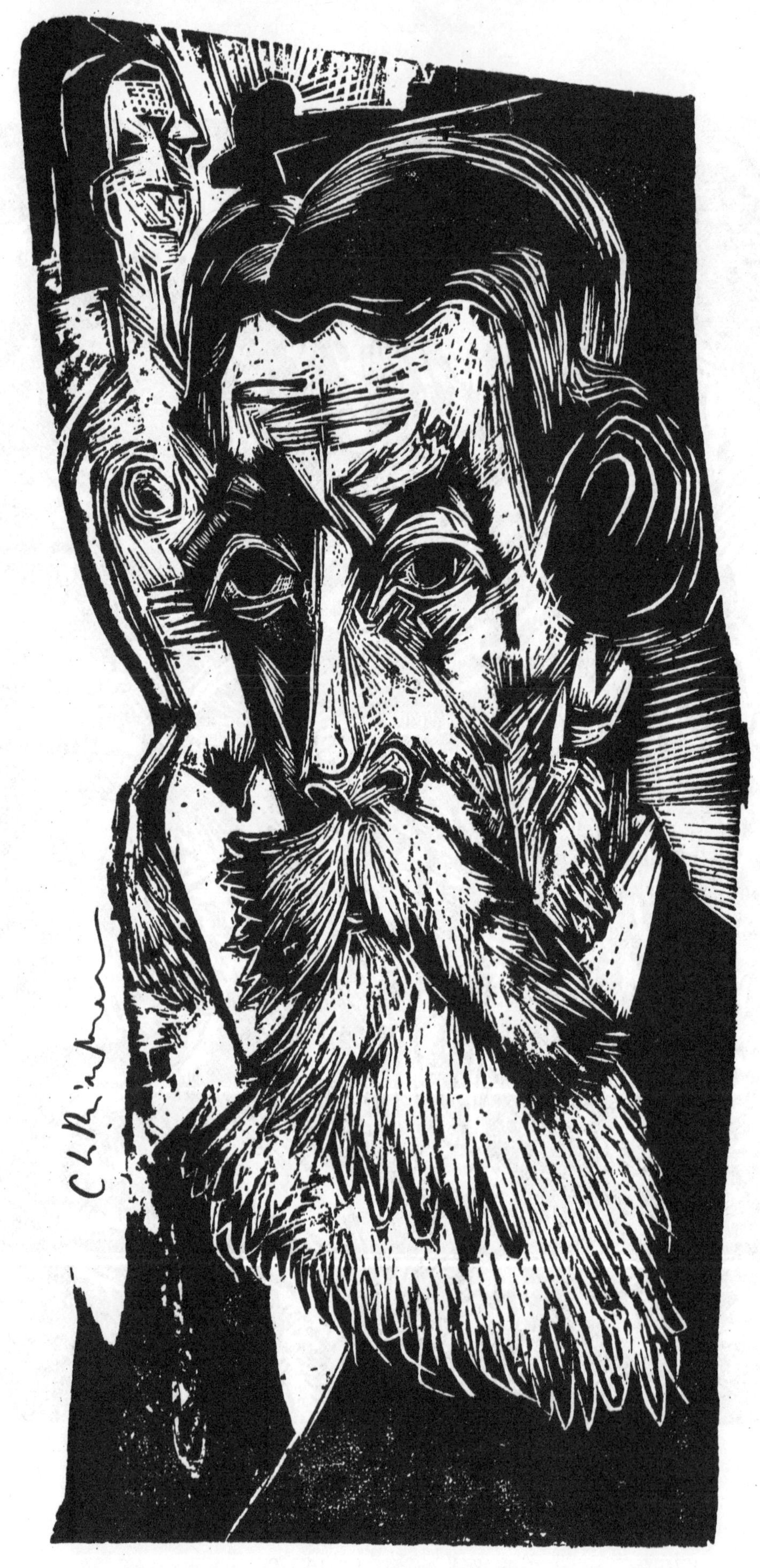

Ernst Ludwig Kirchner. *Head of Ludwig Shames* [Kirchner's Frankfurt dealer], 1918.

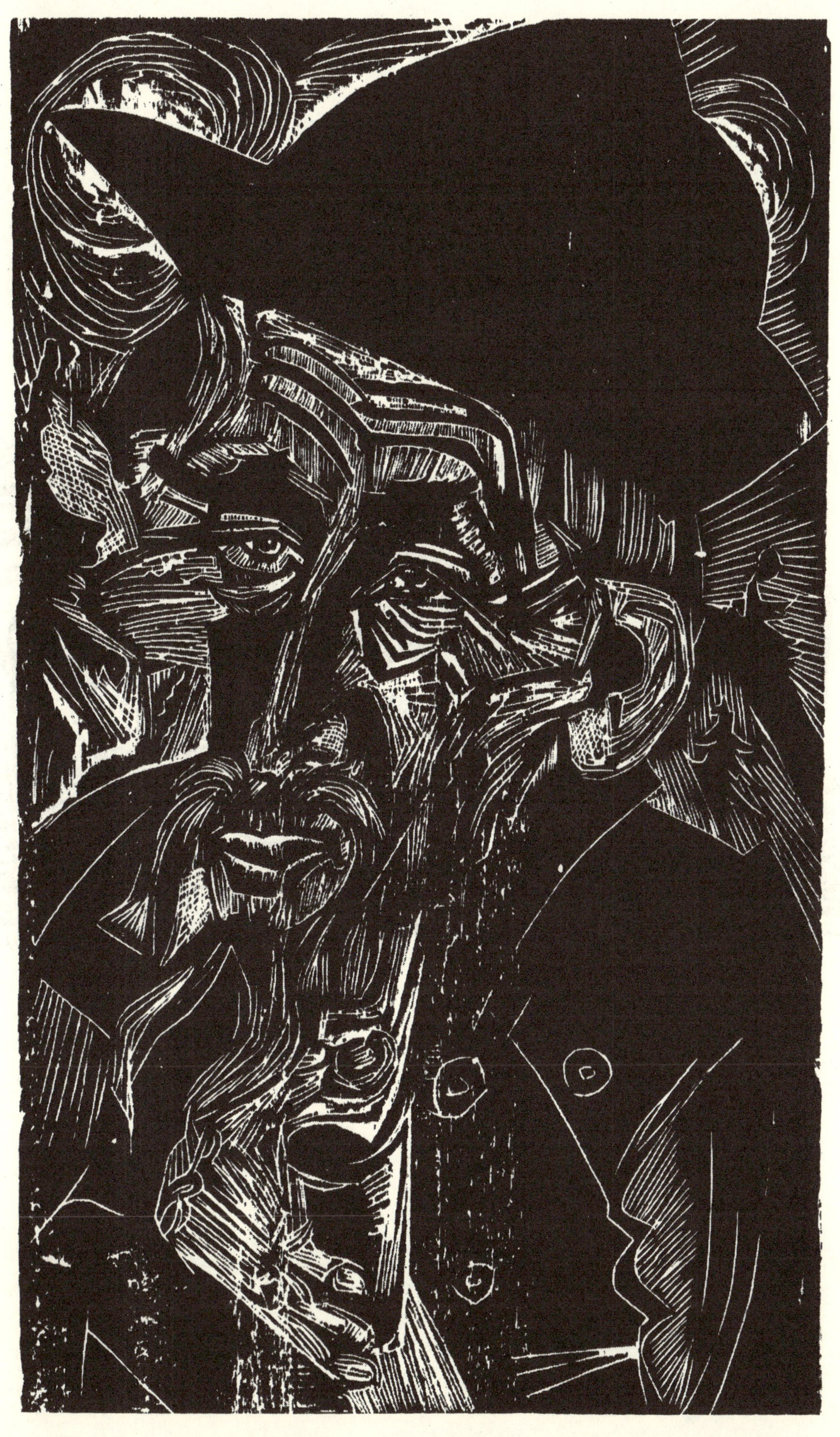

Ernst Ludwig Kirchner. *Old Man from the Alps with Black Hat and Beard*, 1919.

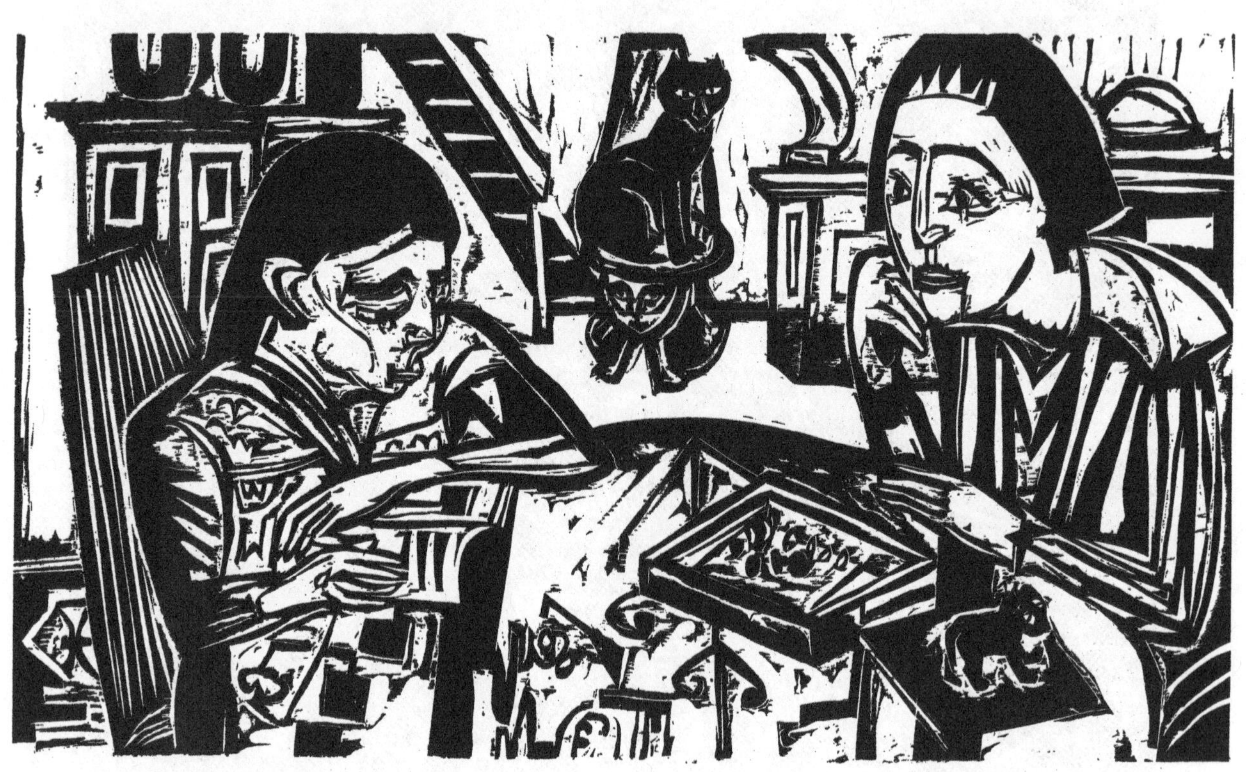

Ernst Ludwig Kirchner. *Work at Table*, 1923.

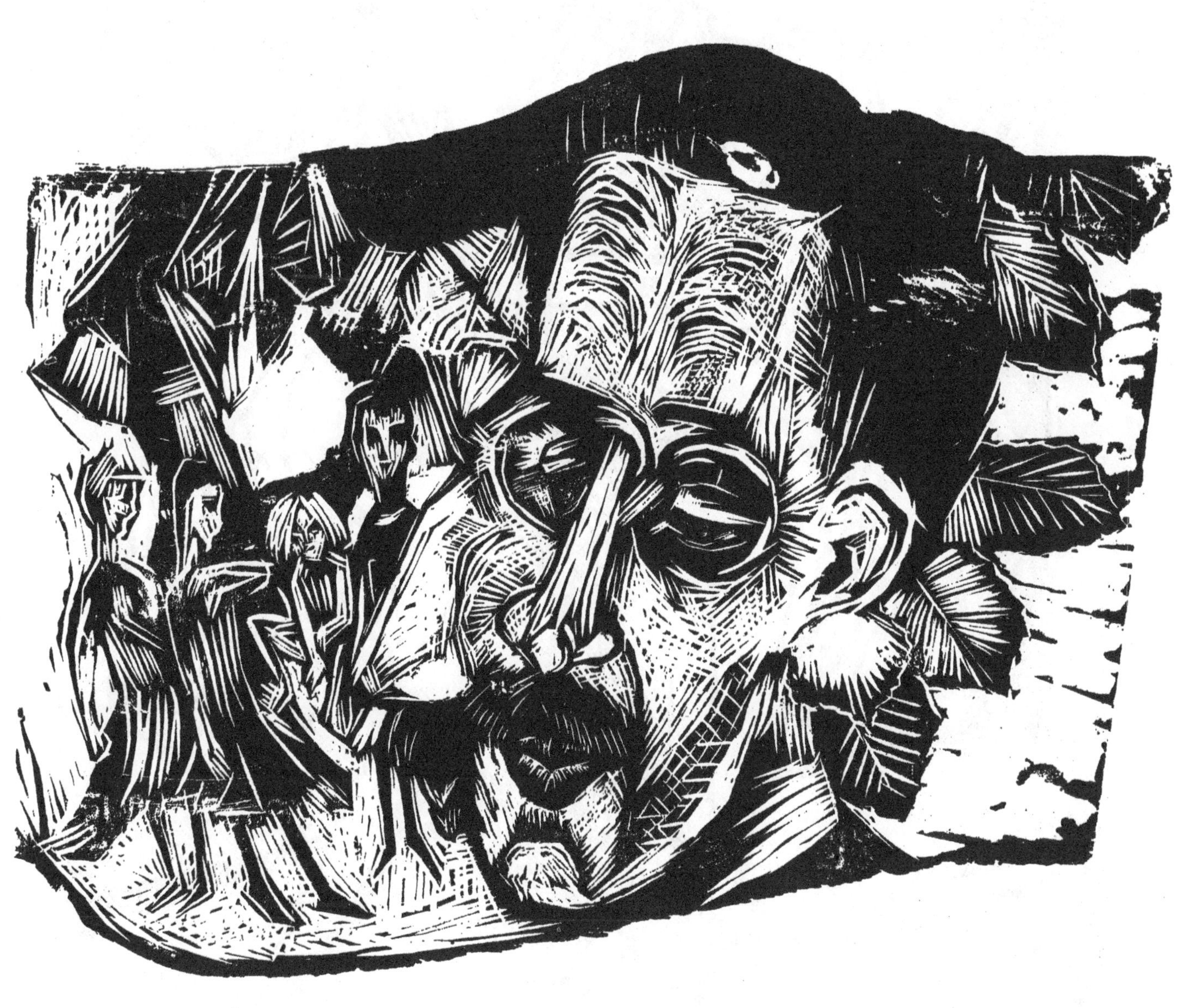

Ernst Ludwig Kirchner. *Head of Dr. Ludwig Binswanger* [director of a sanatorium at which Kirchner stayed] *and Little Girls*, 1917–18.

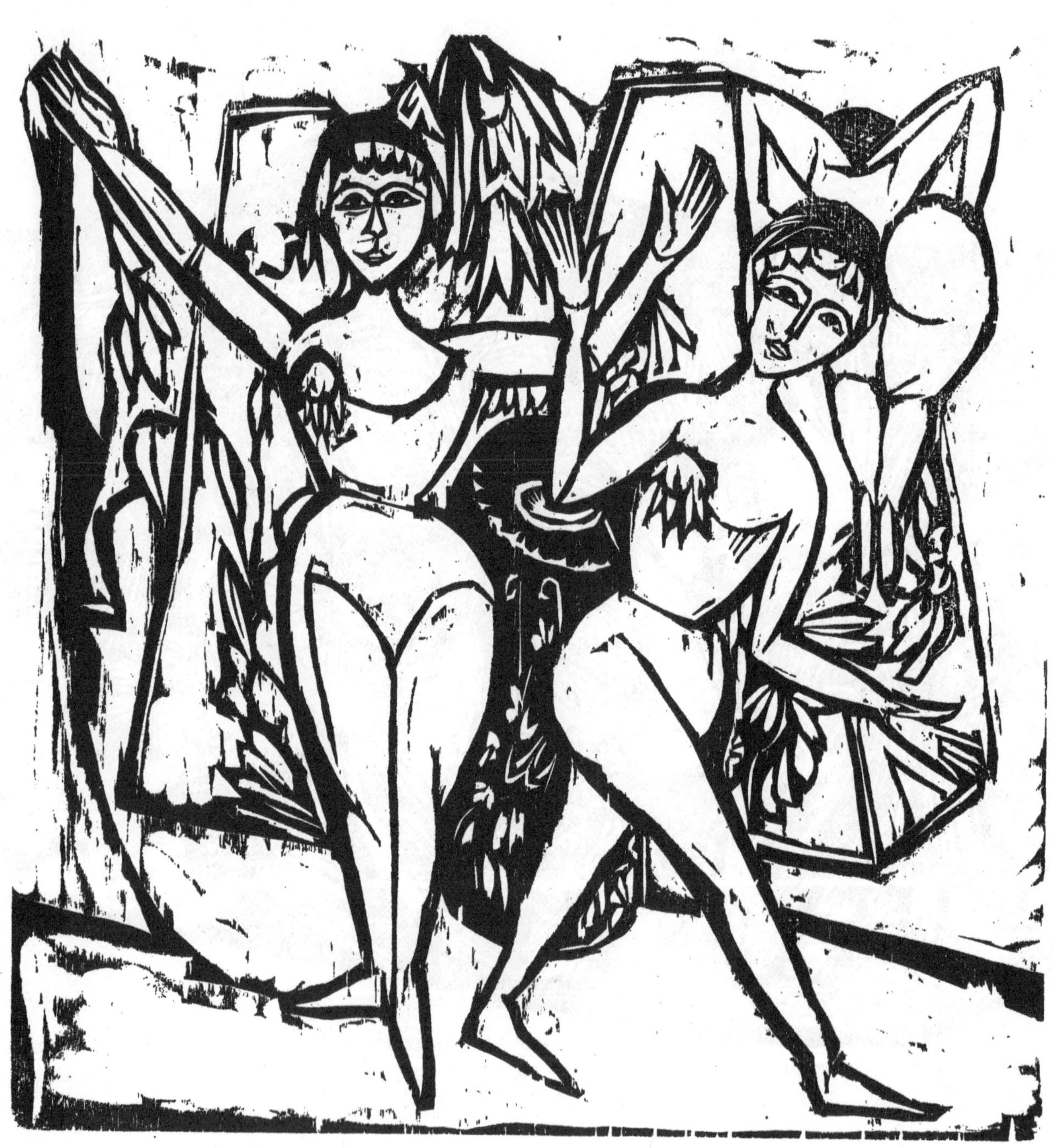

Ernst Ludwig Kirchner. *Vaudeville*, 1916.

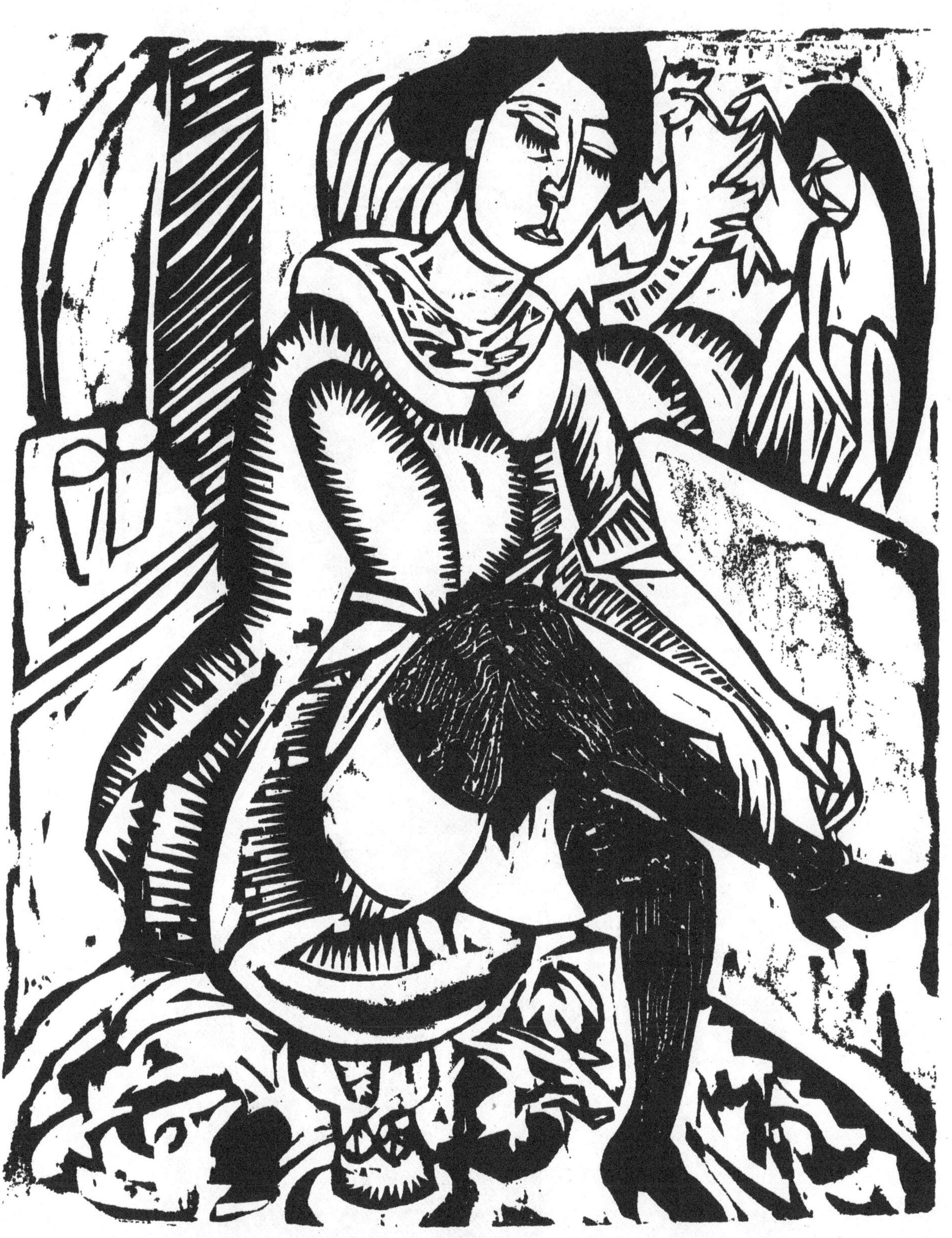

Ernst Ludwig Kirchner. *Woman Buttoning Shoe*, 1912.

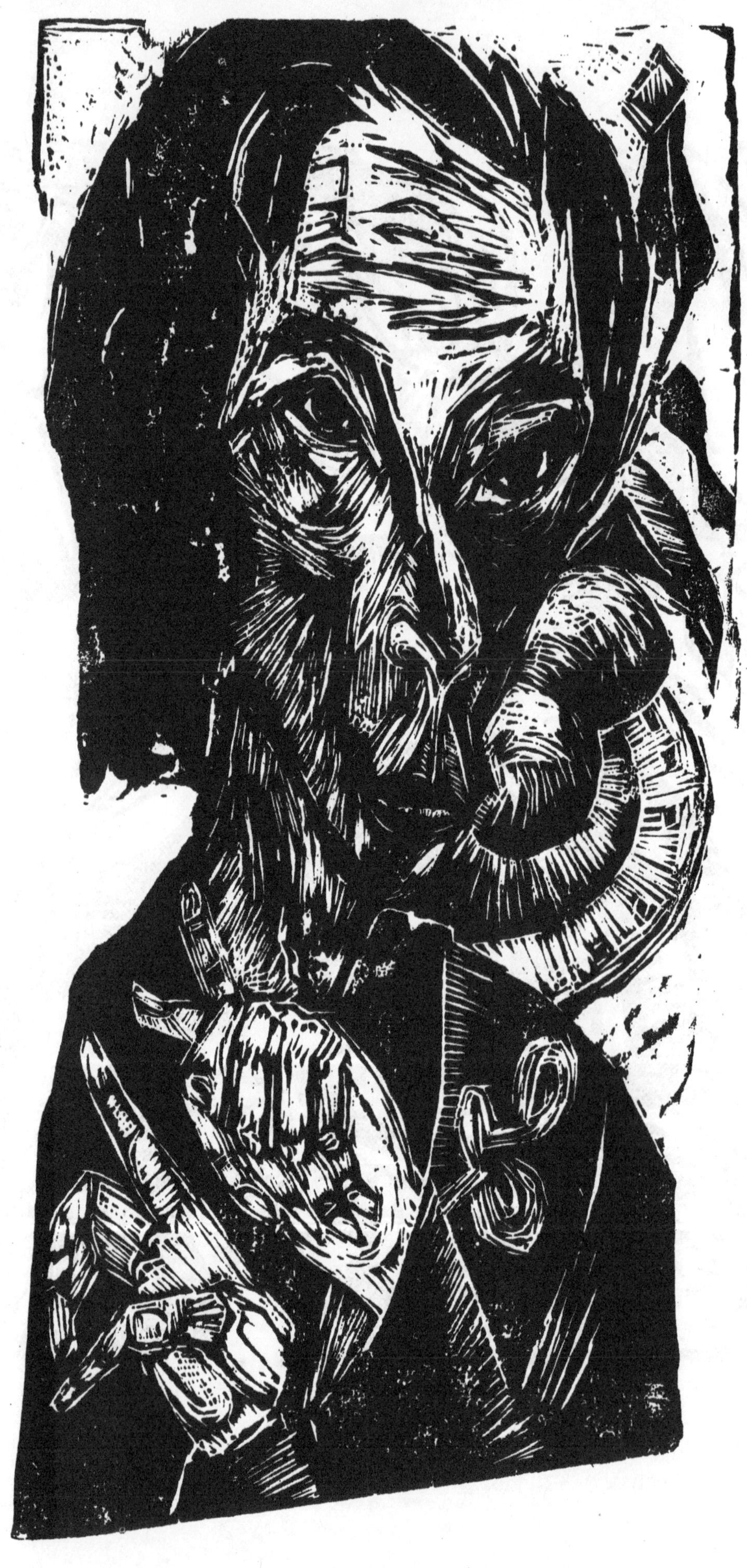

Ernst Ludwig Kirchner. *Head of the Sick Man (Self-portrait)*, 1917.

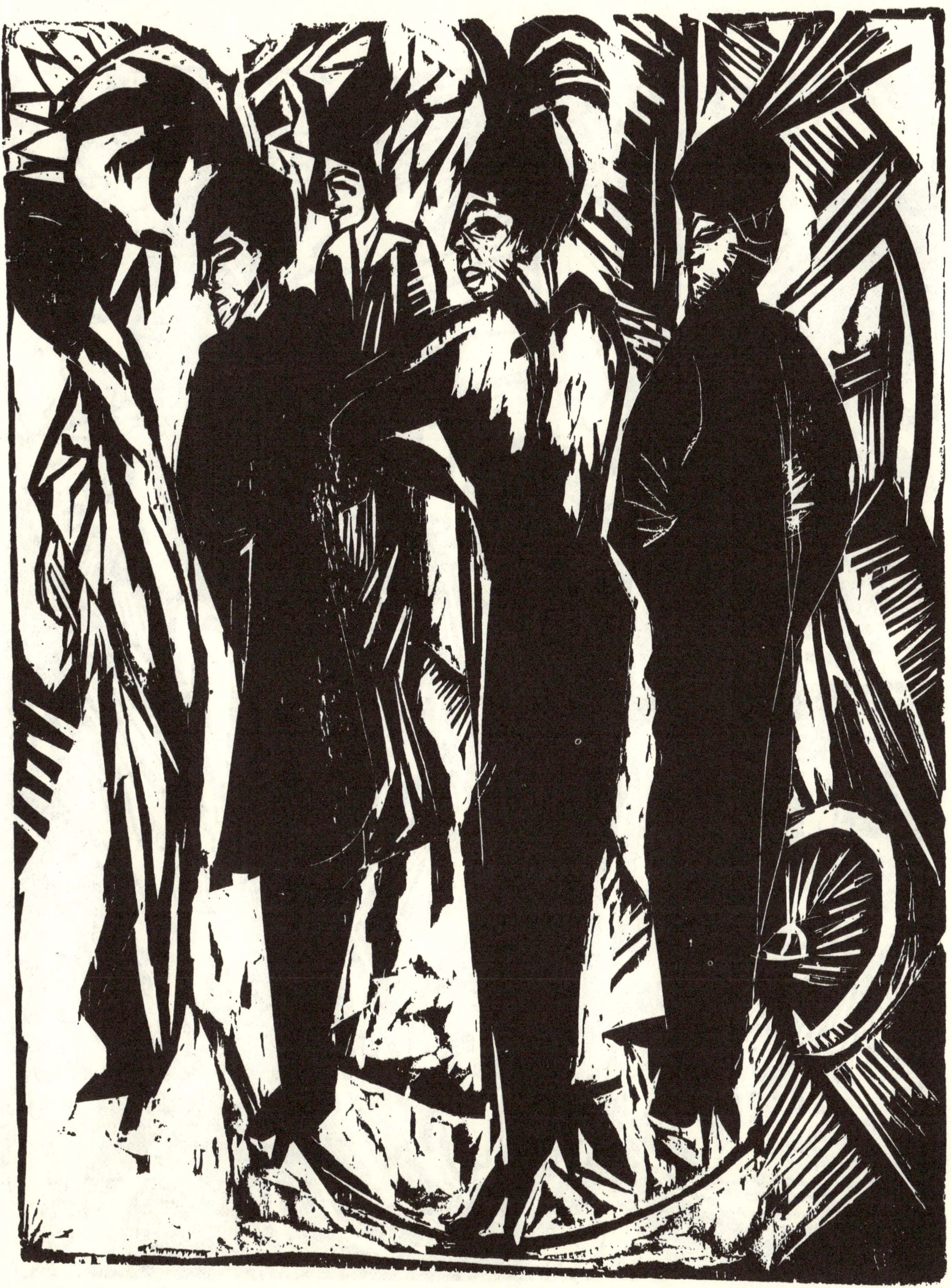

Ernst Ludwig Kirchner. *Street Scene*, 1922.

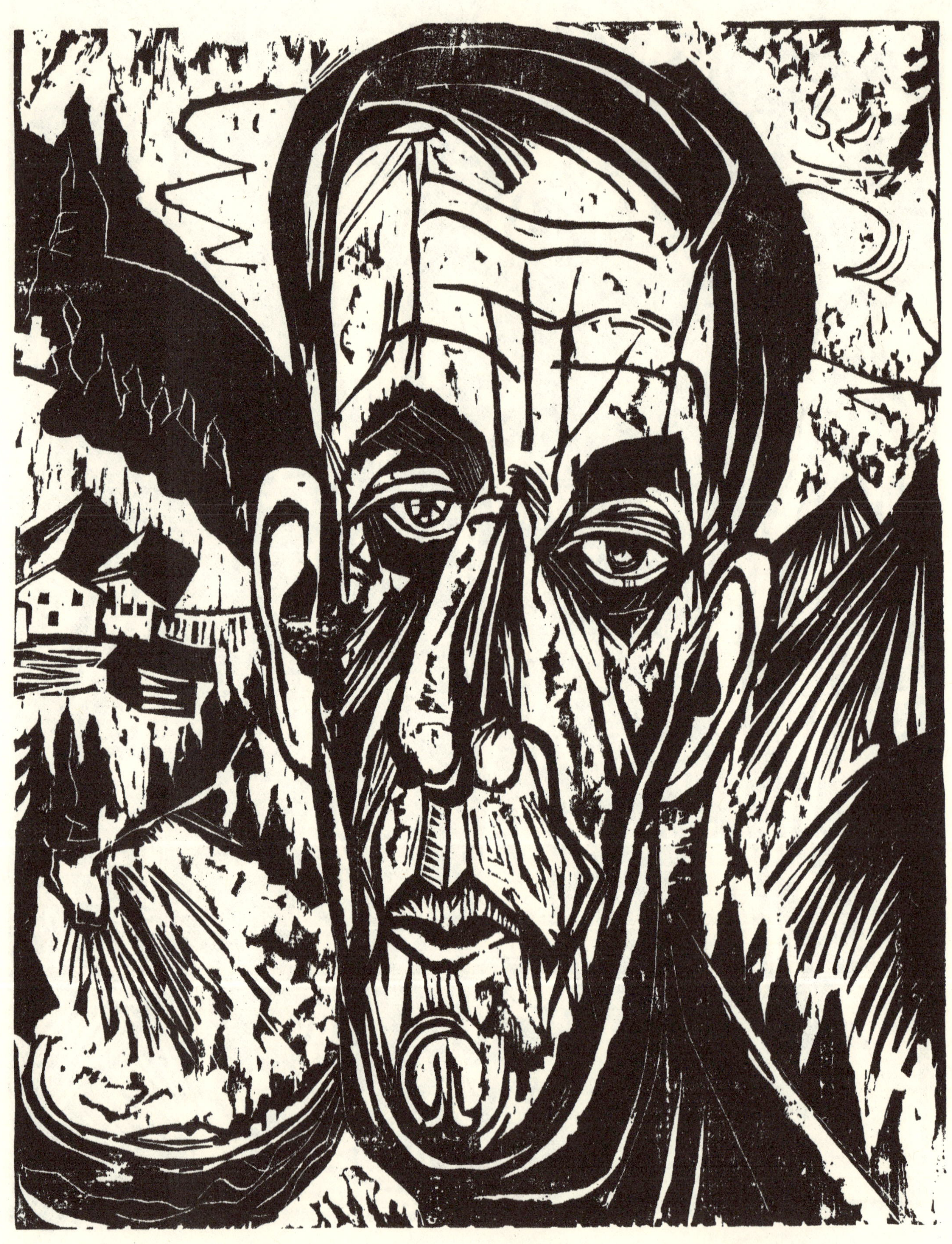

Ernst Ludwig Kirchner. *Head of Henry van de Velde* [Belgian artist and architect, 1863–1957], *Light*, 1917.

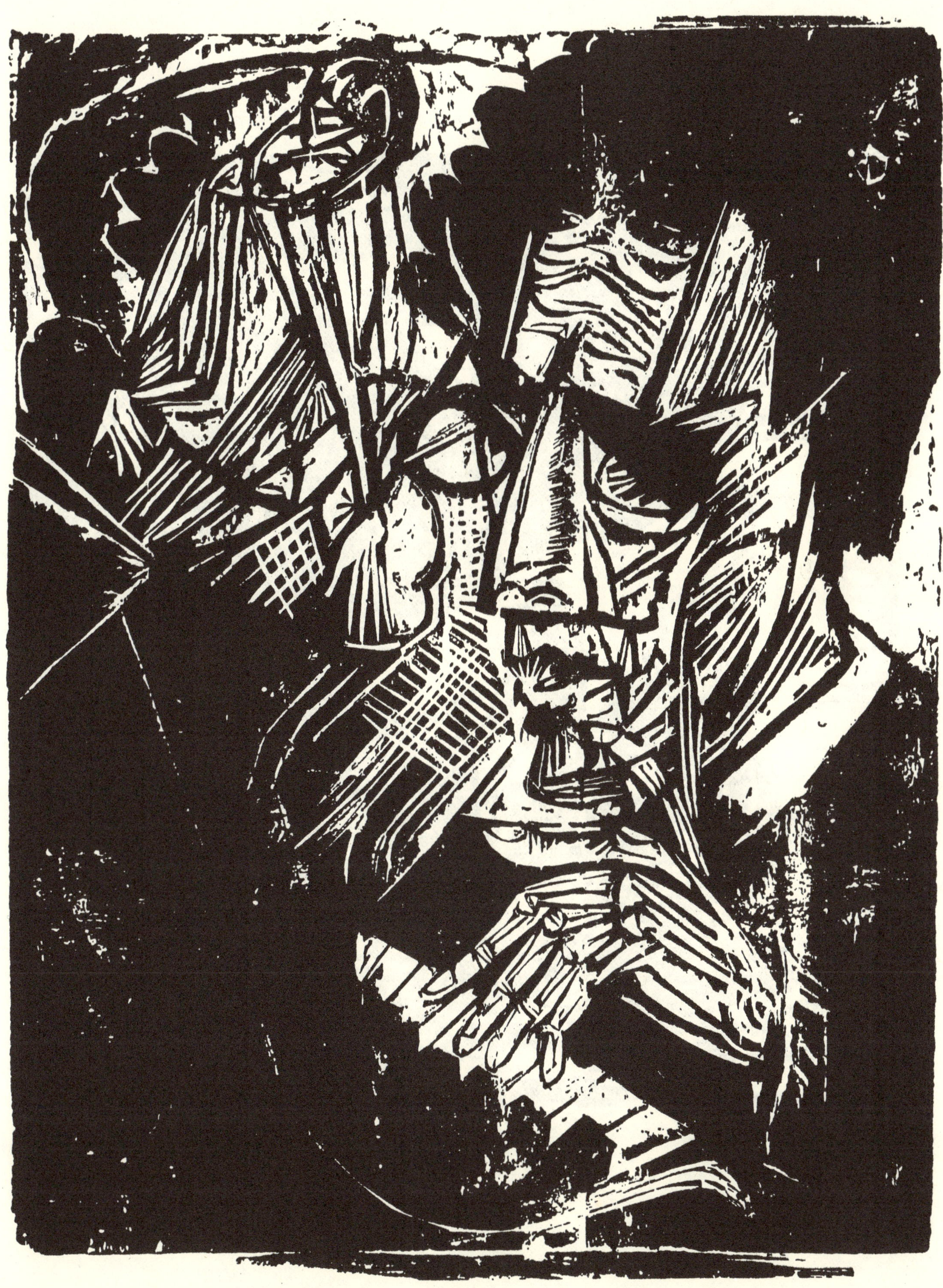

Ernst Ludwig Kirchner. *The Composer Otto Klemperer* [conductor, 1885–1973], 1916.

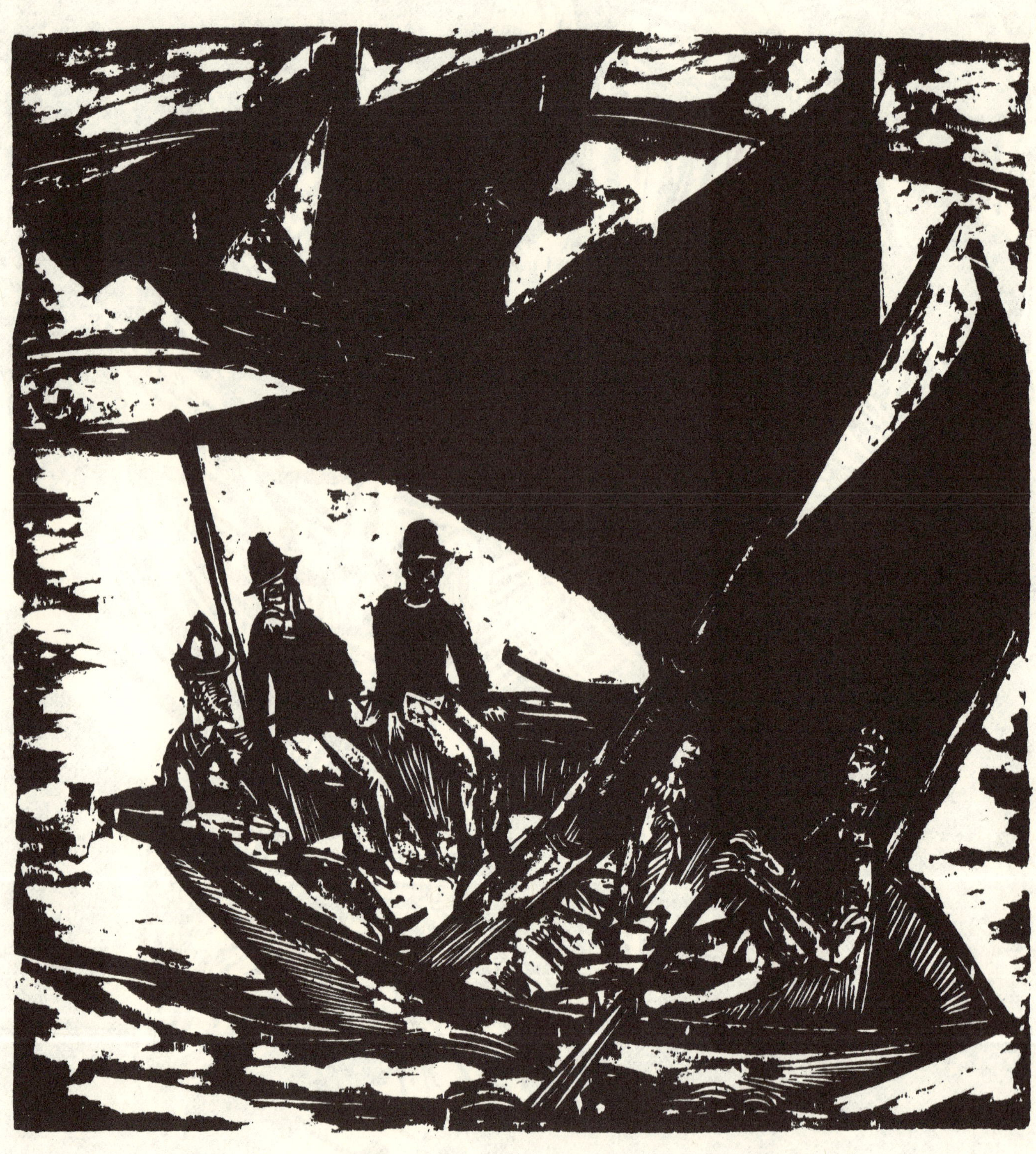

 Ernst Ludwig Kirchner. *Sailboats at Fehmarn*, 1914.

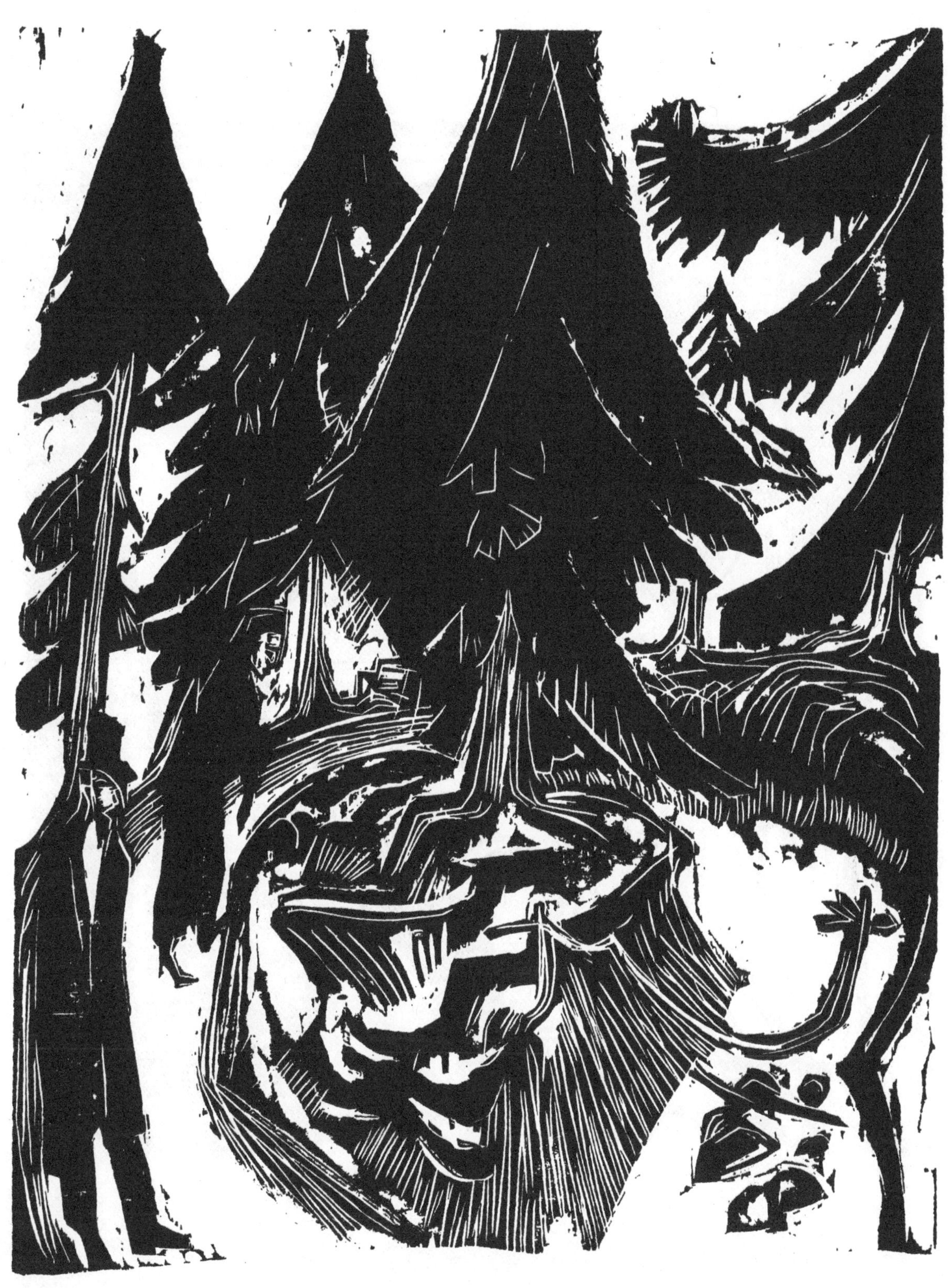

Ernst Ludwig Kirchner. *Stroll at the Sanatorium*, 1916.

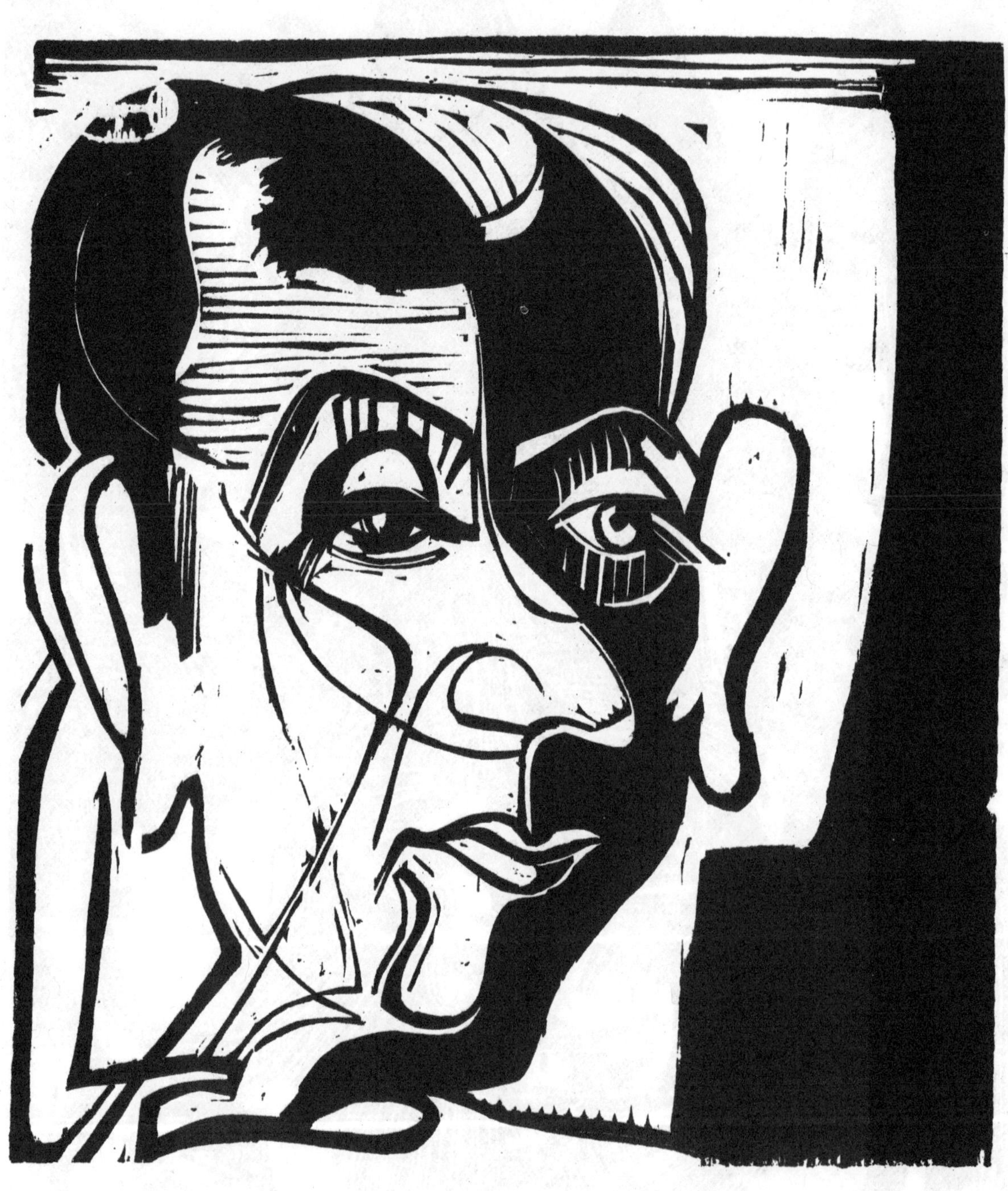

Ernst Ludwig Kirchner. *Portrait of Jean Arp* [French painter, sculptor and poet, 1887–1966], 1933.

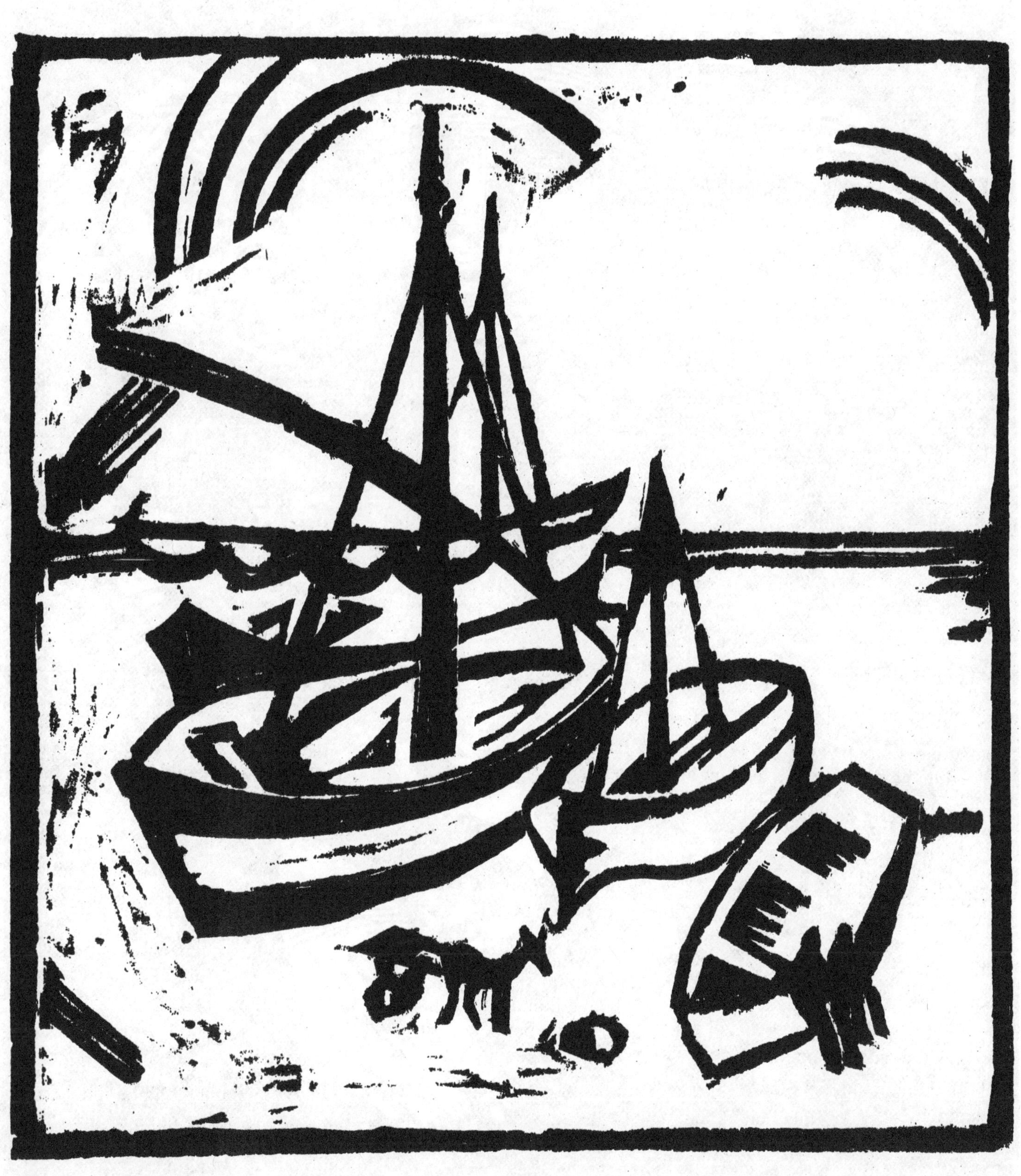

César Klein. *Fishing Boats on the Beach*, n.d.

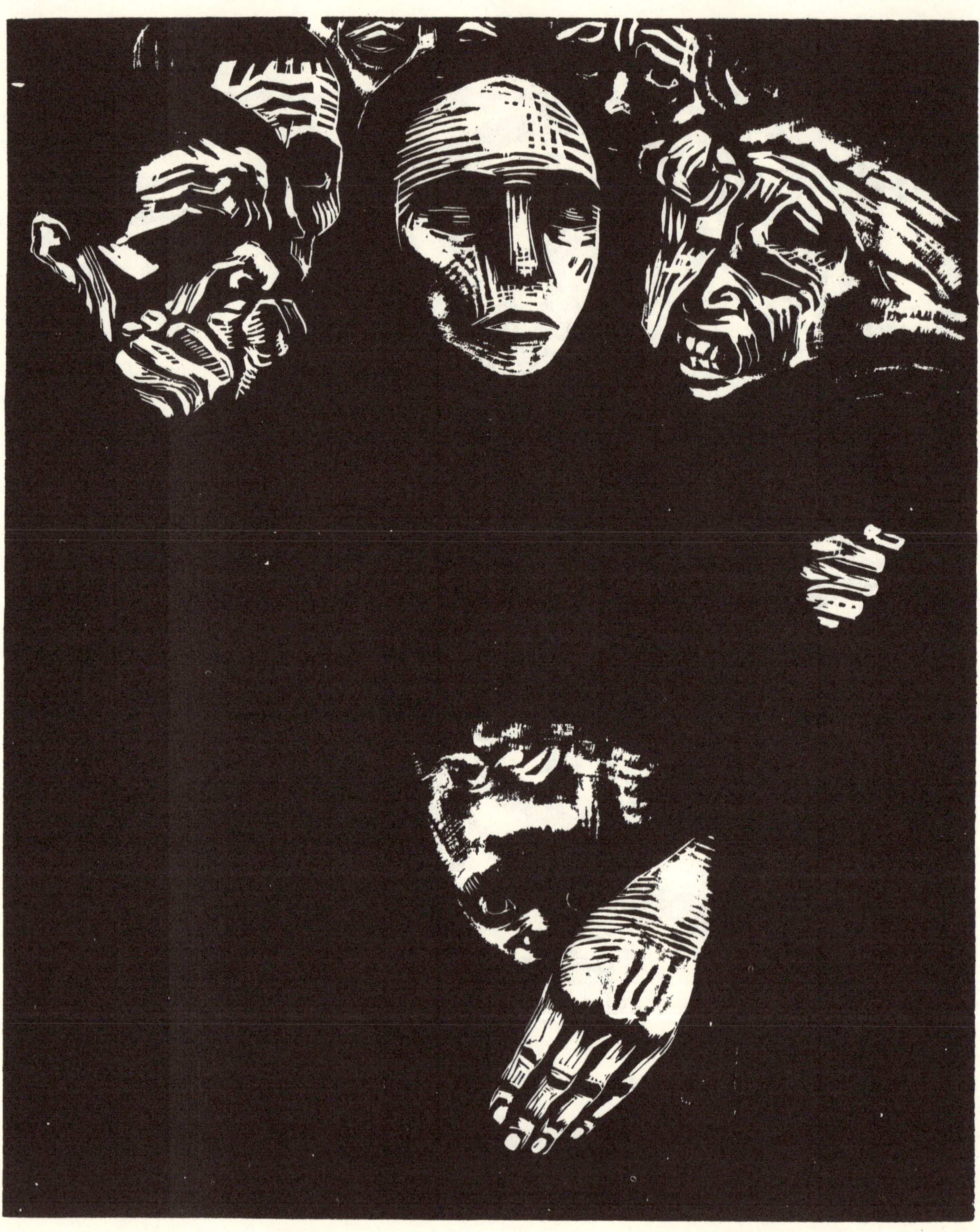

Käthe Kollwitz. *The People*, 1923.

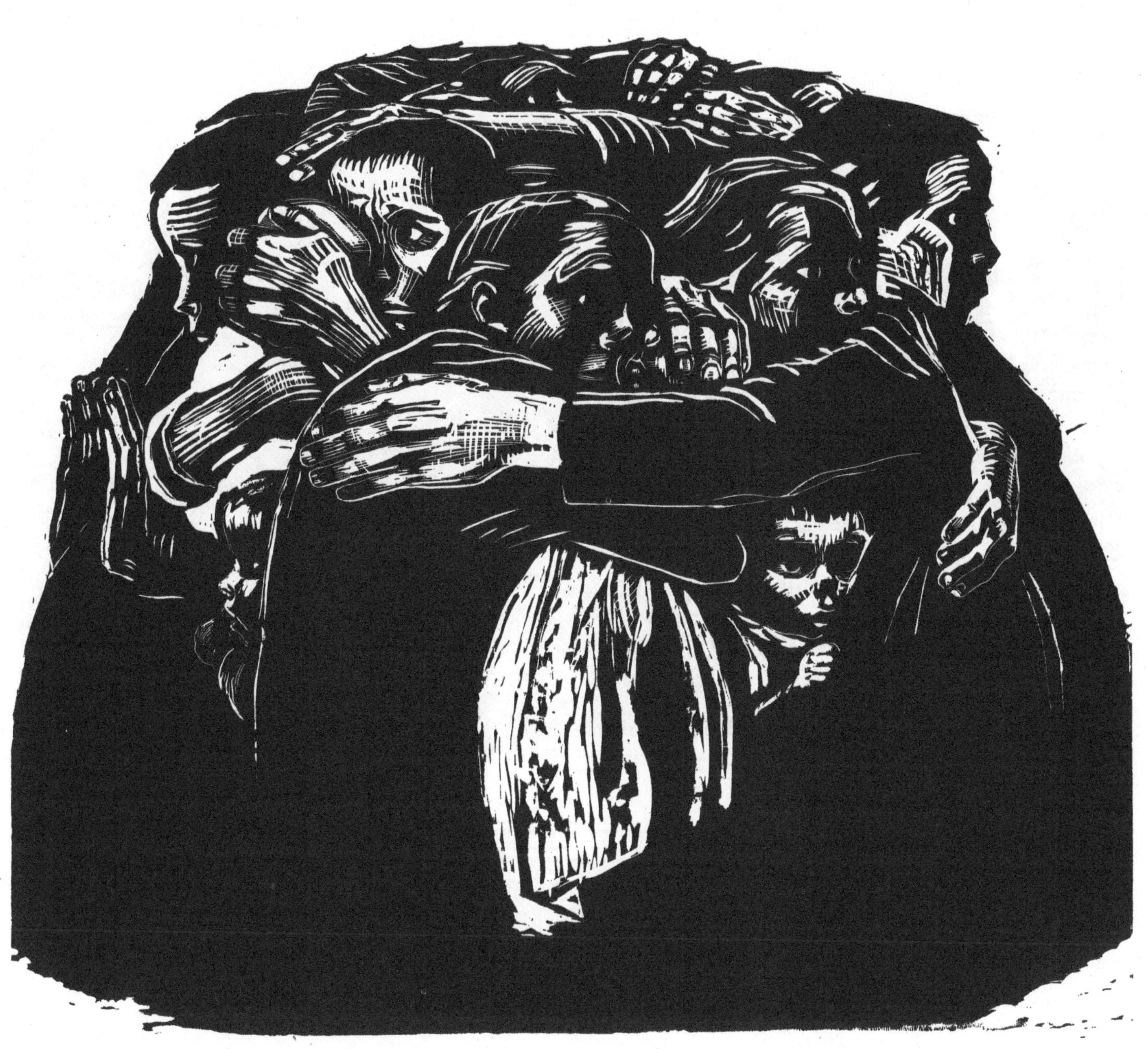

Käthe Kollwitz. *The Mothers*, 1923.

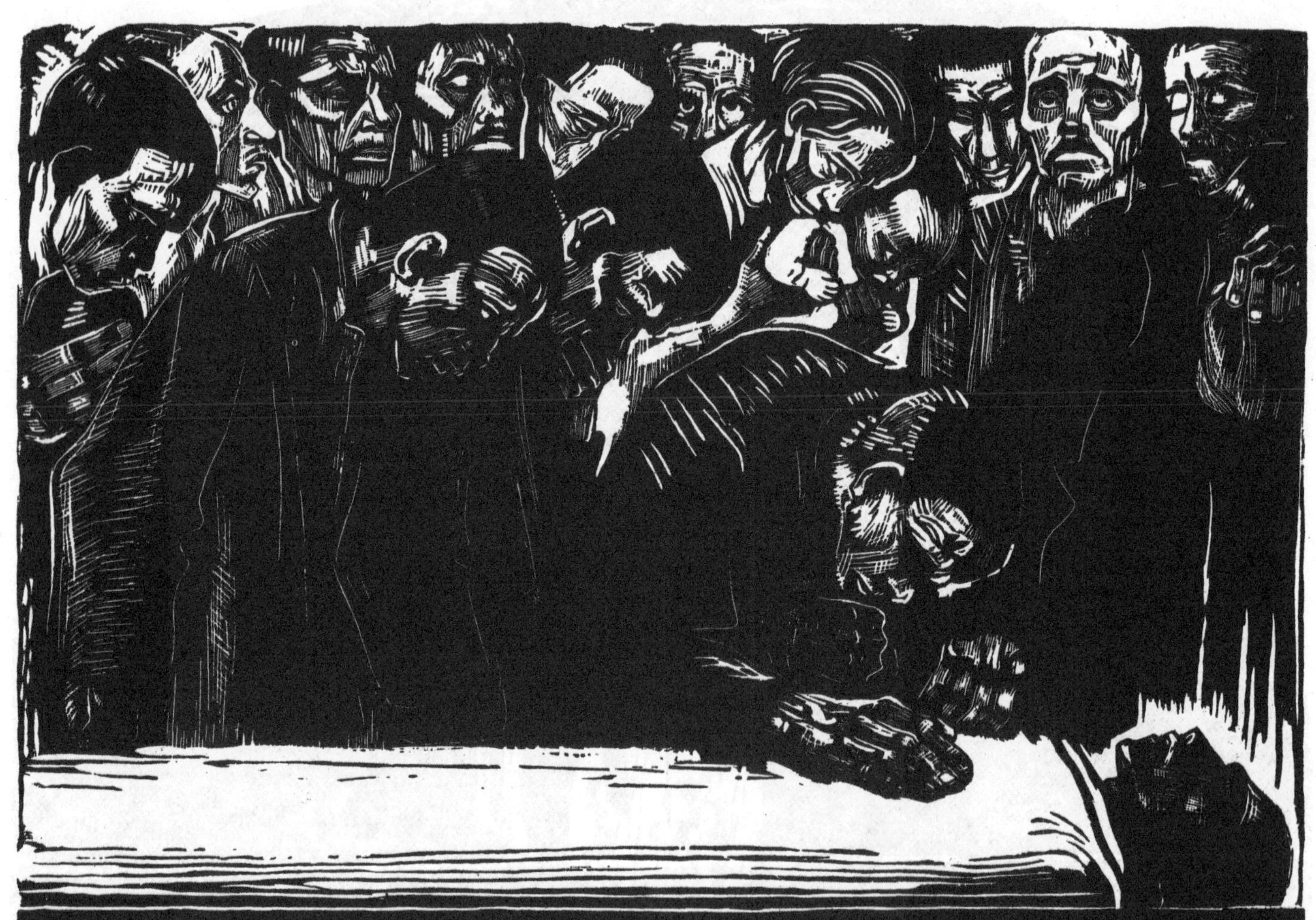

Käthe Kollwitz. *Memorial to Karl Liebknecht*, 1919. ["The living to the dead. In memory of 15 January 1919." Liebknecht, 1871–1919, was a Marxist leader killed with Rosa Luxemburg as a result of the putsch of 1919.]

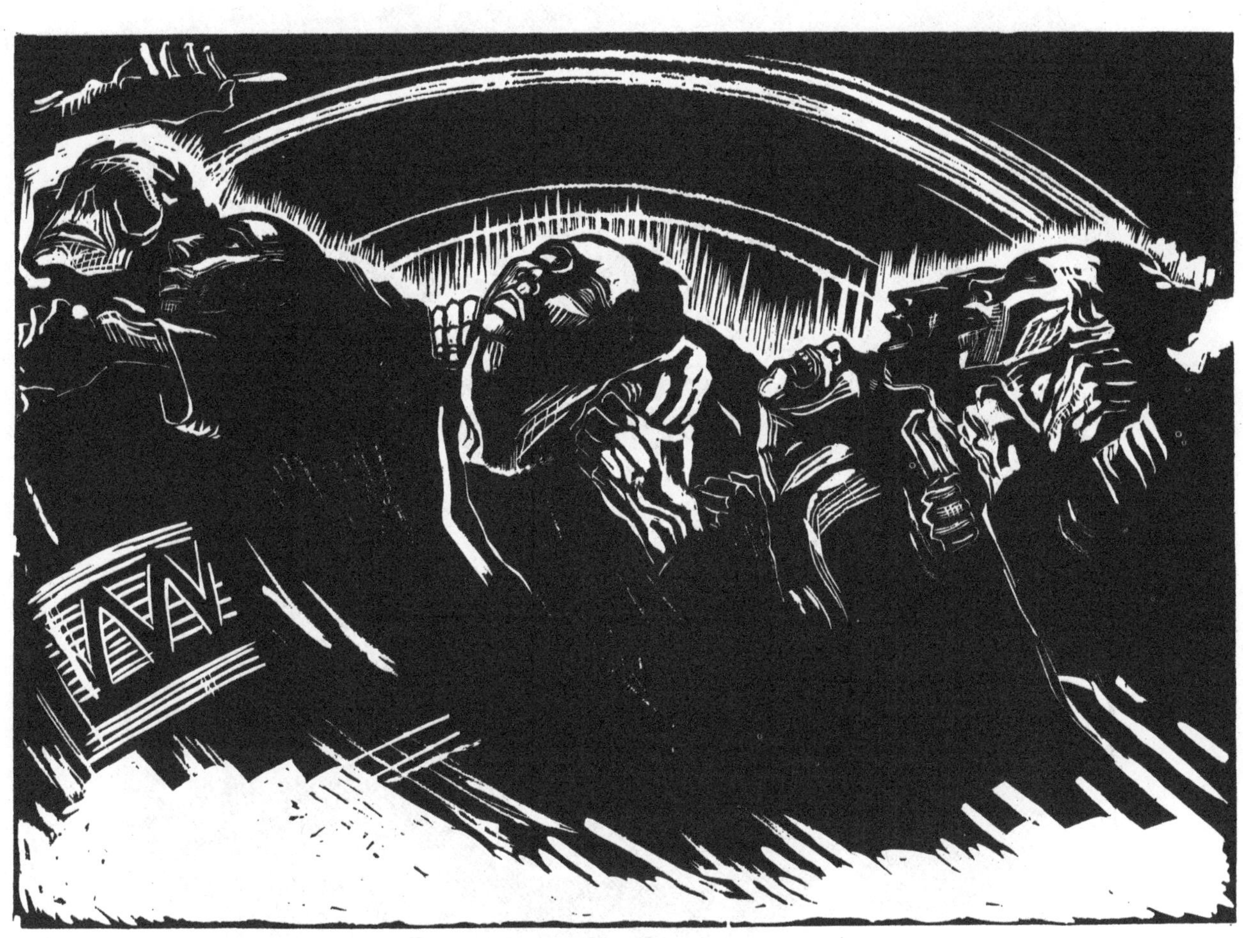

Käthe Kollwitz. *The Volunteers*, 1923.

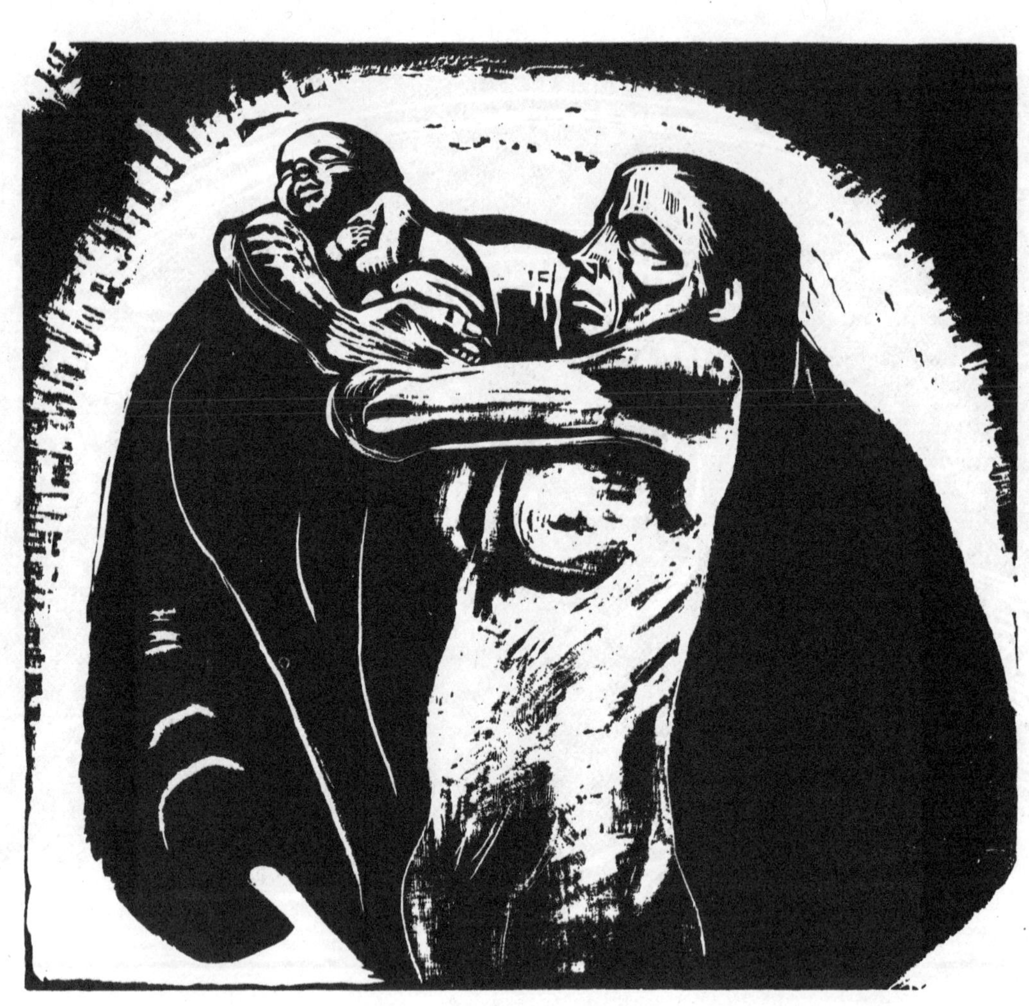

Käthe Kollwitz. *The Sacrifice*, 1923.

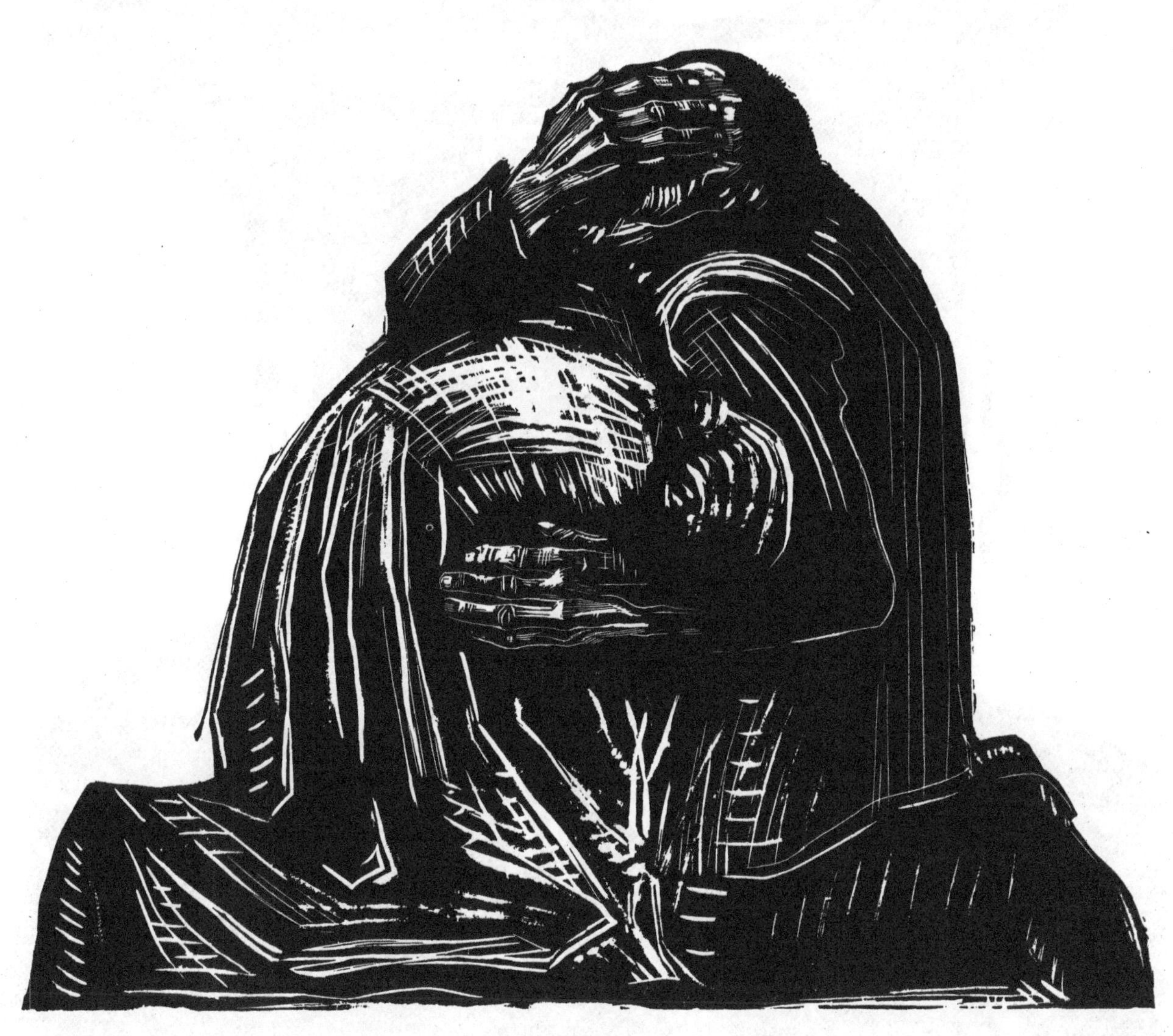

Käthe Kollwitz. *The Parents*, 1923.

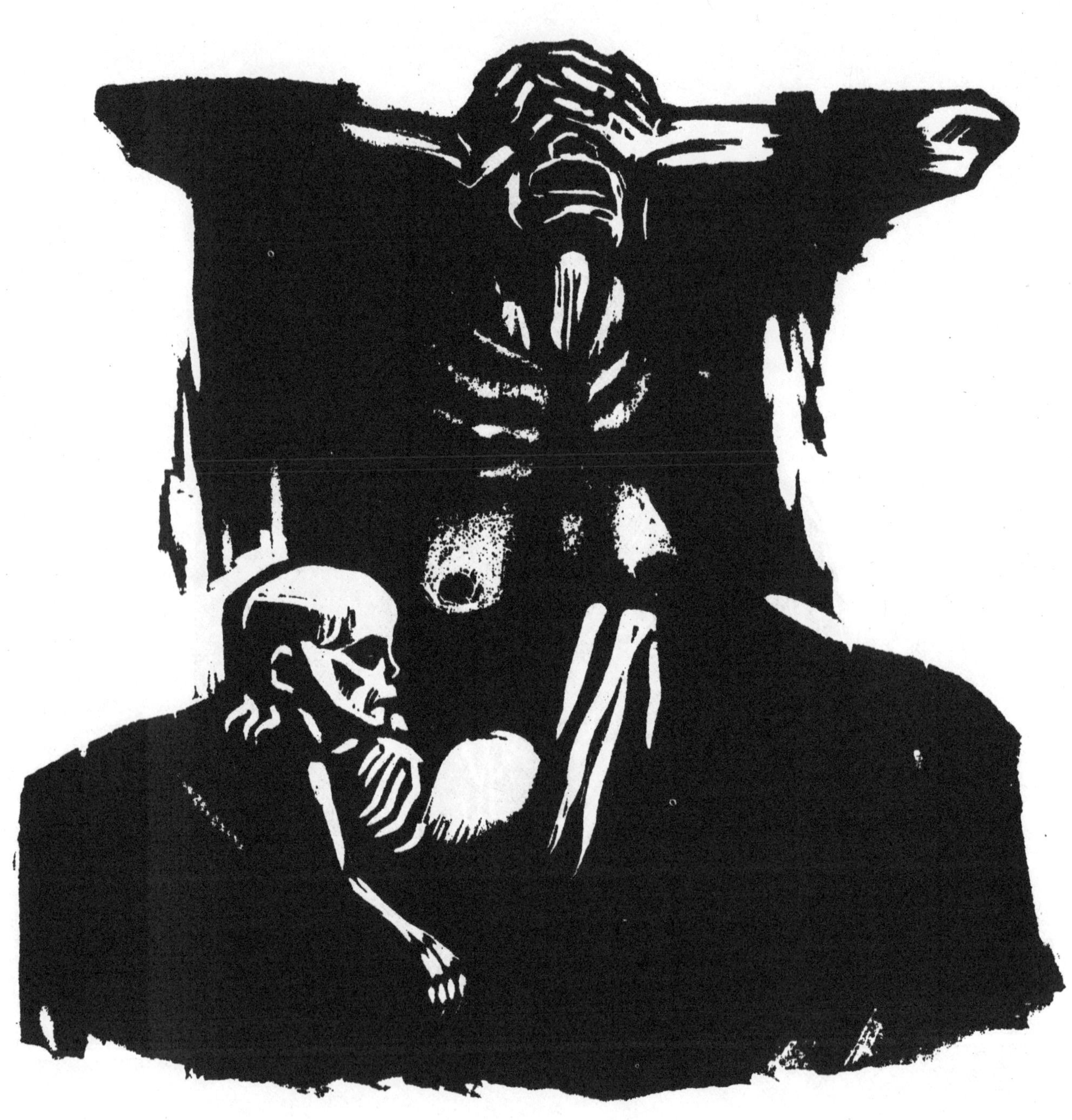

Käthe Kollwitz. *Hunger*, 1923.

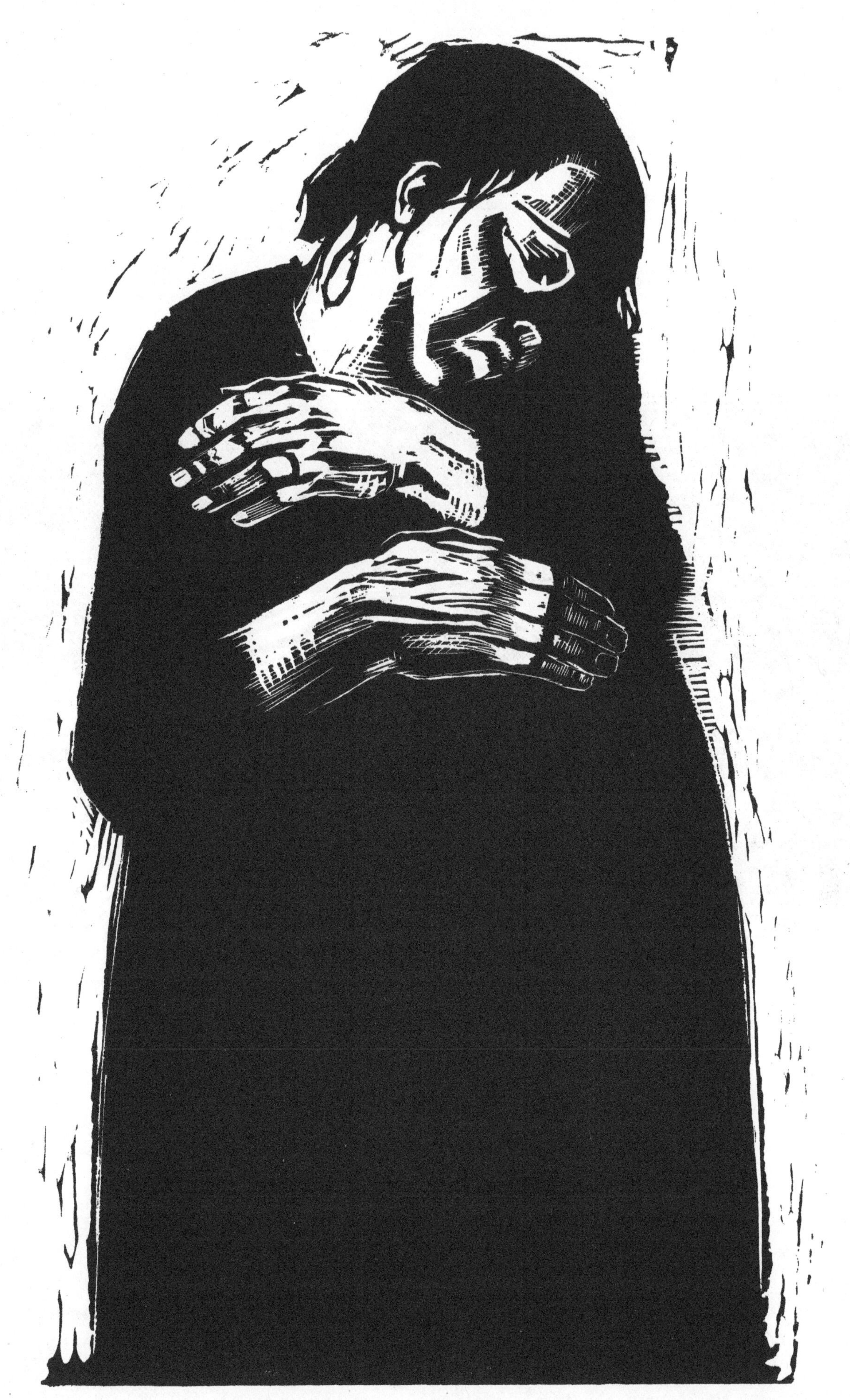

Käthe Kollwitz. *The Widow I*, 1923.

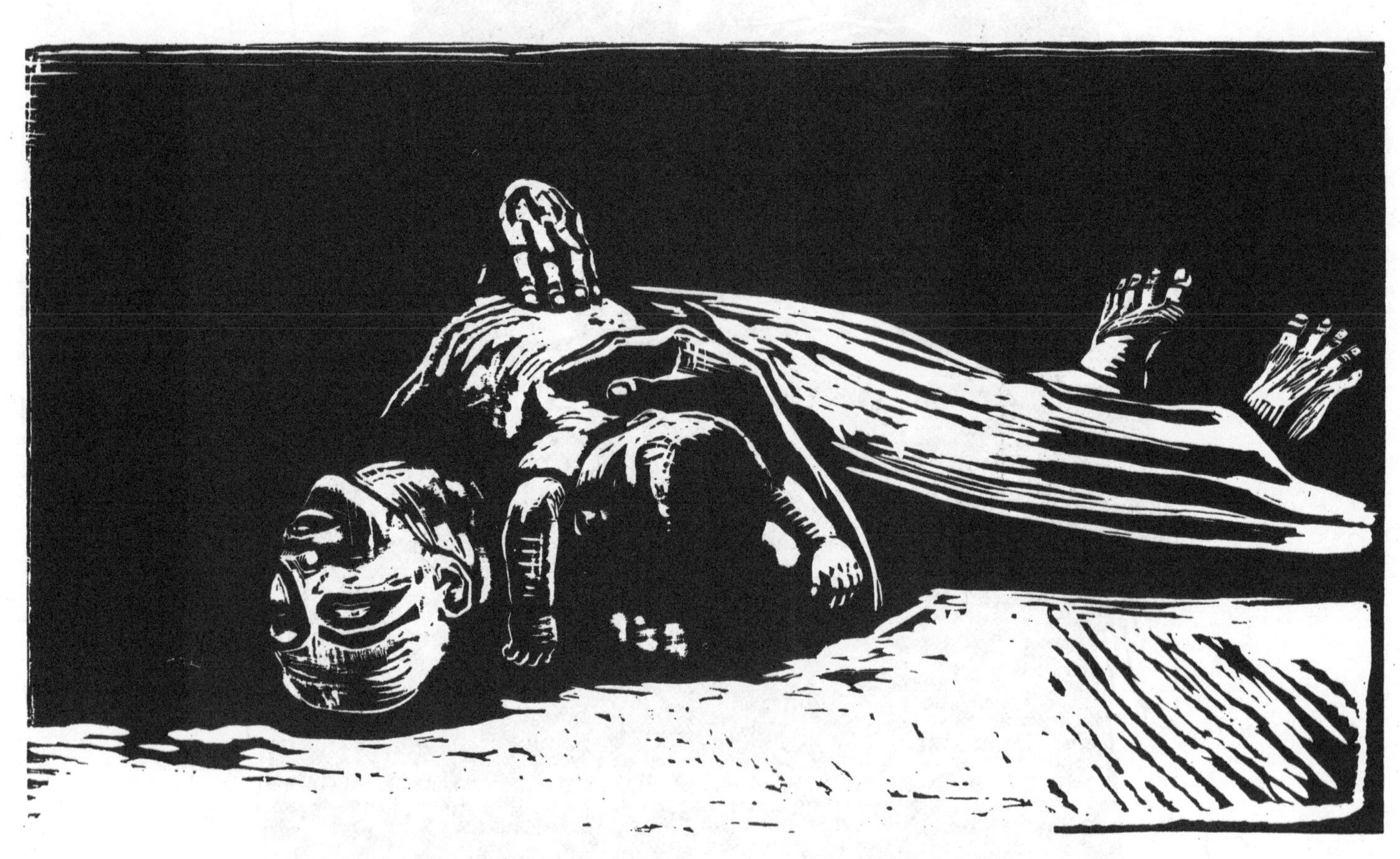

Käthe Kollwitz. *The Widow II*, 1923.

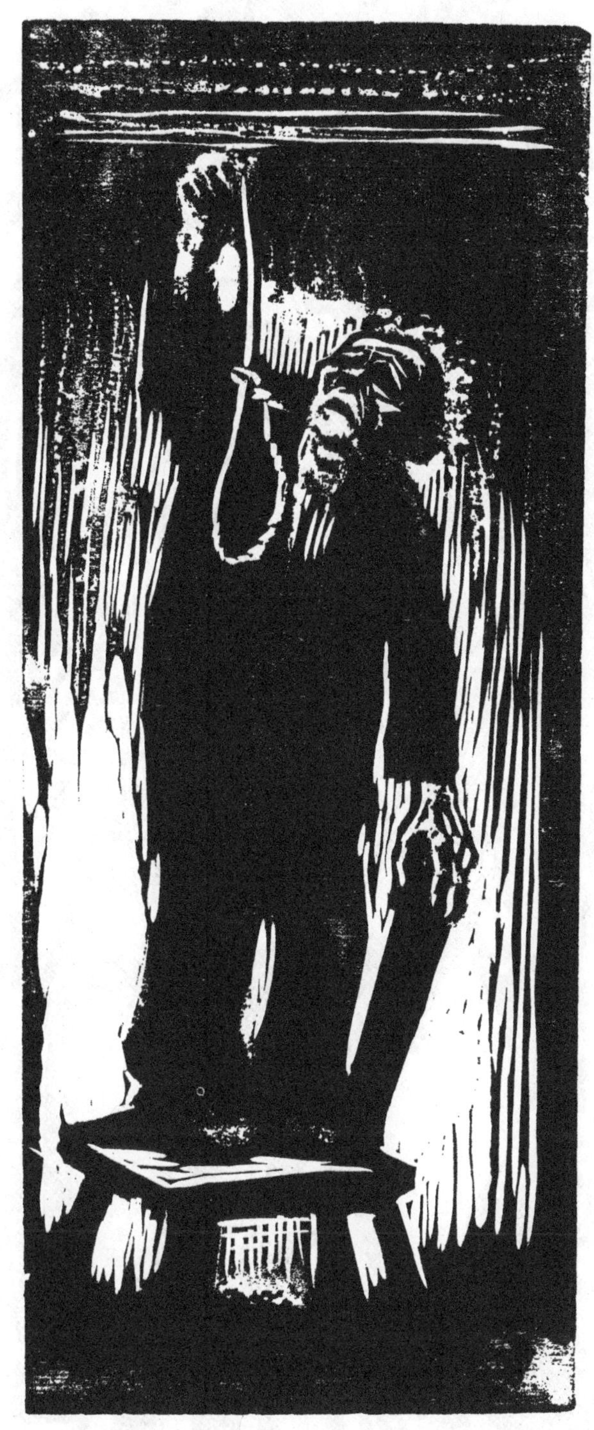

Käthe Kollwitz. *Old Man with Noose*, 1923.

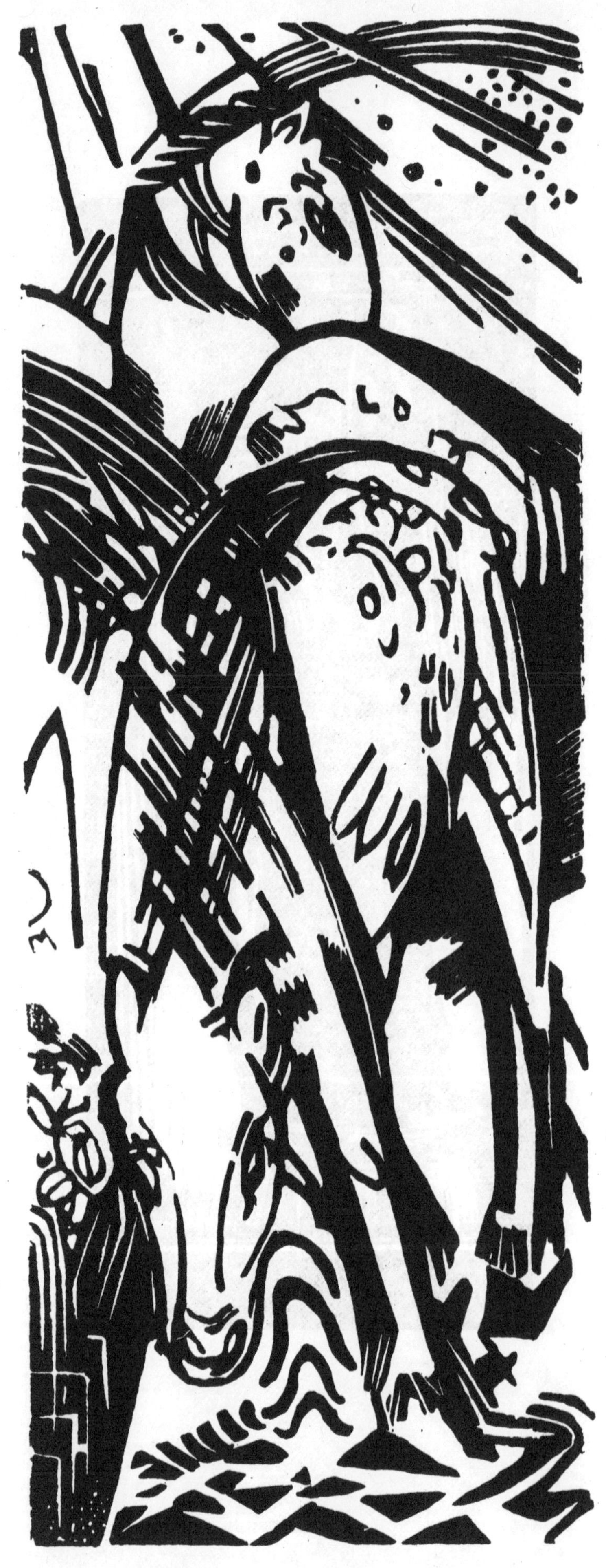

Franz Marc. *Horse Drinking*, 1912.

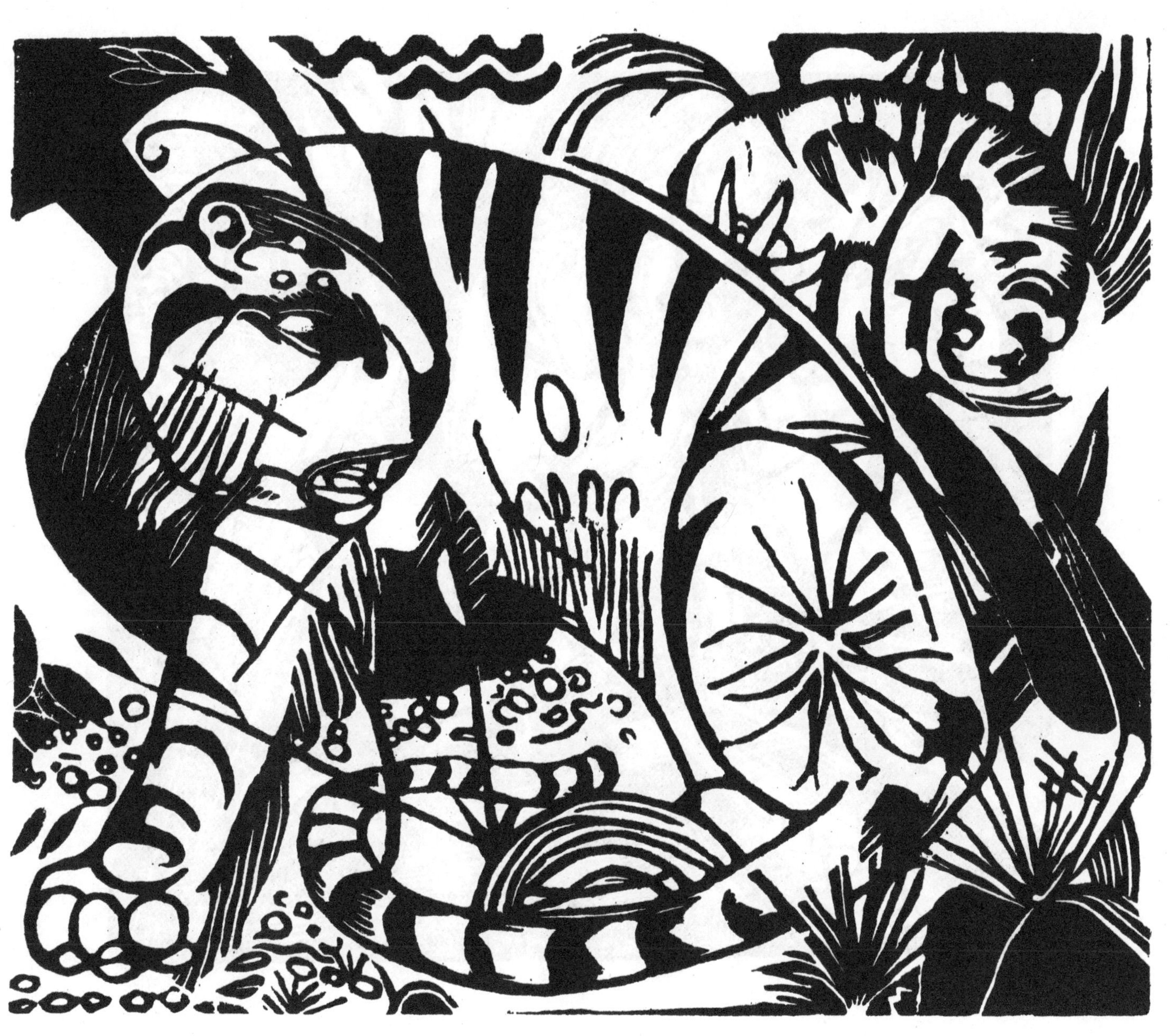

Franz Marc. *Tigers*, 1912.

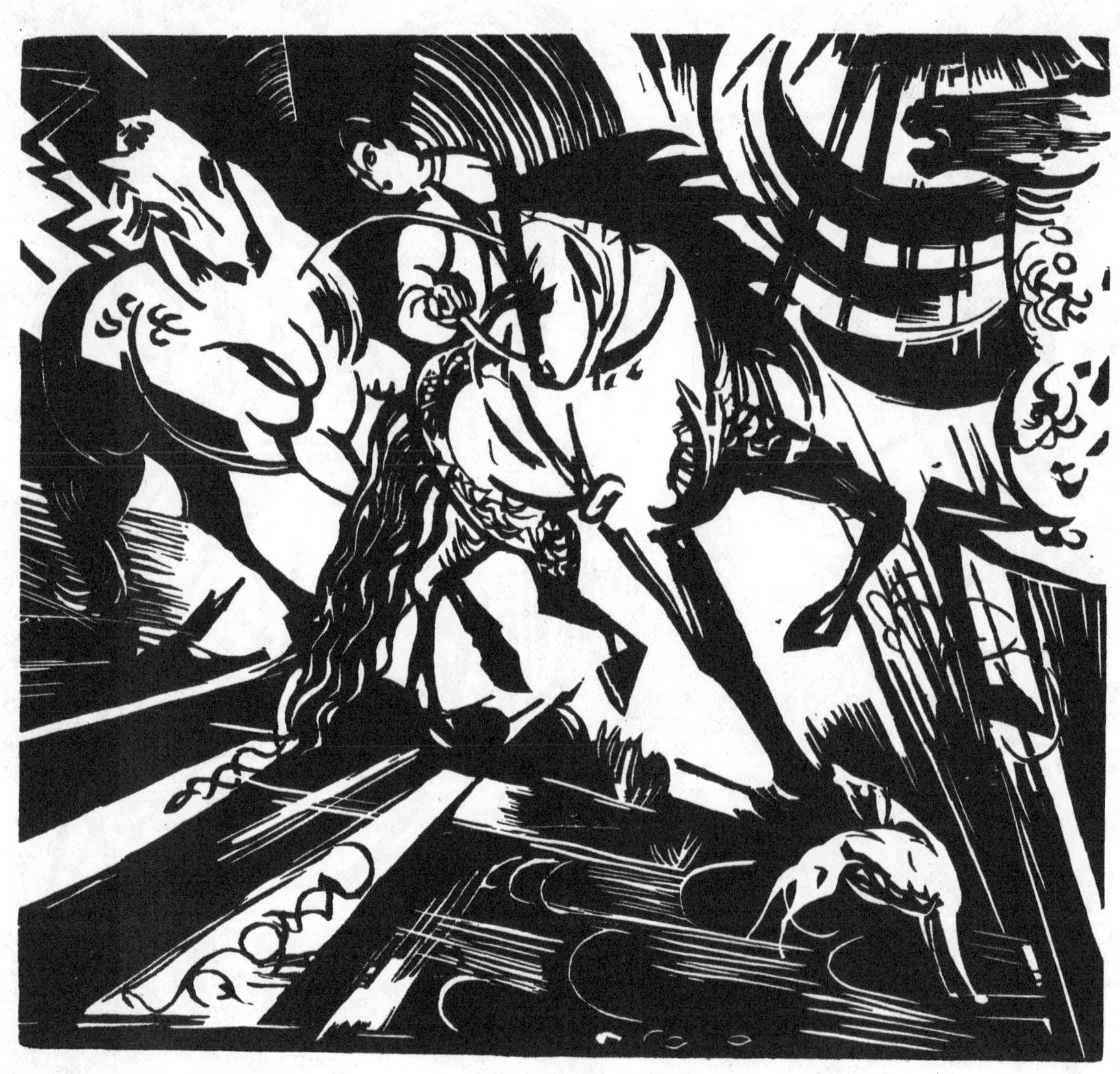

 Franz Marc. *Riding School*, 1913.

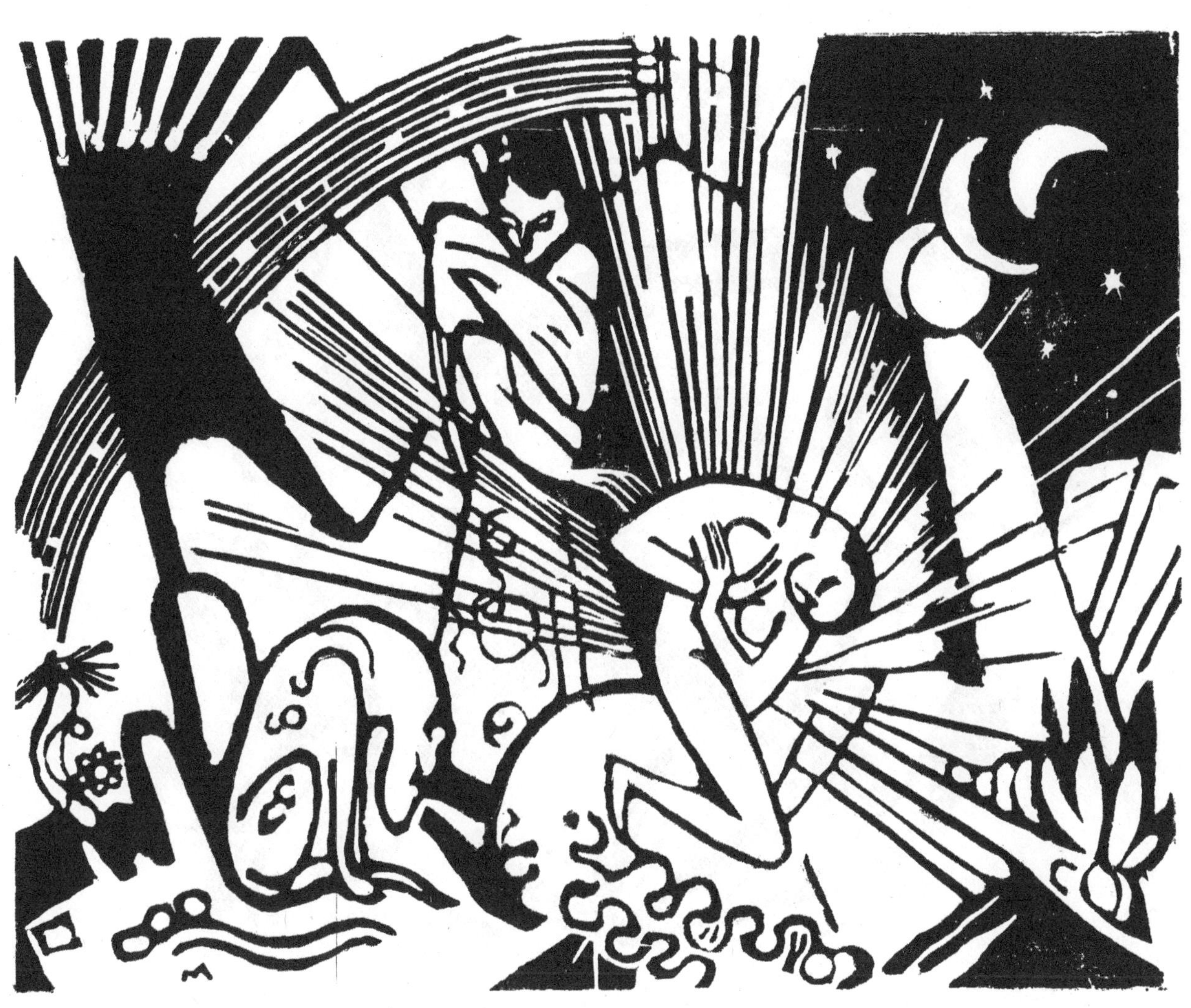

Franz Marc. *Annunciation*, 1912.

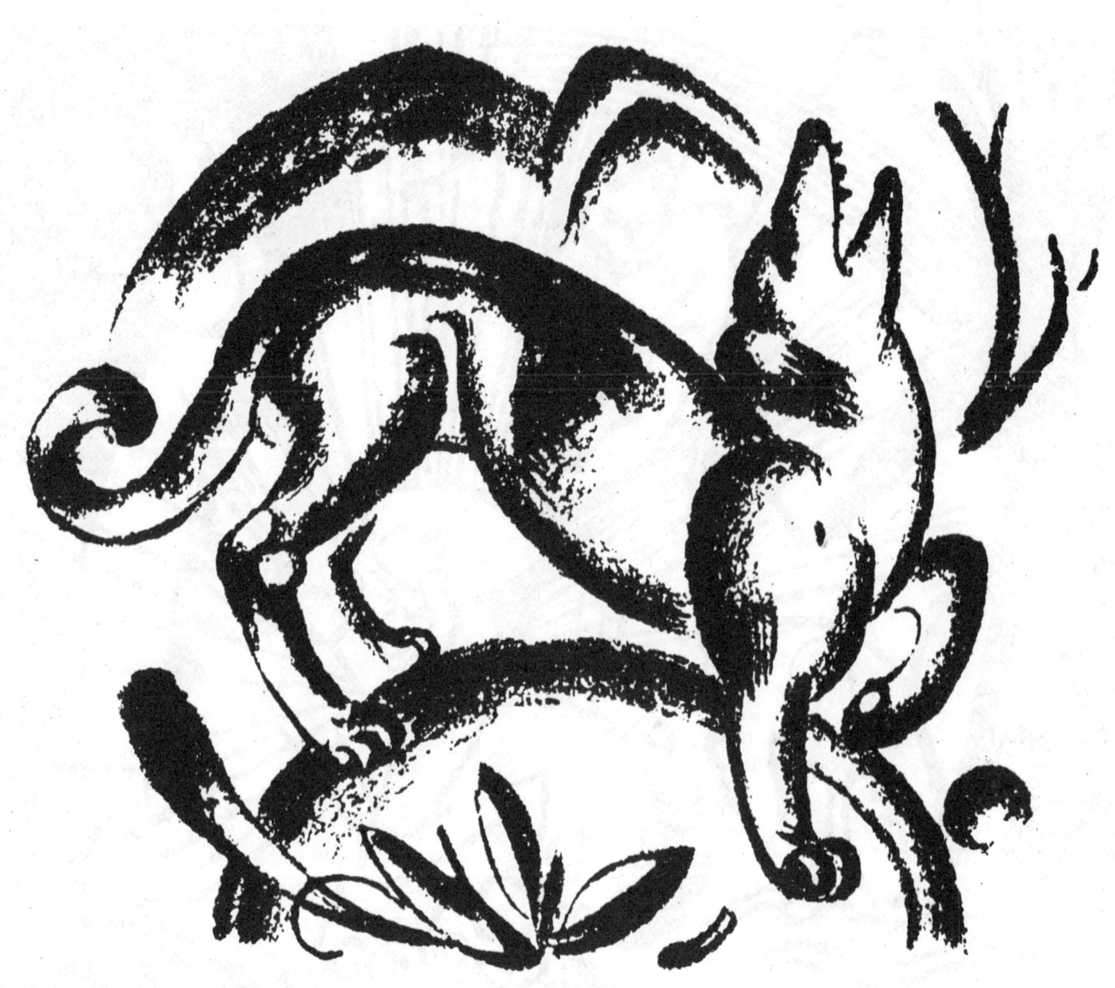

Franz Marc. Untitled, 1913.

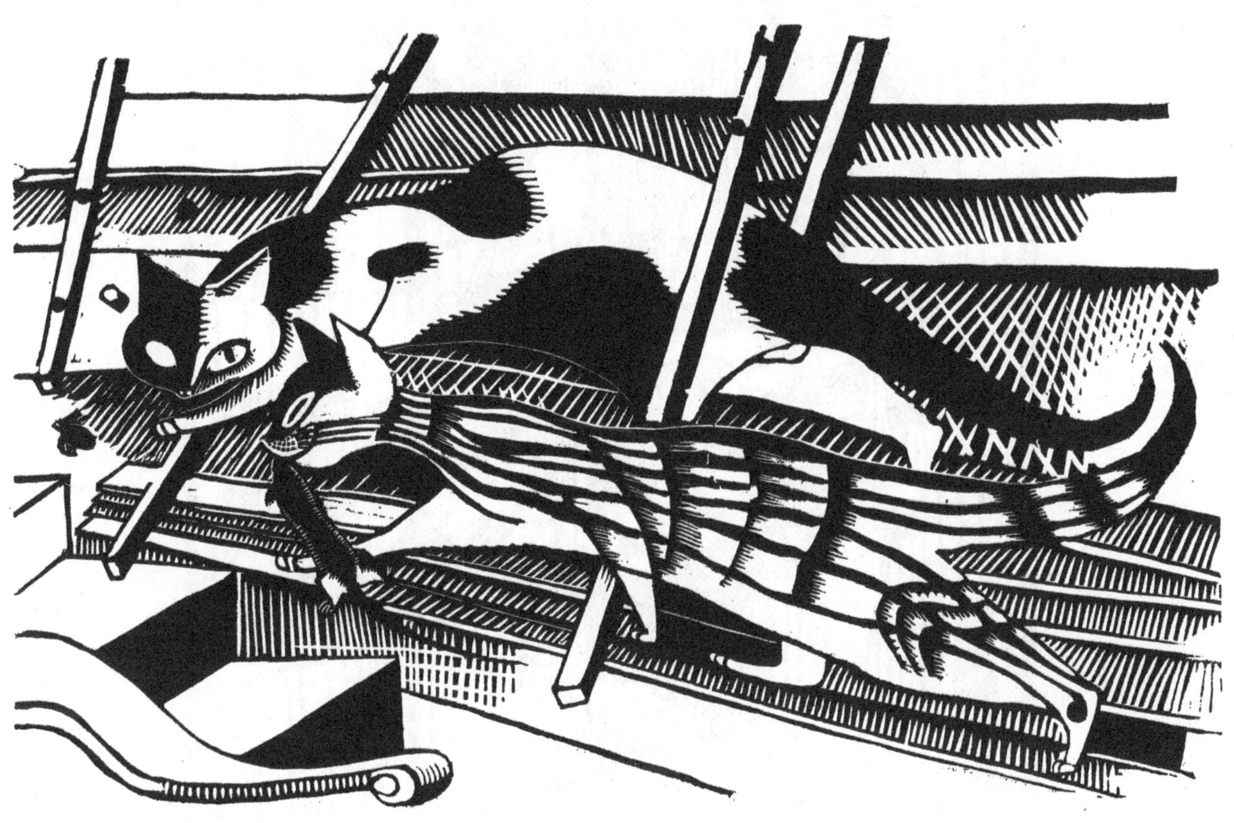

Gerhard Marcks. *Cats*, 1921.

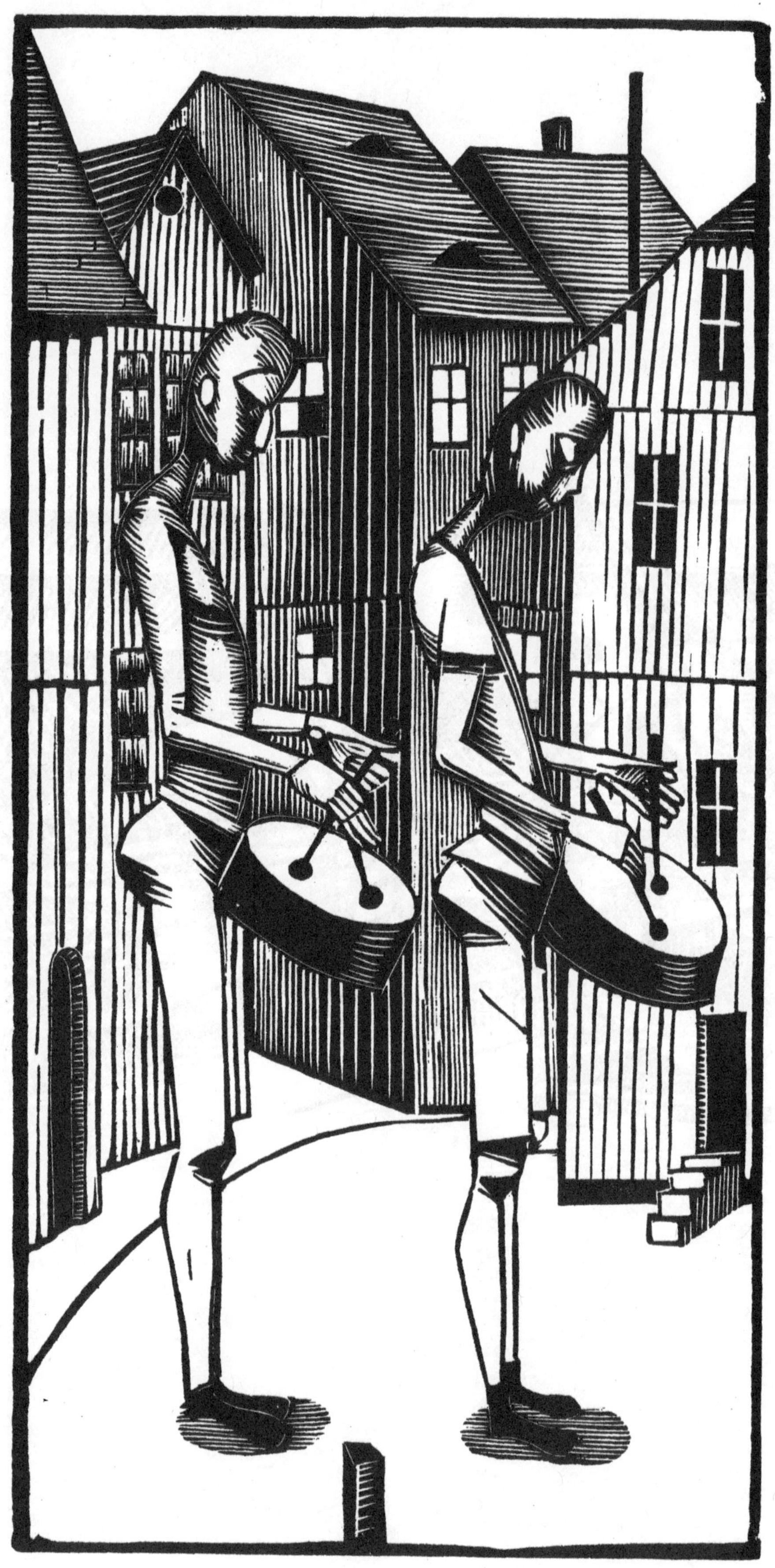

Gerhard Marcks. *Drummers*, 1921.

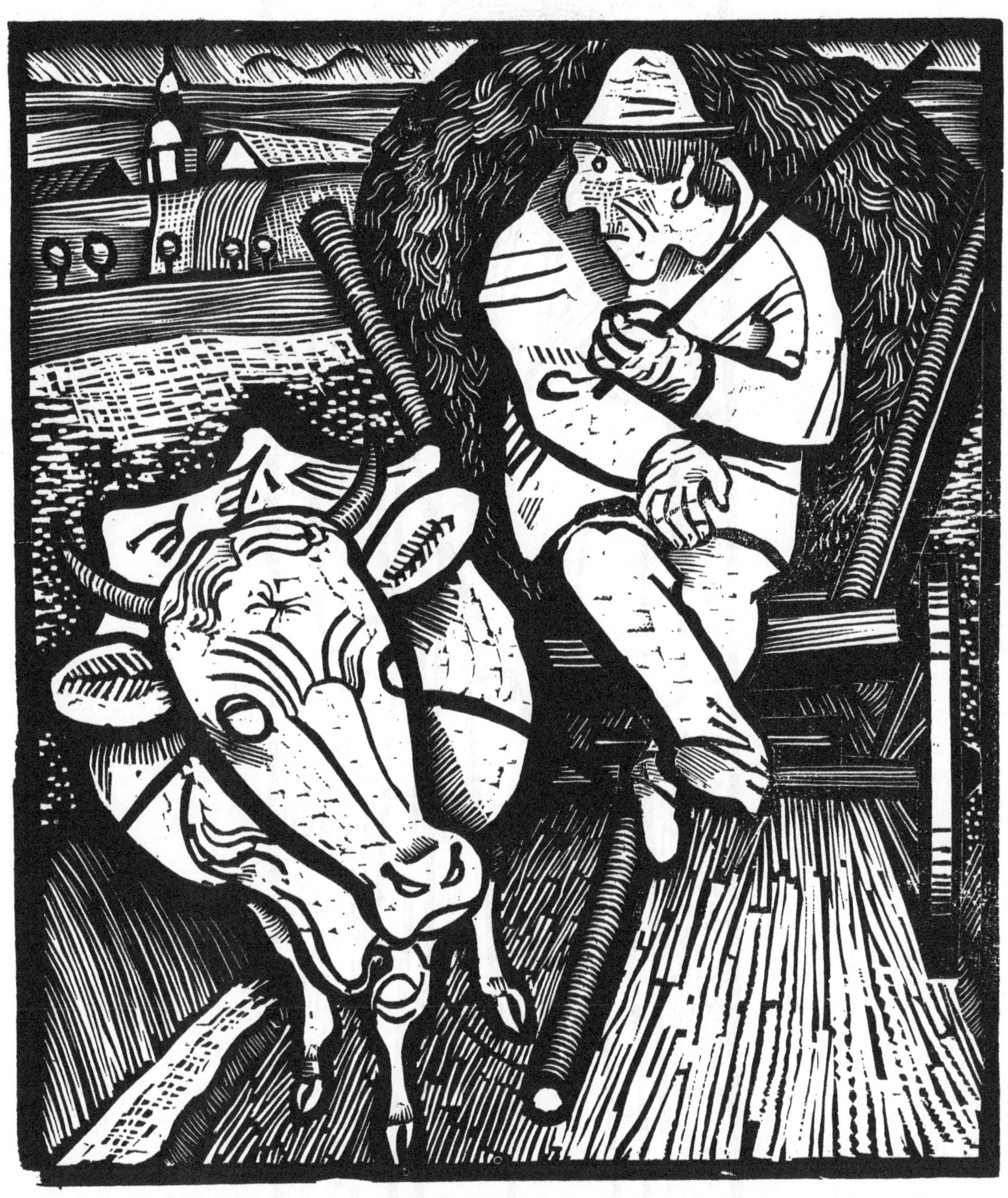

Gerhard Marcks. *Peasant with Cow*, 1924.

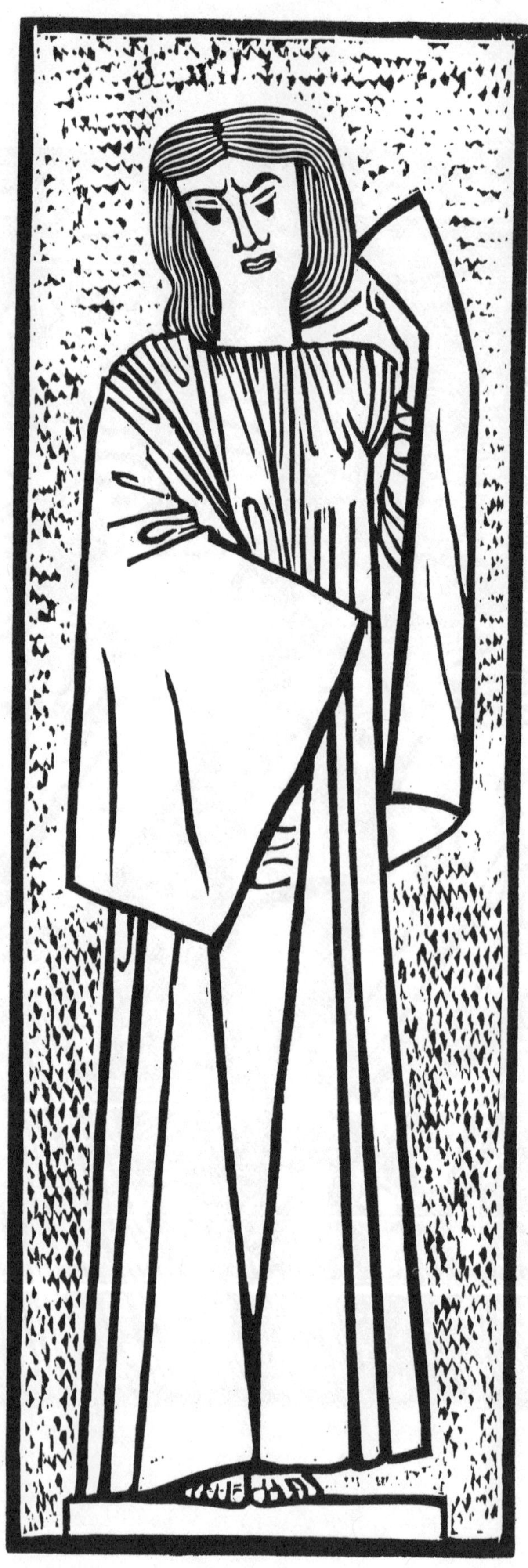

Gerhard Marcks. *Angel of Cologne*, 1946.

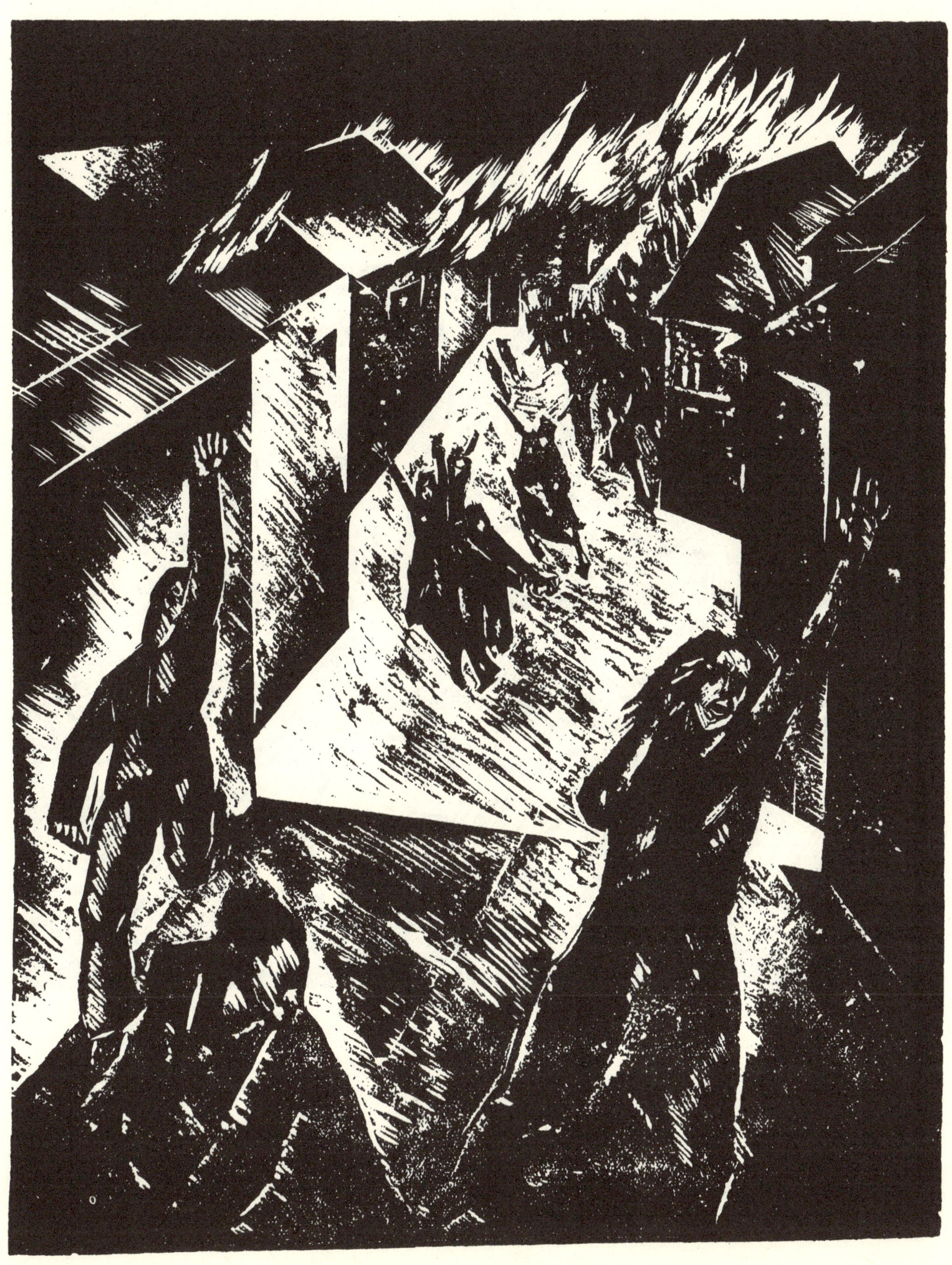

Georg A. Mathéy. *Burning Town*, 1916.

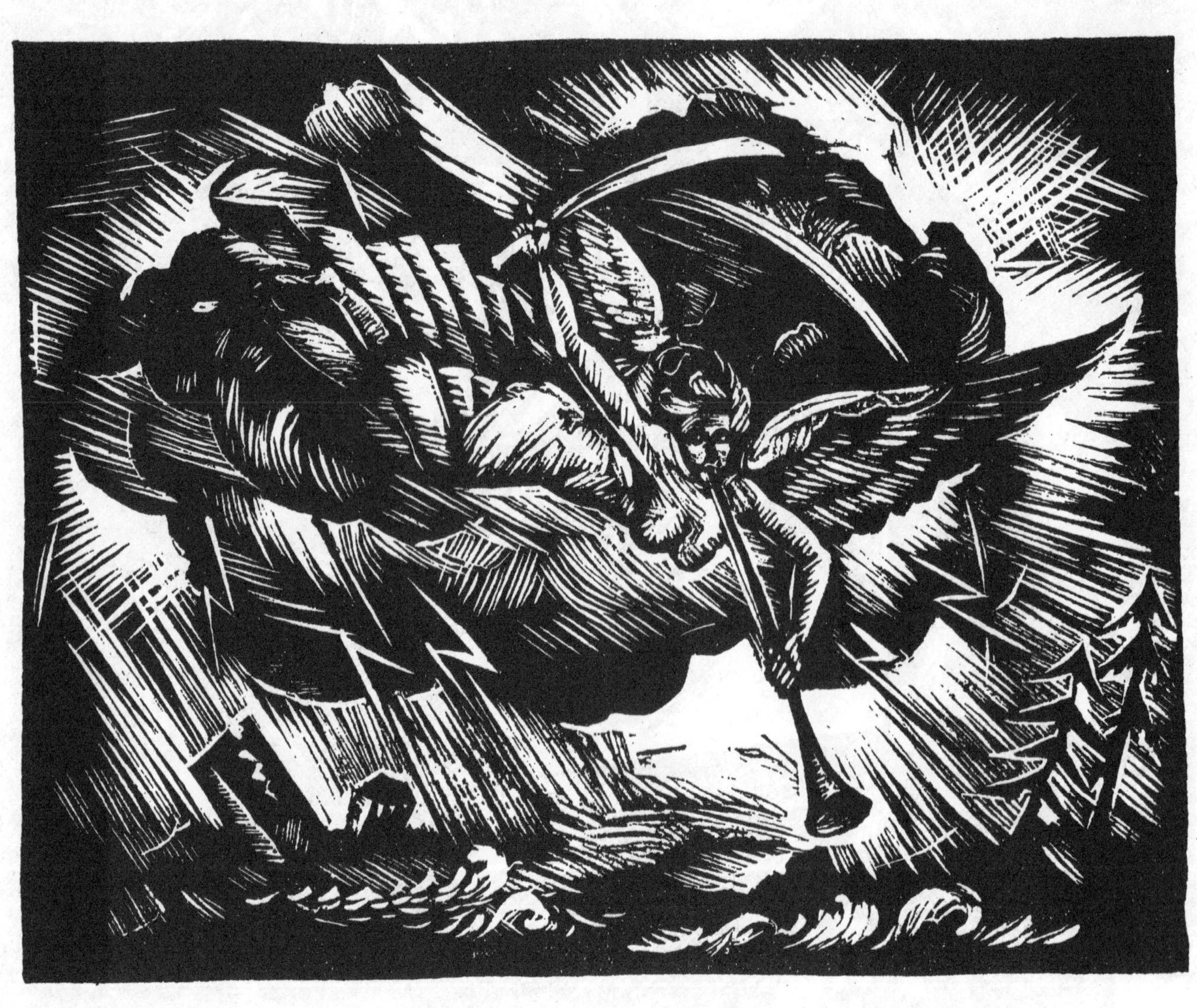

Georg A. Mathéy. *Storm*, 1916. [Dedicated to Paul Adler, author and translator, 1878–1946.]

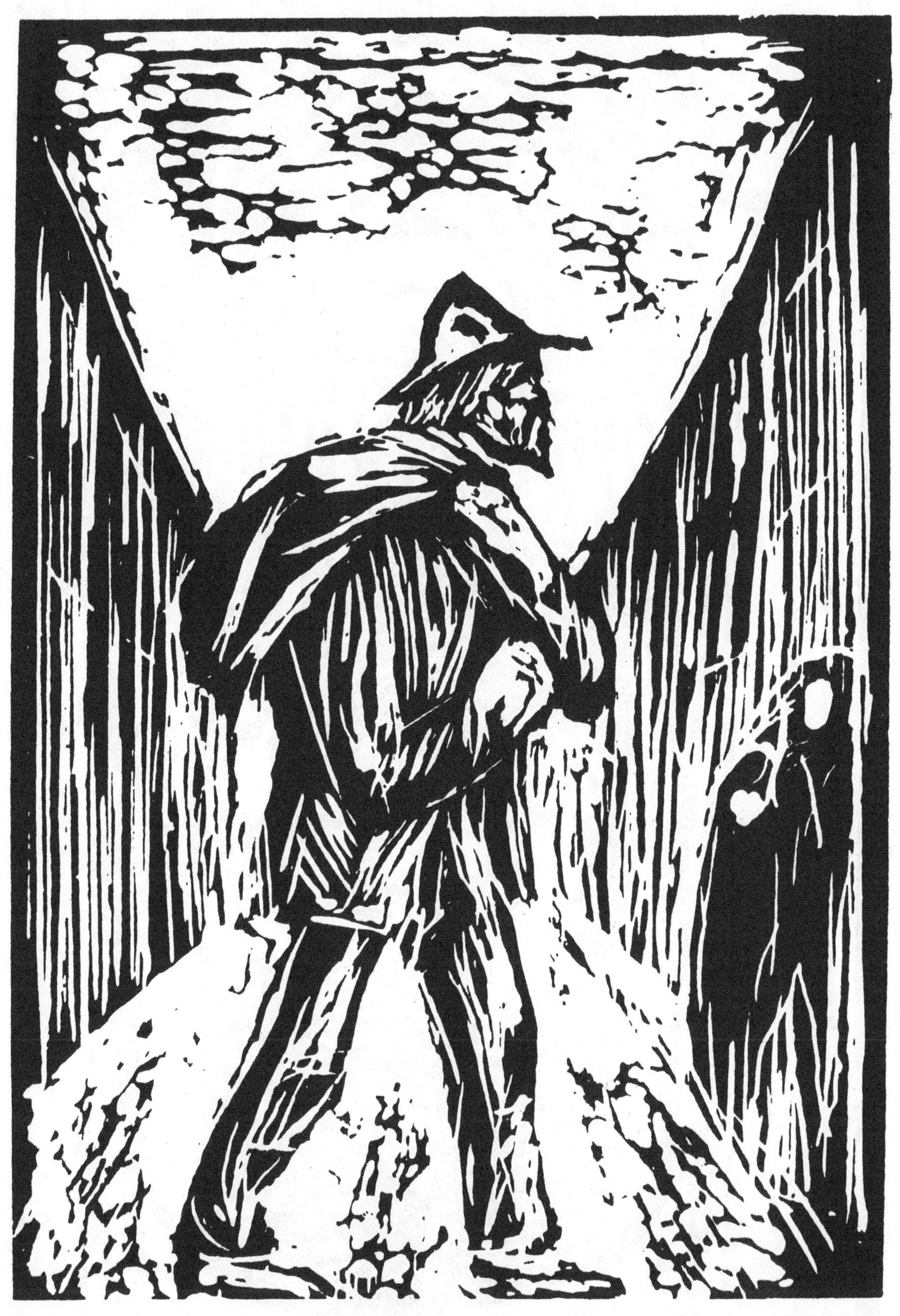

Edvard Munch. *The Ragpicker (The Wanderer)*, 1908–09.

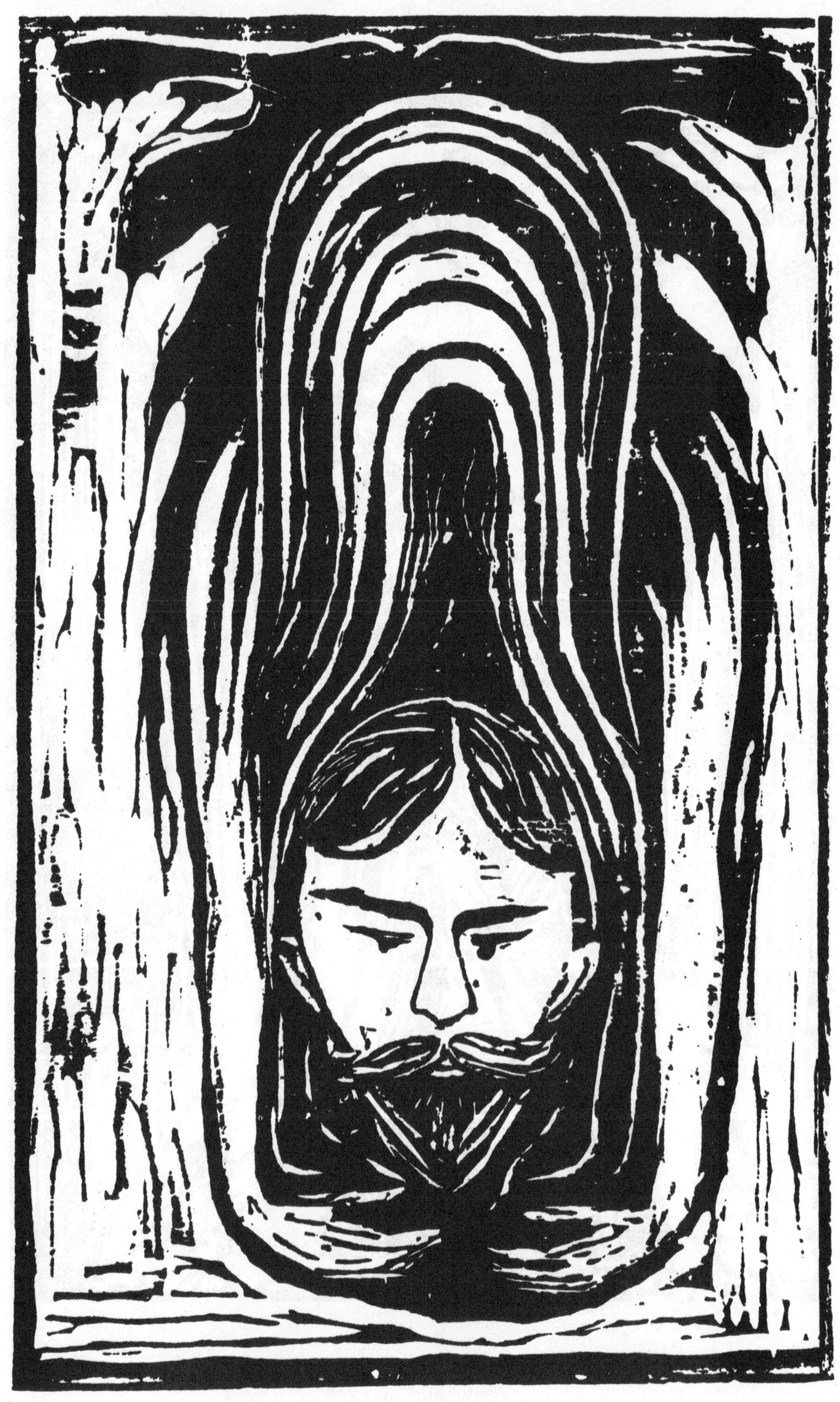

Edvard Munch. *Salome Paraphrase*, 1898.

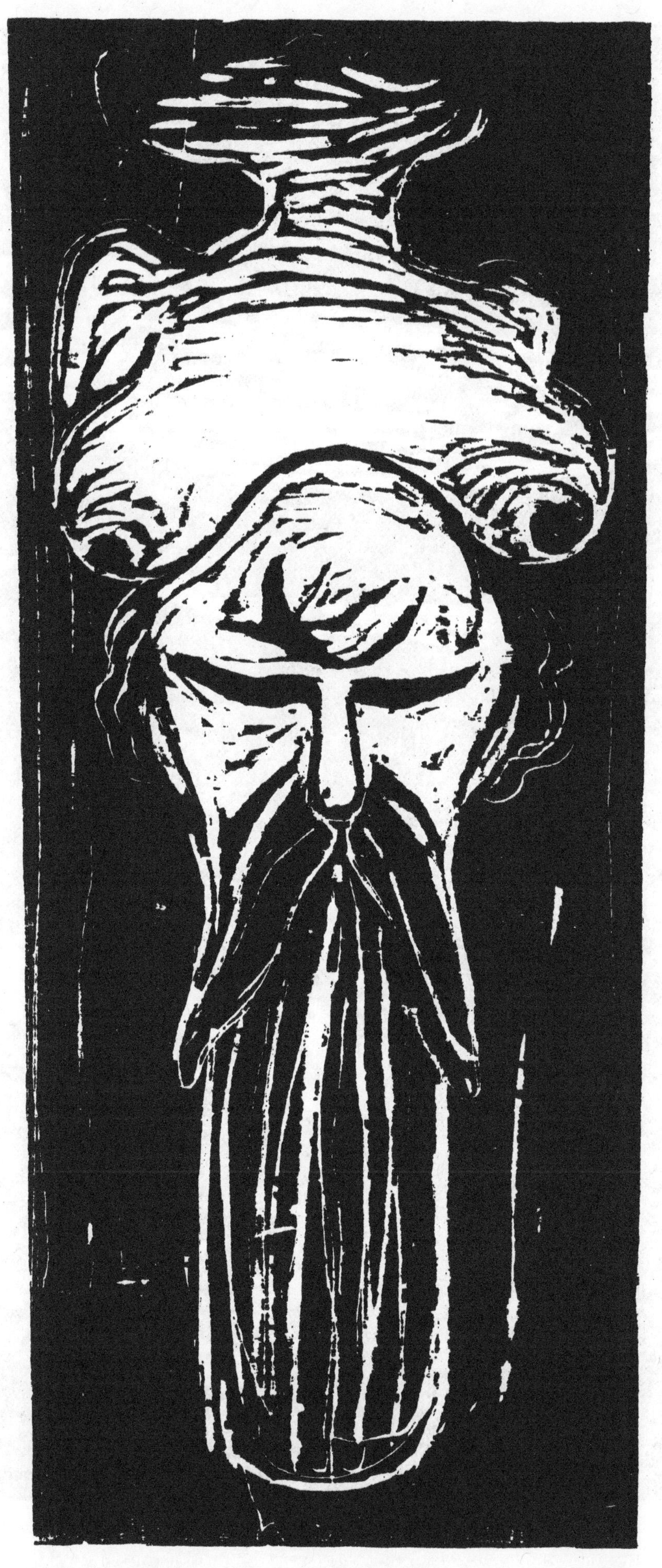

Edvard Munch. *Head of a Man below a Woman's Breast*, ca. 1898–1908/09.

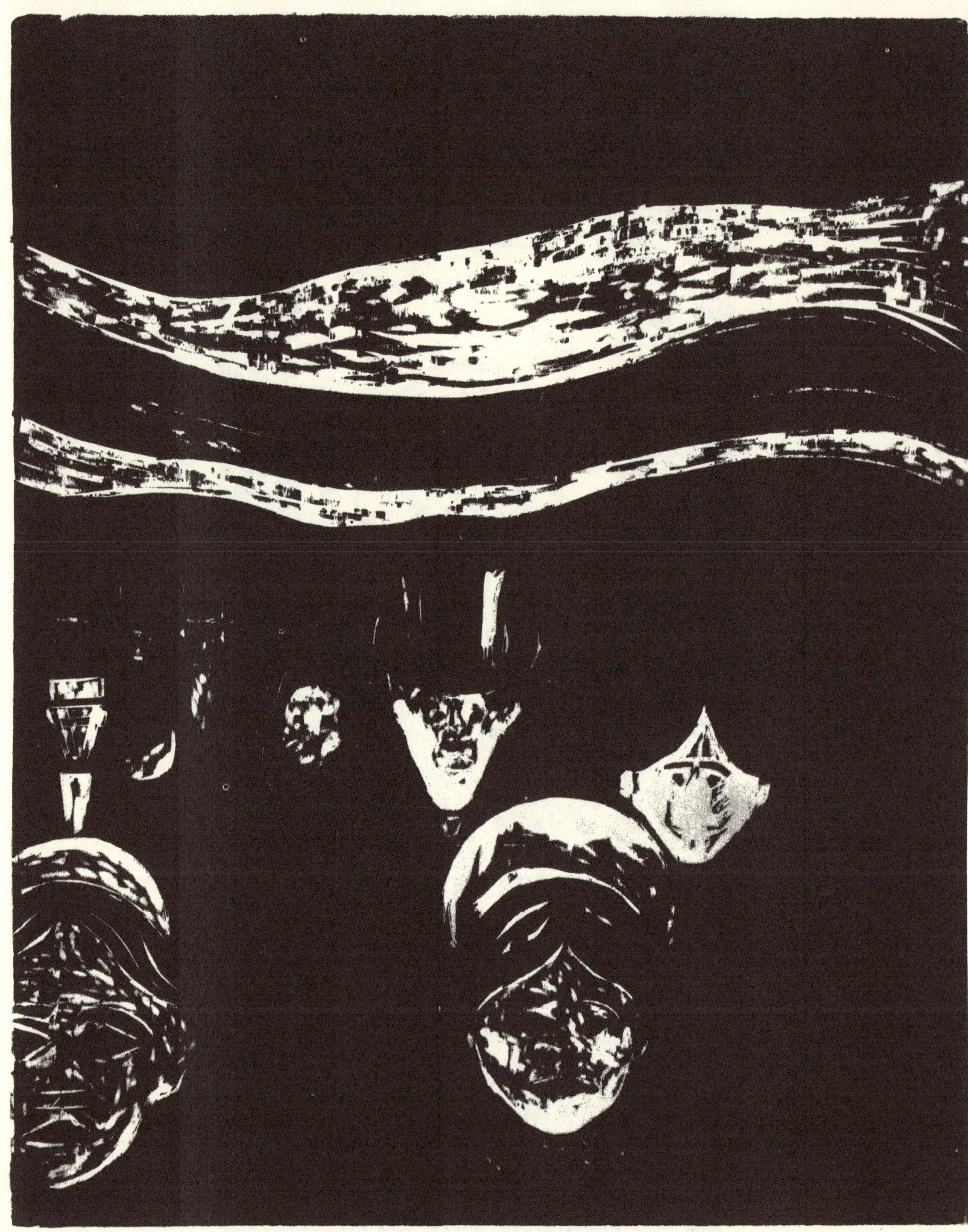

Edvard Munch. *Anxiety*, 1896.

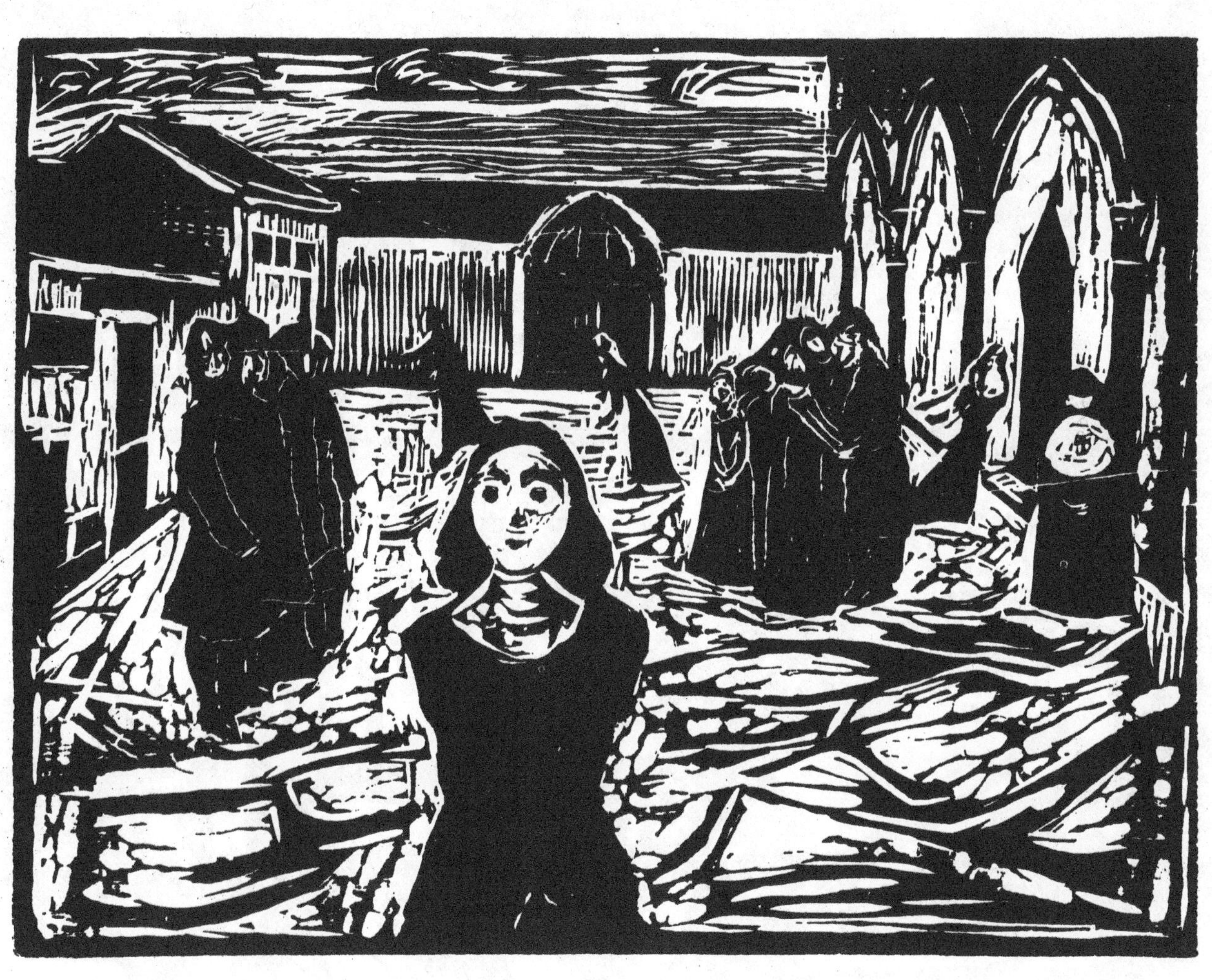

Edvard Munch. *The Last Hour (Skule in a Nunnery)*, 1919–20.

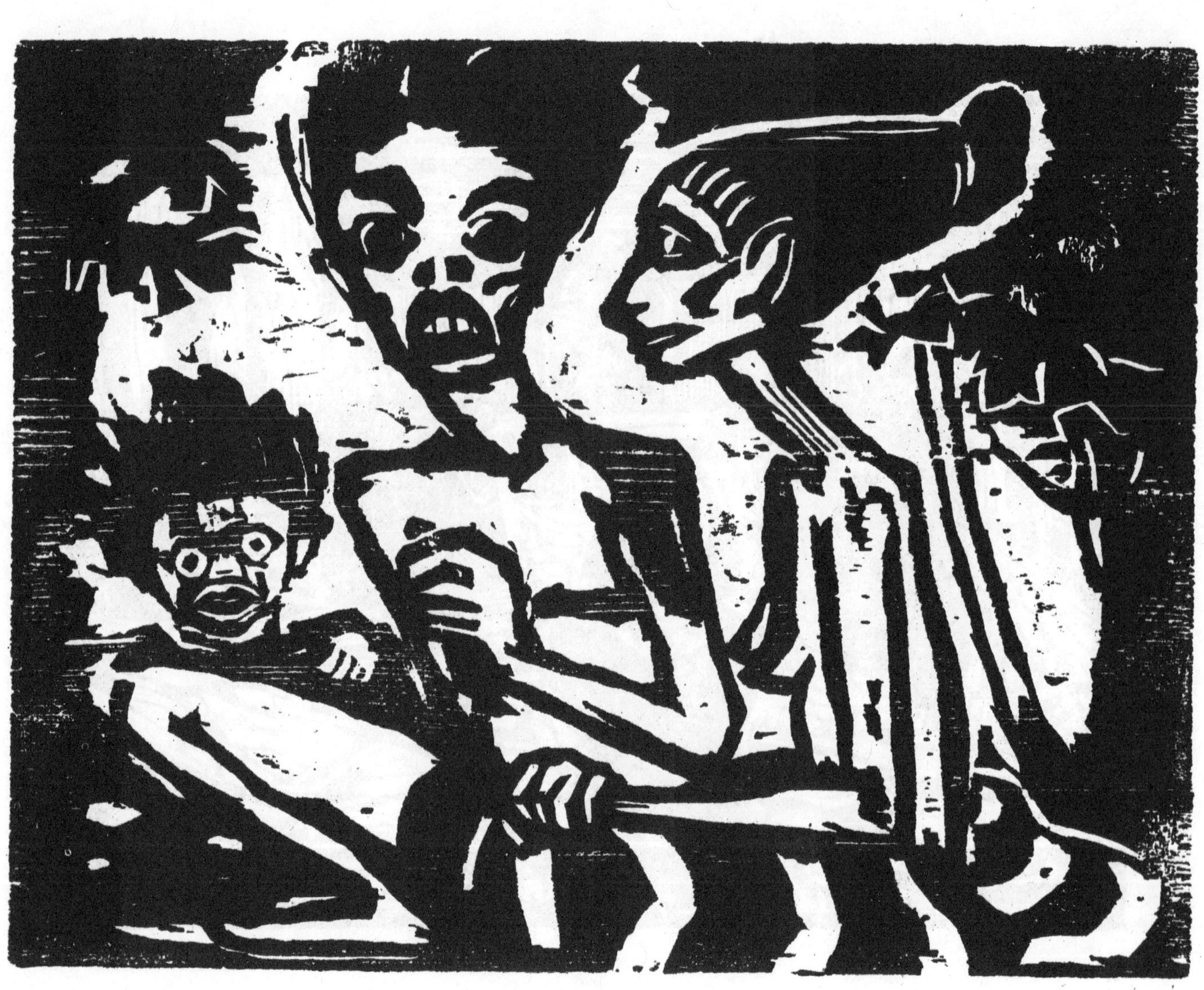

Emil Nolde. *Family*, 1917.

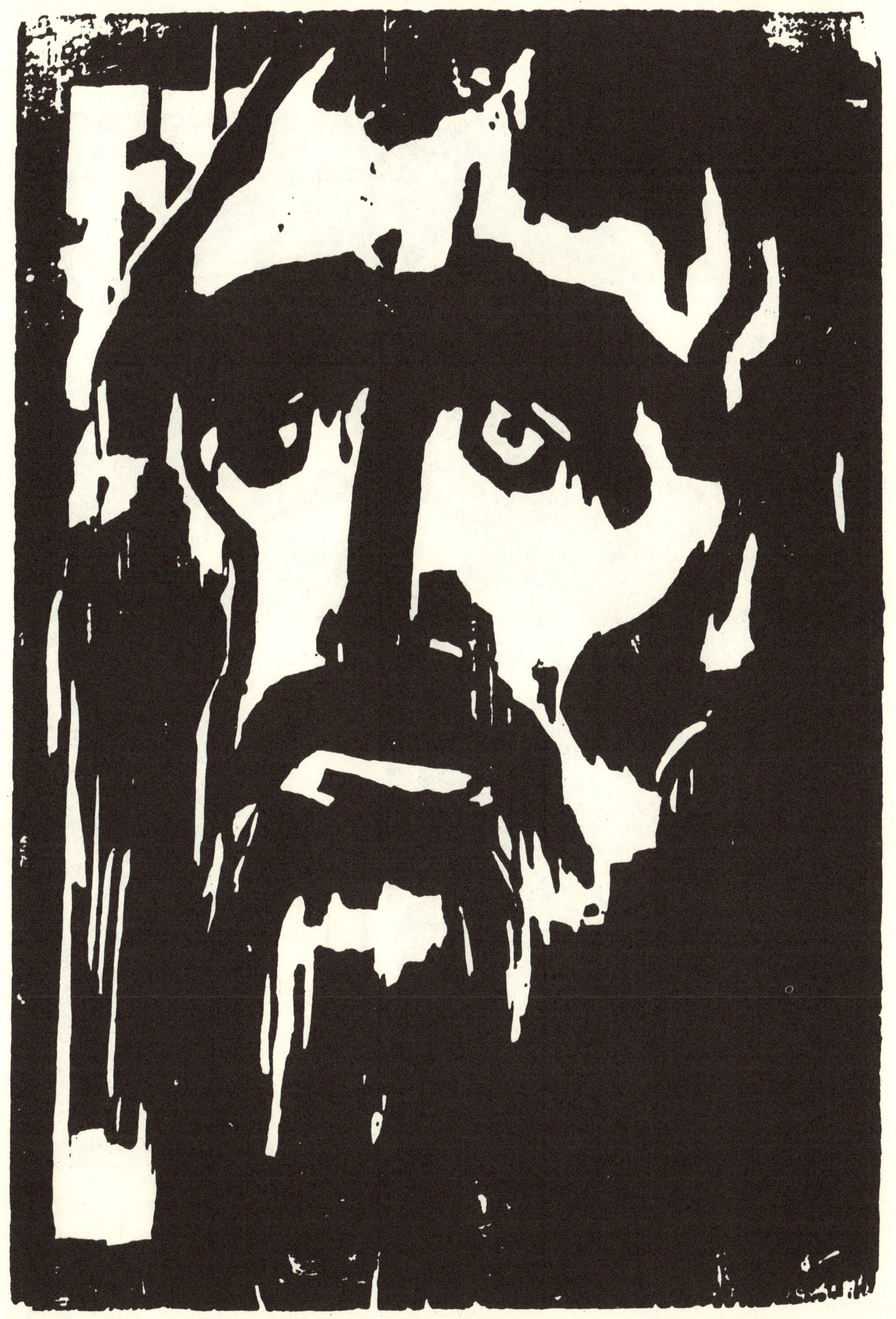

Emil Nolde. *Prophet*, 1912.

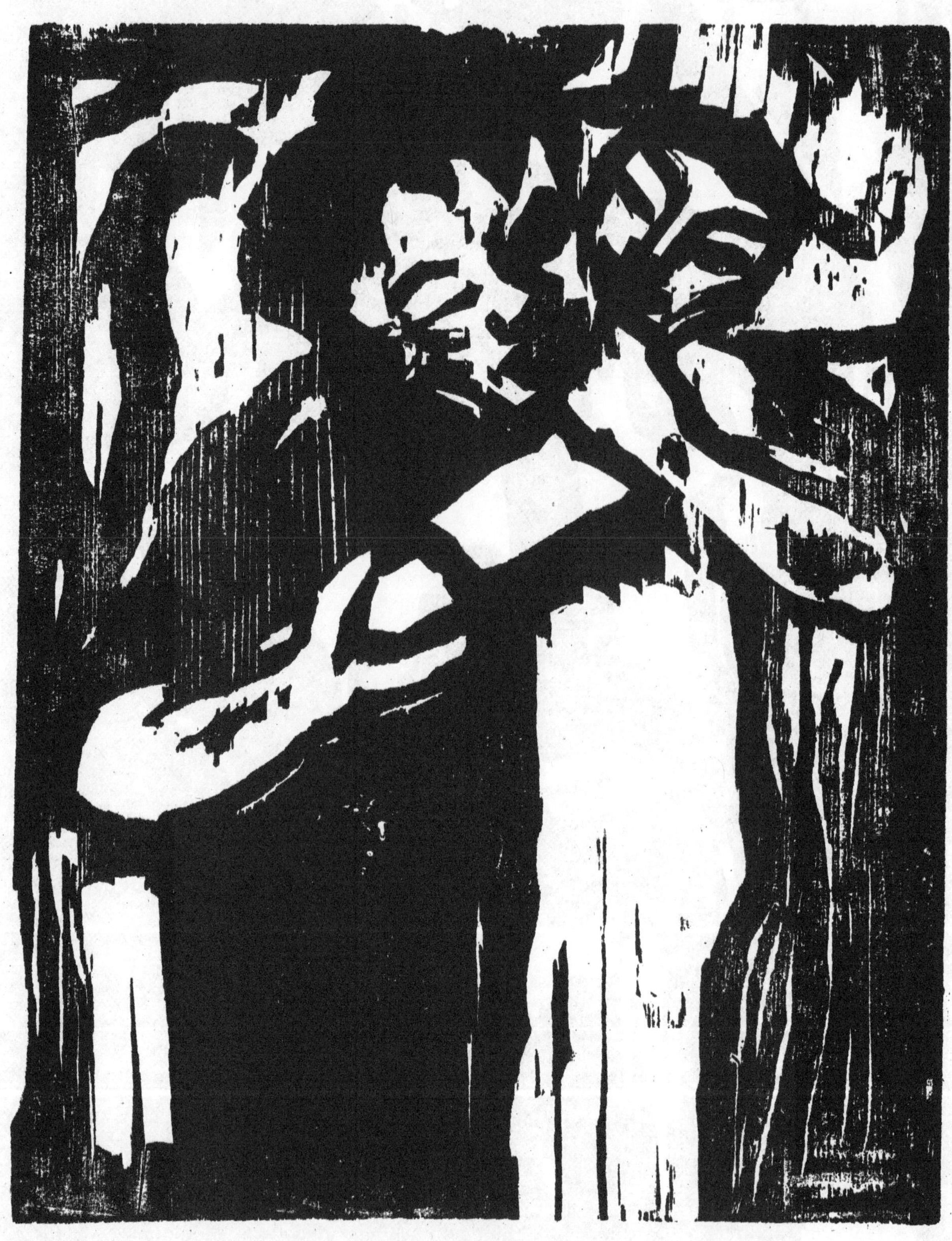

Emil Nolde. *Young Couple*, 1917.

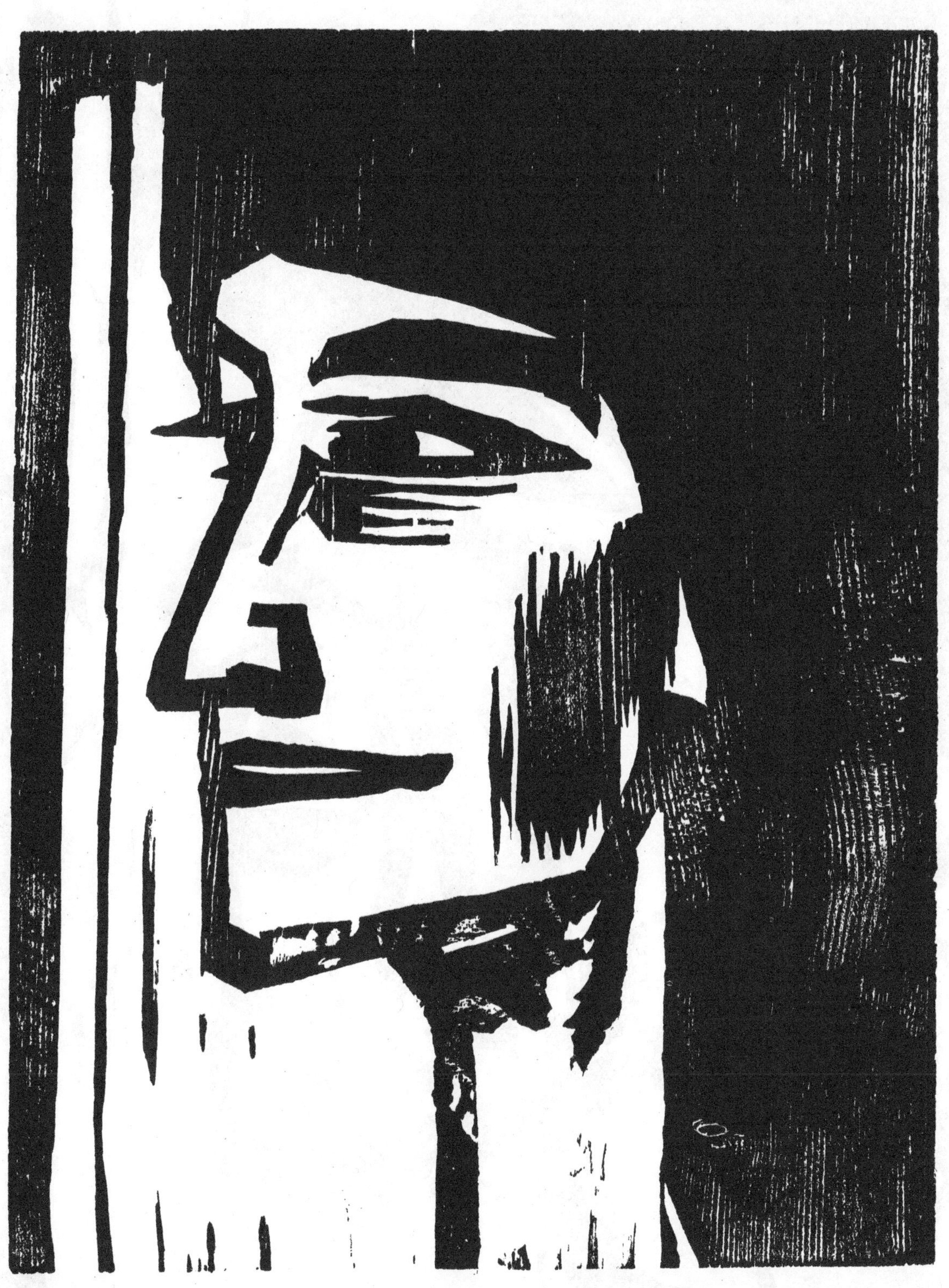

Emil Nolde. *Jestri*, 1917.

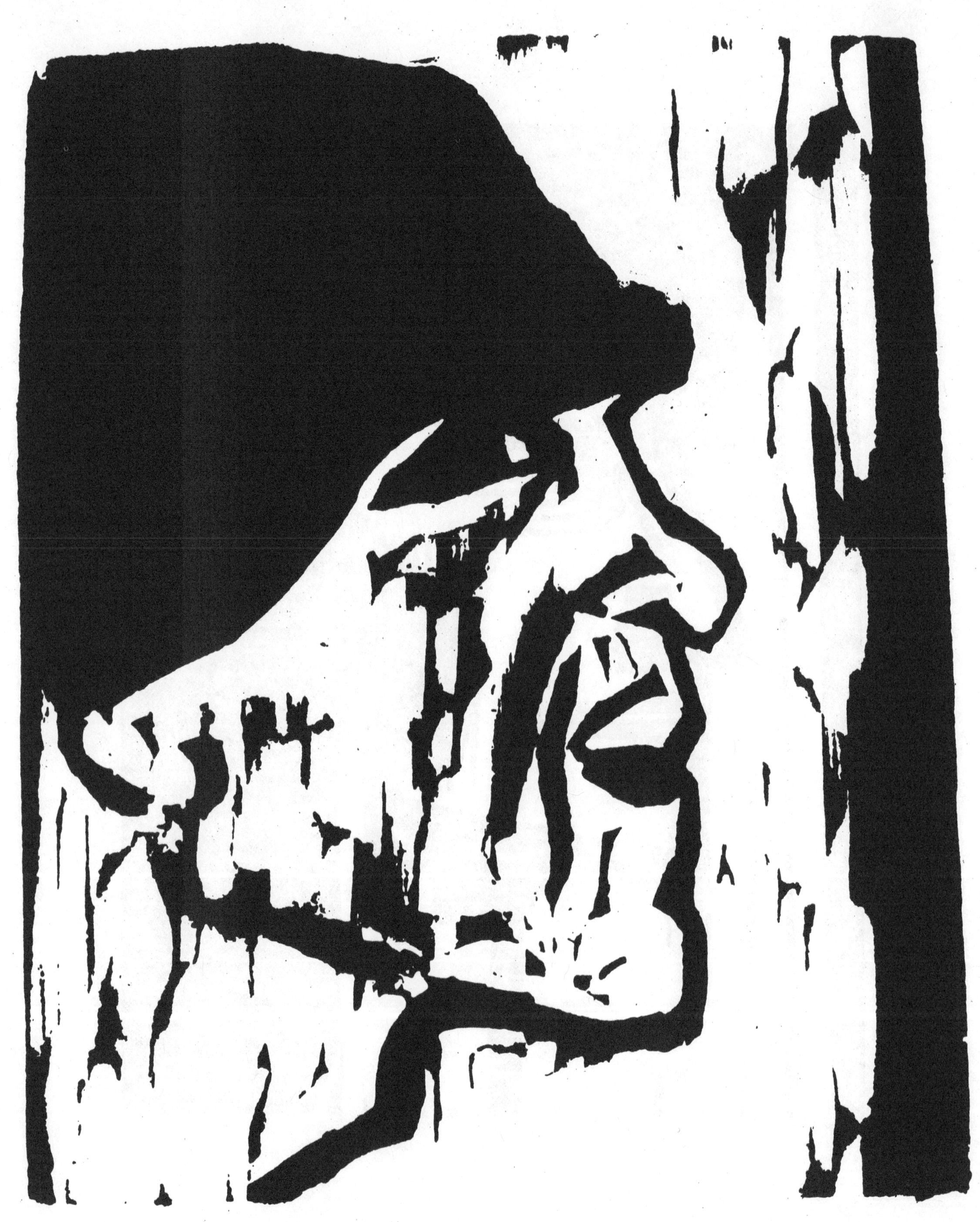

Max Pechstein. *Man's Head with Hat*, 1911.

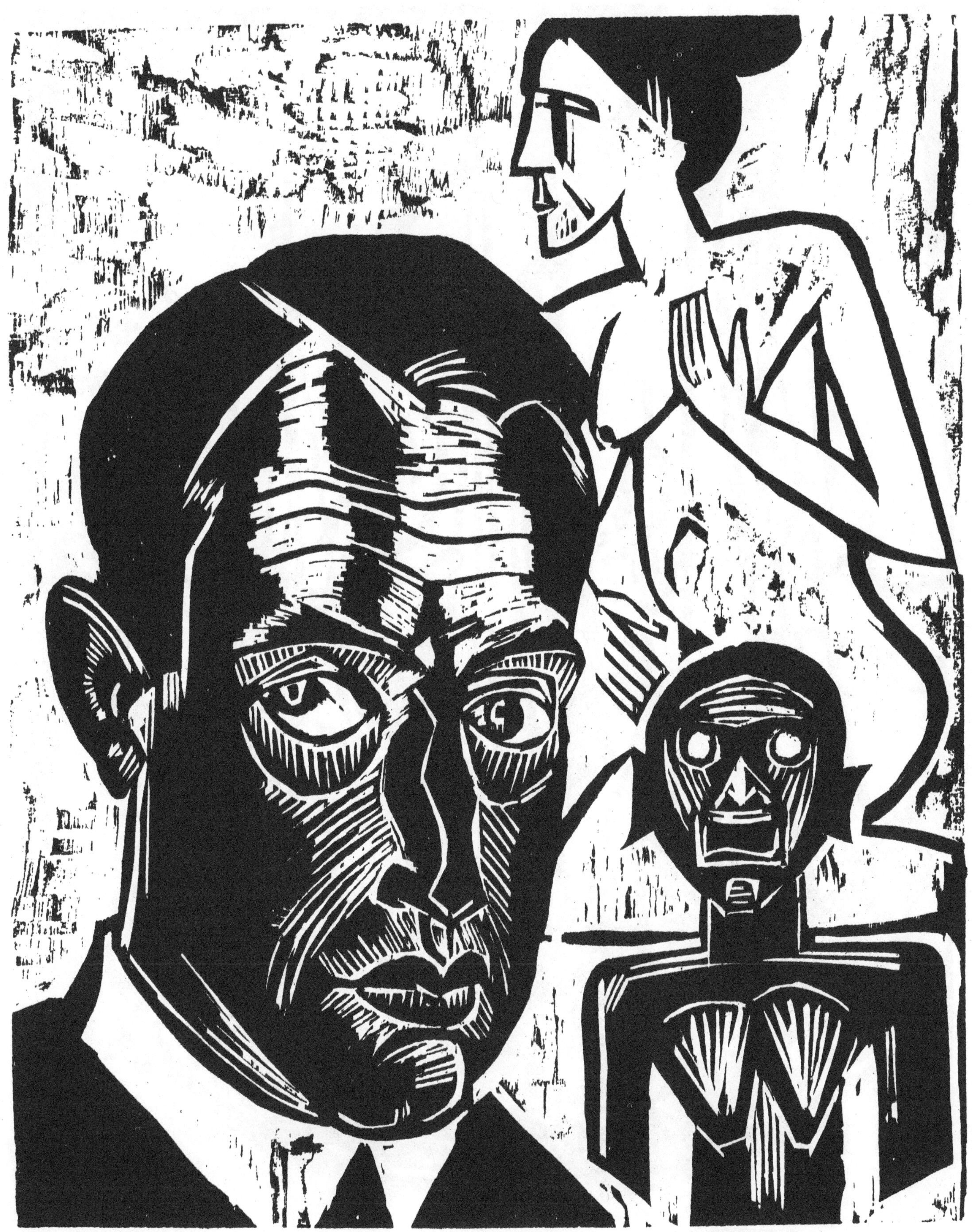

Max Pechstein. *Self-portrait,* 1922.

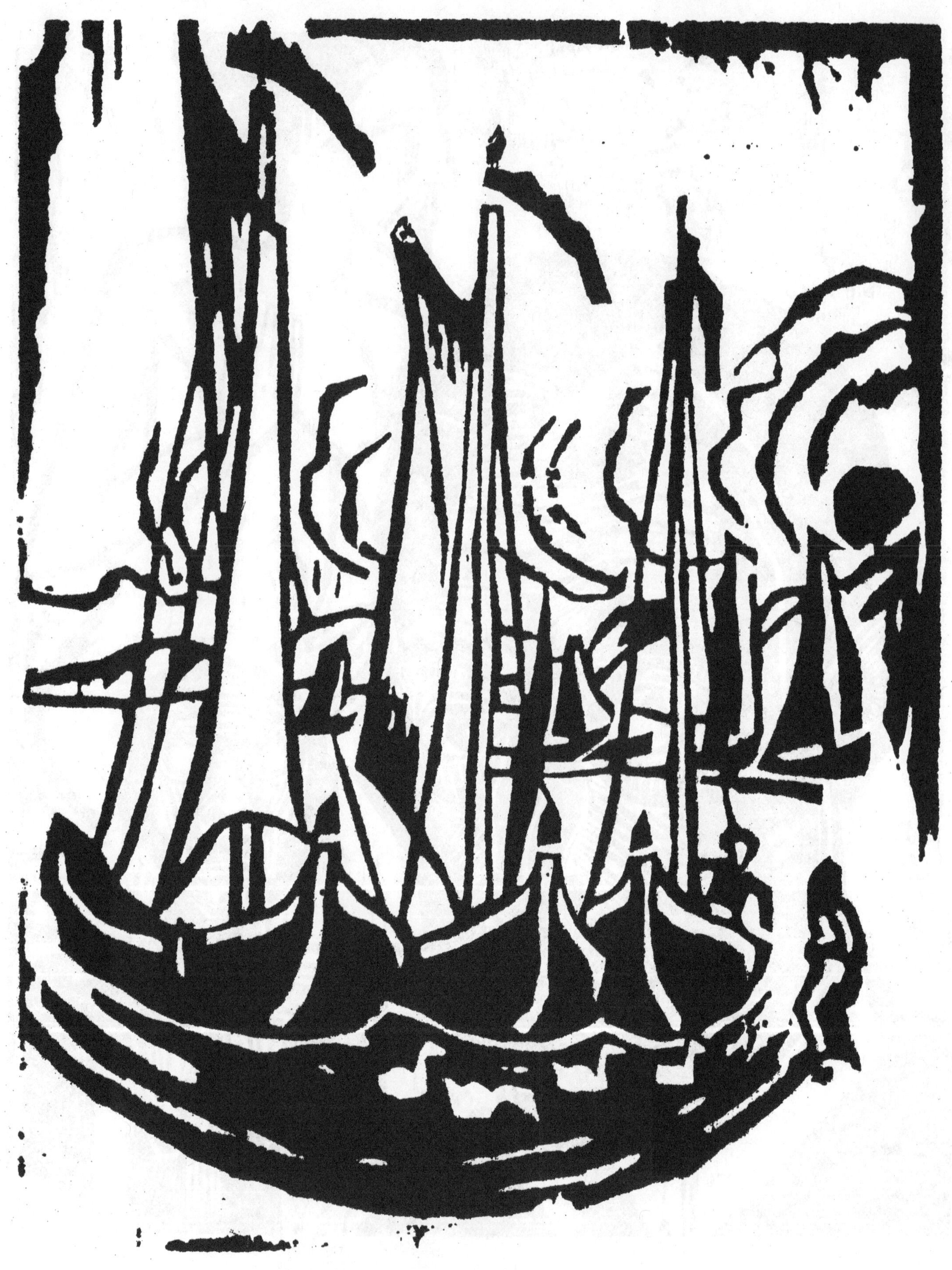

Max Pechstein. *Three Fishing Boats*, 1912.

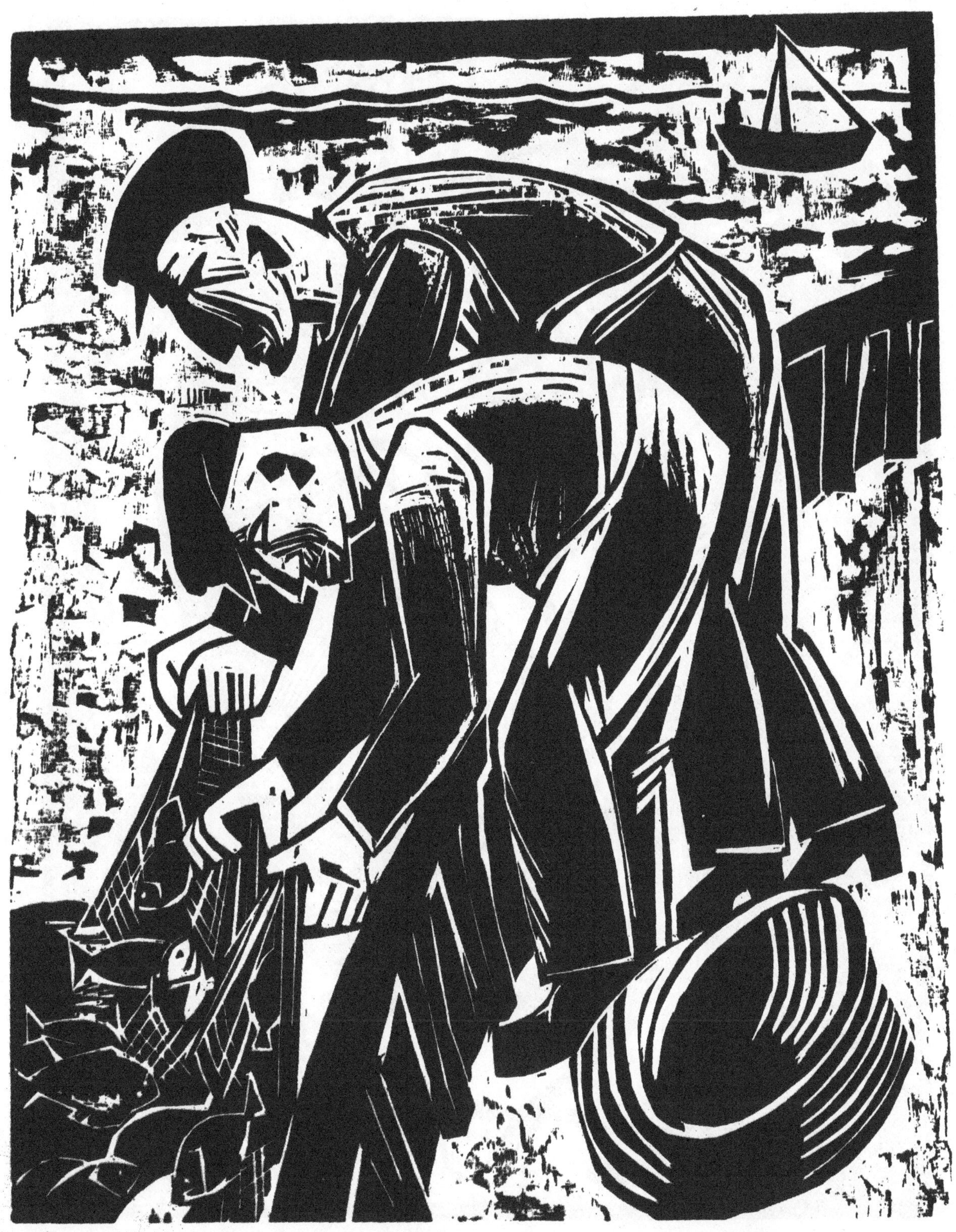

Max Pechstein. *Two Fishermen*, 1923.

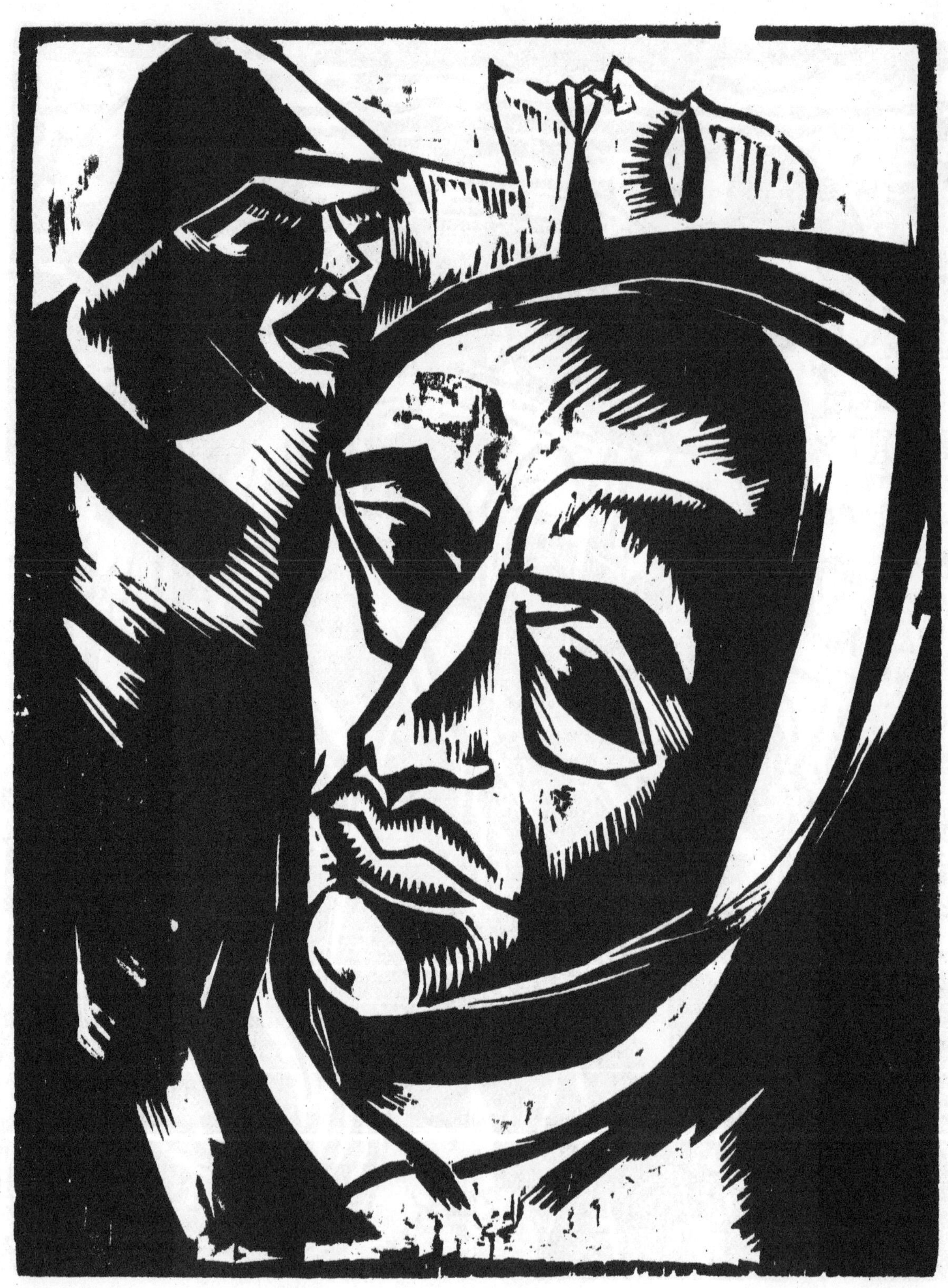

Max Pechstein. *Wounded Man*, 1919.

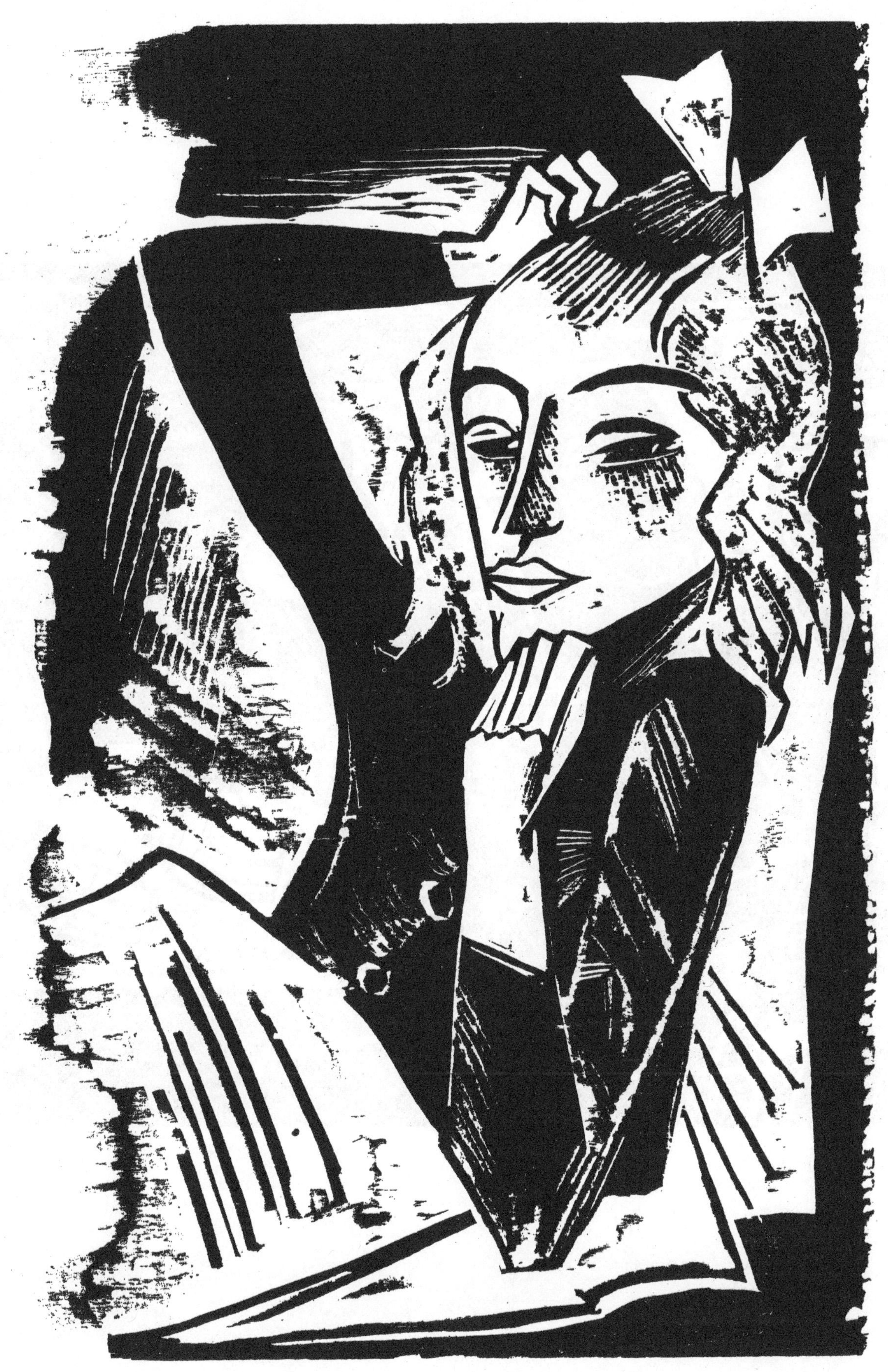

Max Pechstein. *The Convalescent*, n.d.

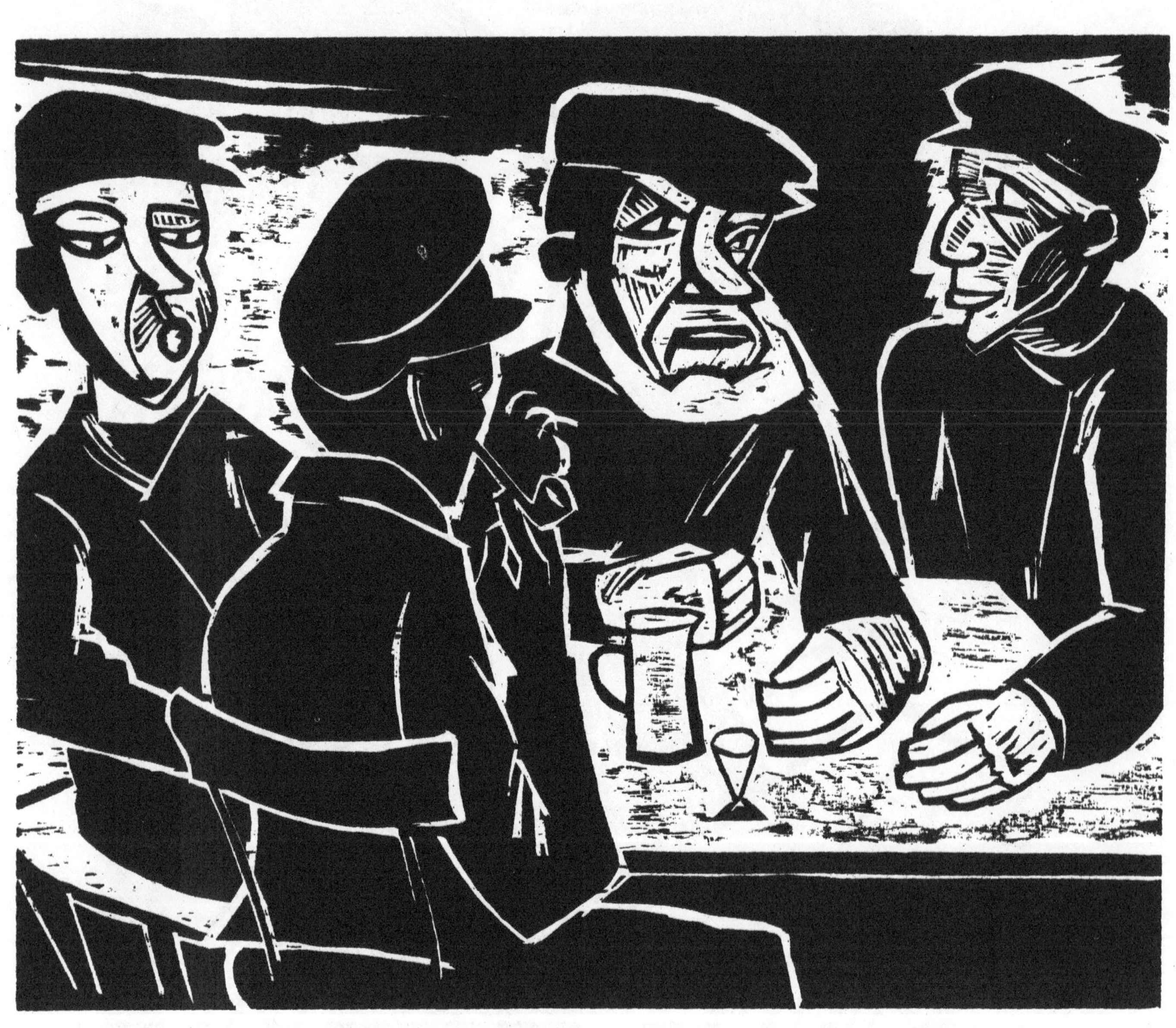

Max Pechstein. *Four Men at Table*, 1923.

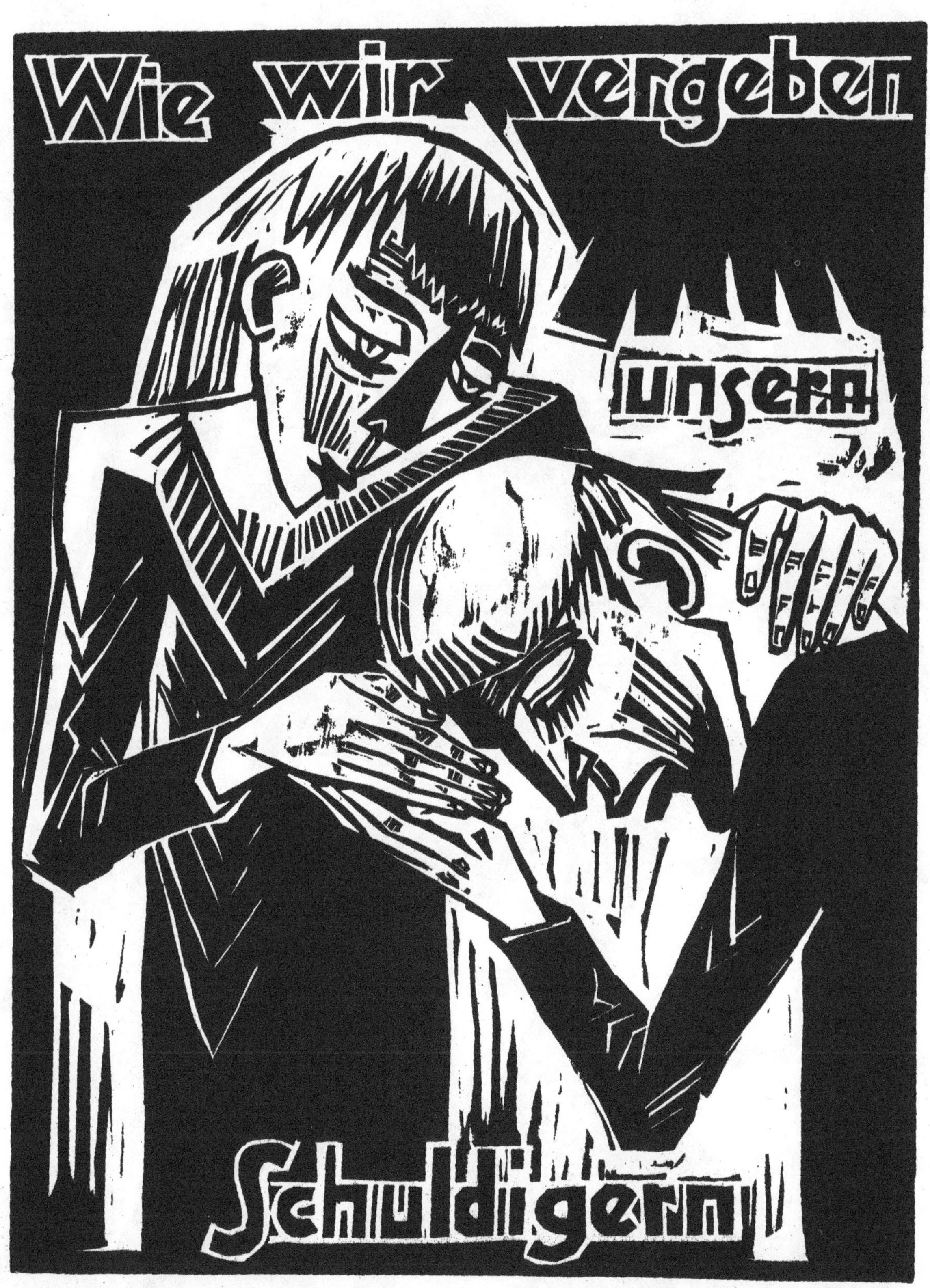

Max Pechstein. *As we forgive those who trespass against us*, 1921.

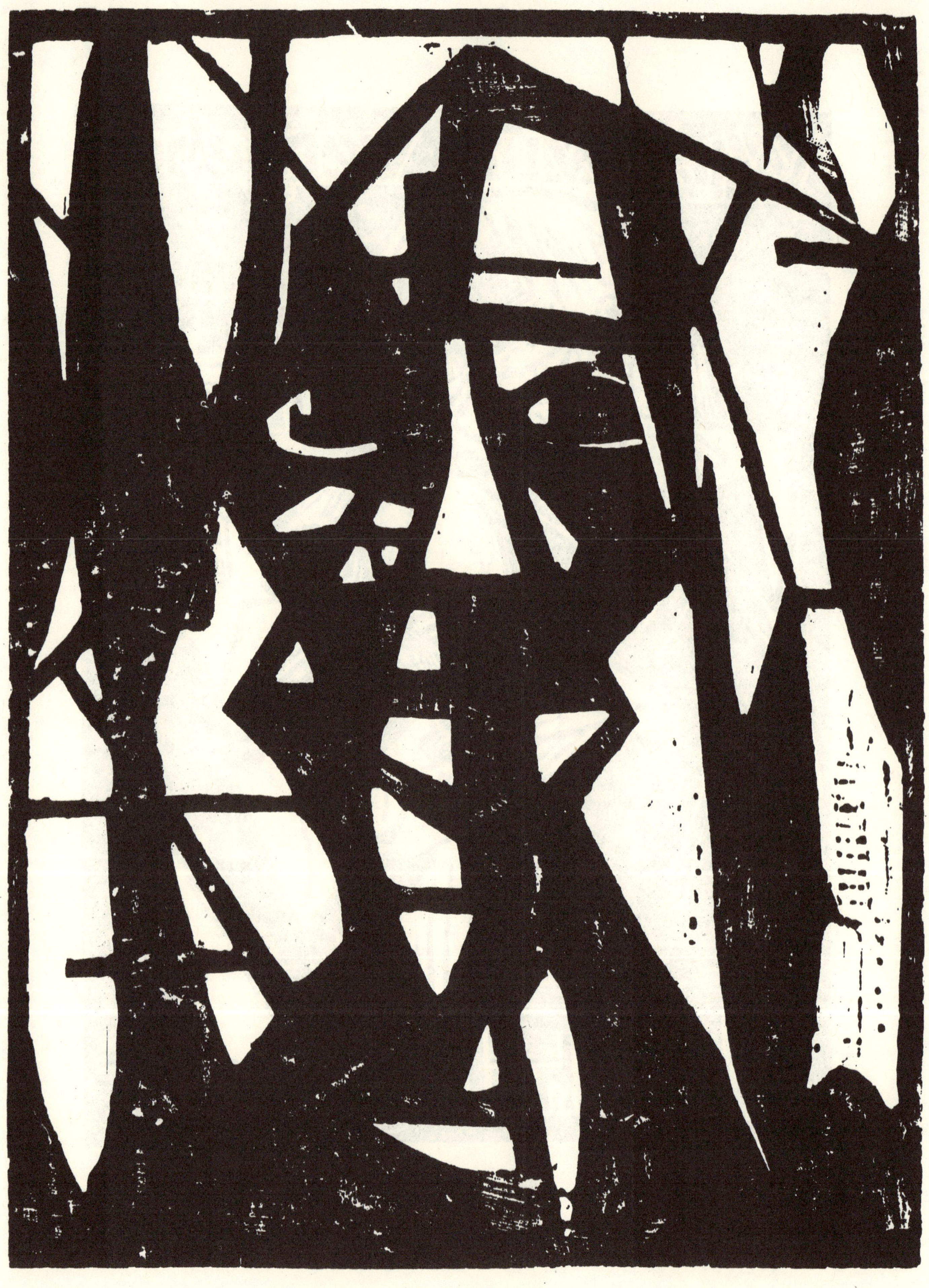

Christian Rohlfs. *Large Head*, 1922.

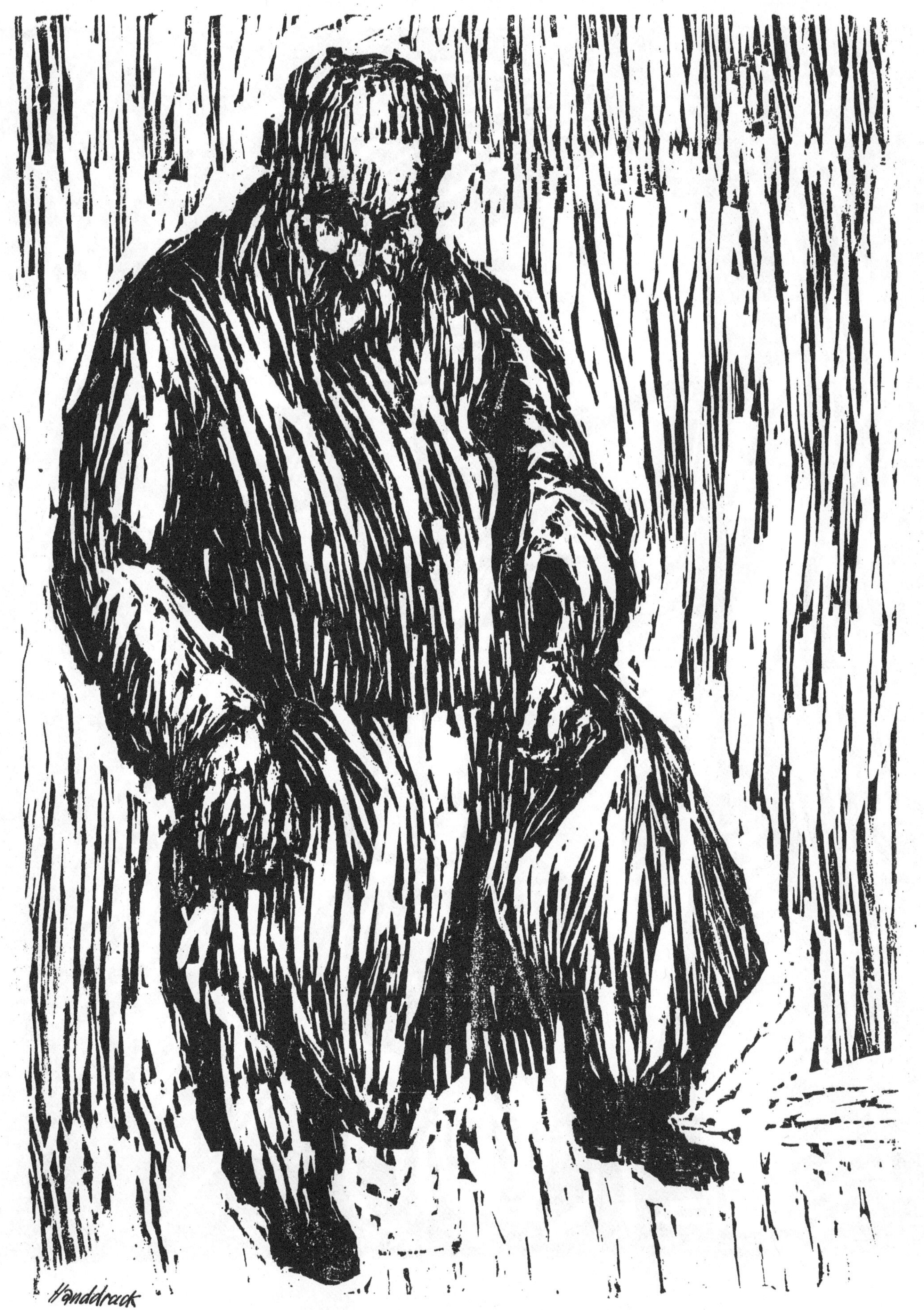

Wilhelm Rudolph. *Old Man*, n.d.

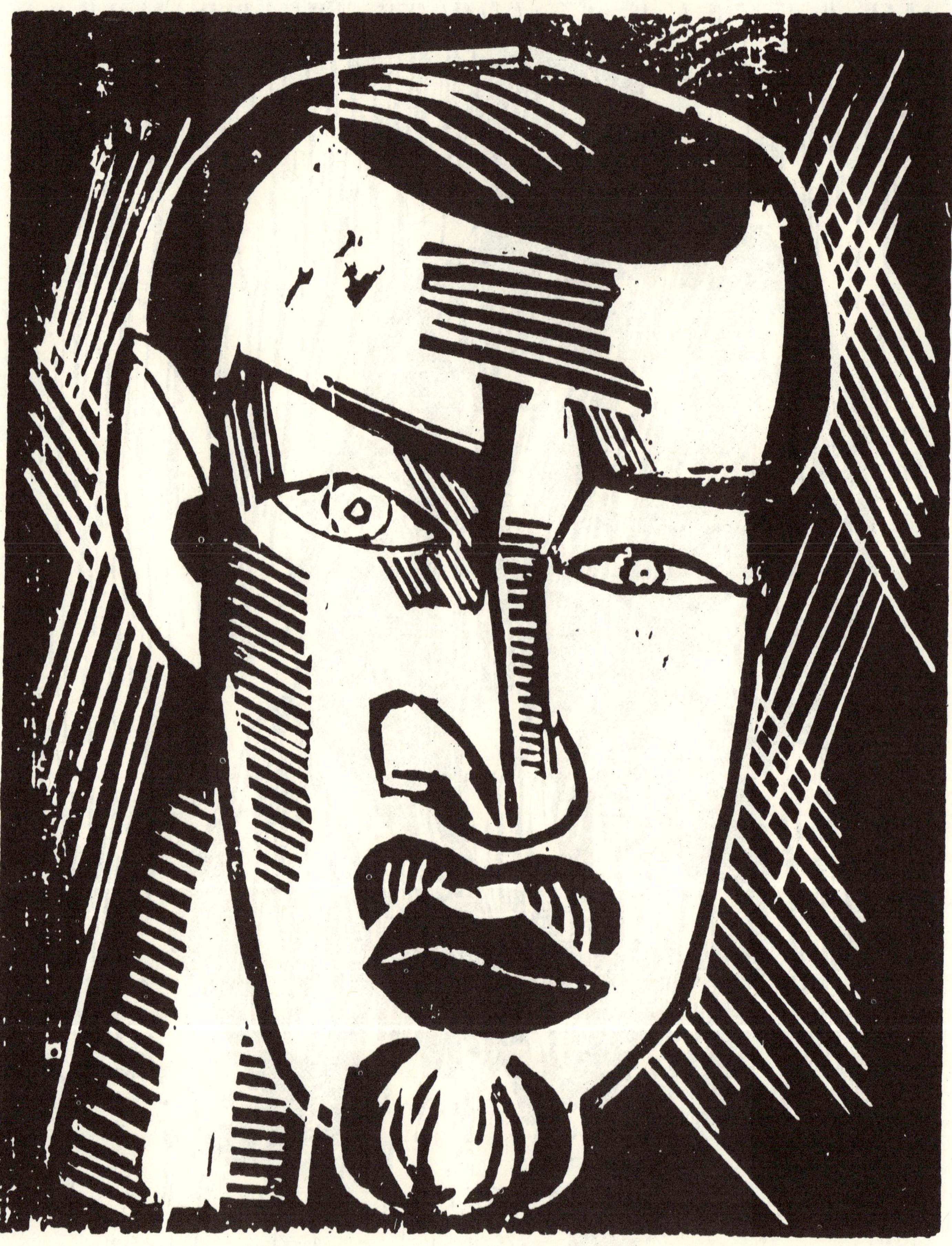

Karl Schmidt-Rottluff. *Self-portrait*, 1916.

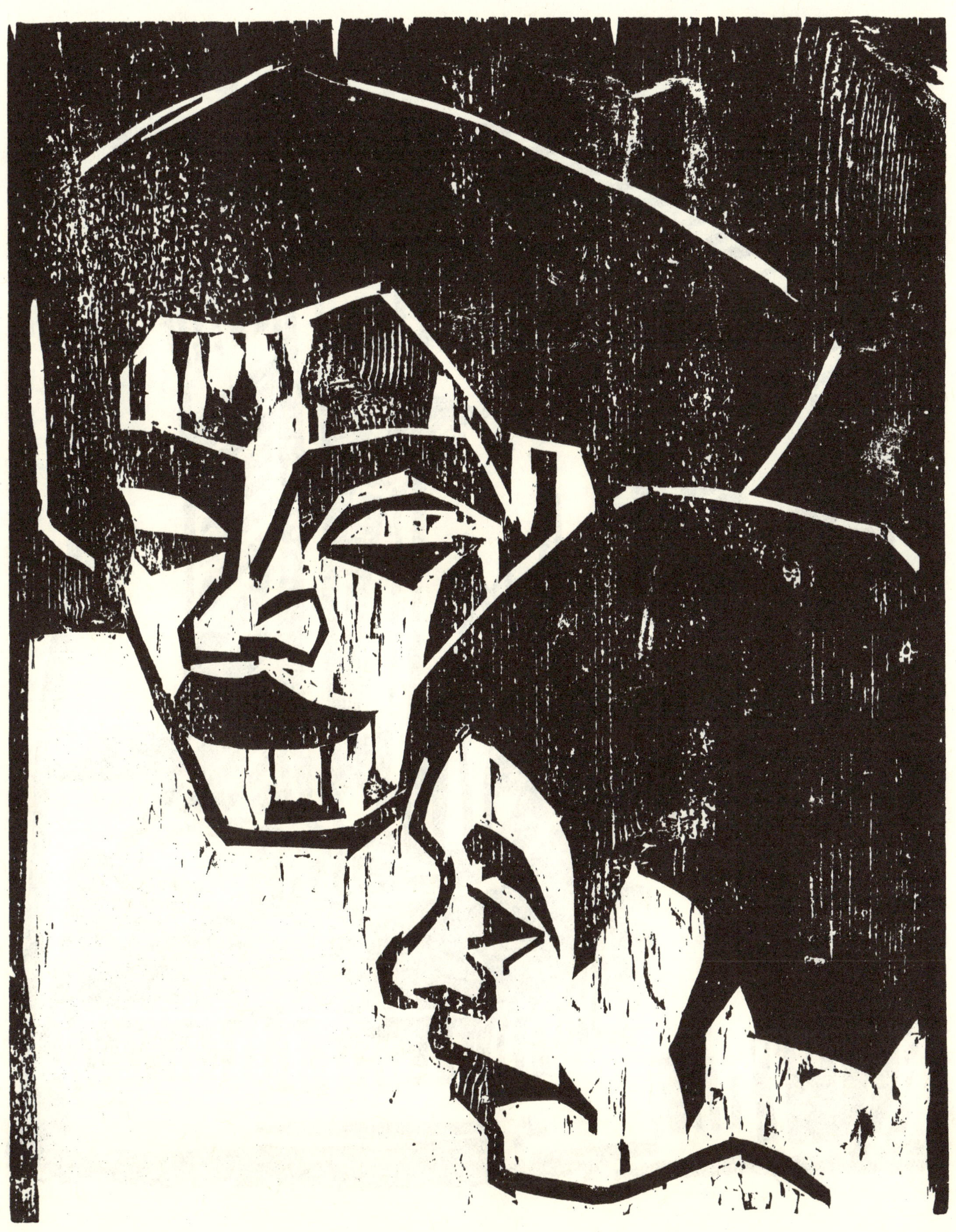

Karl Schmidt-Rottluff. *Heads I*, 1911.

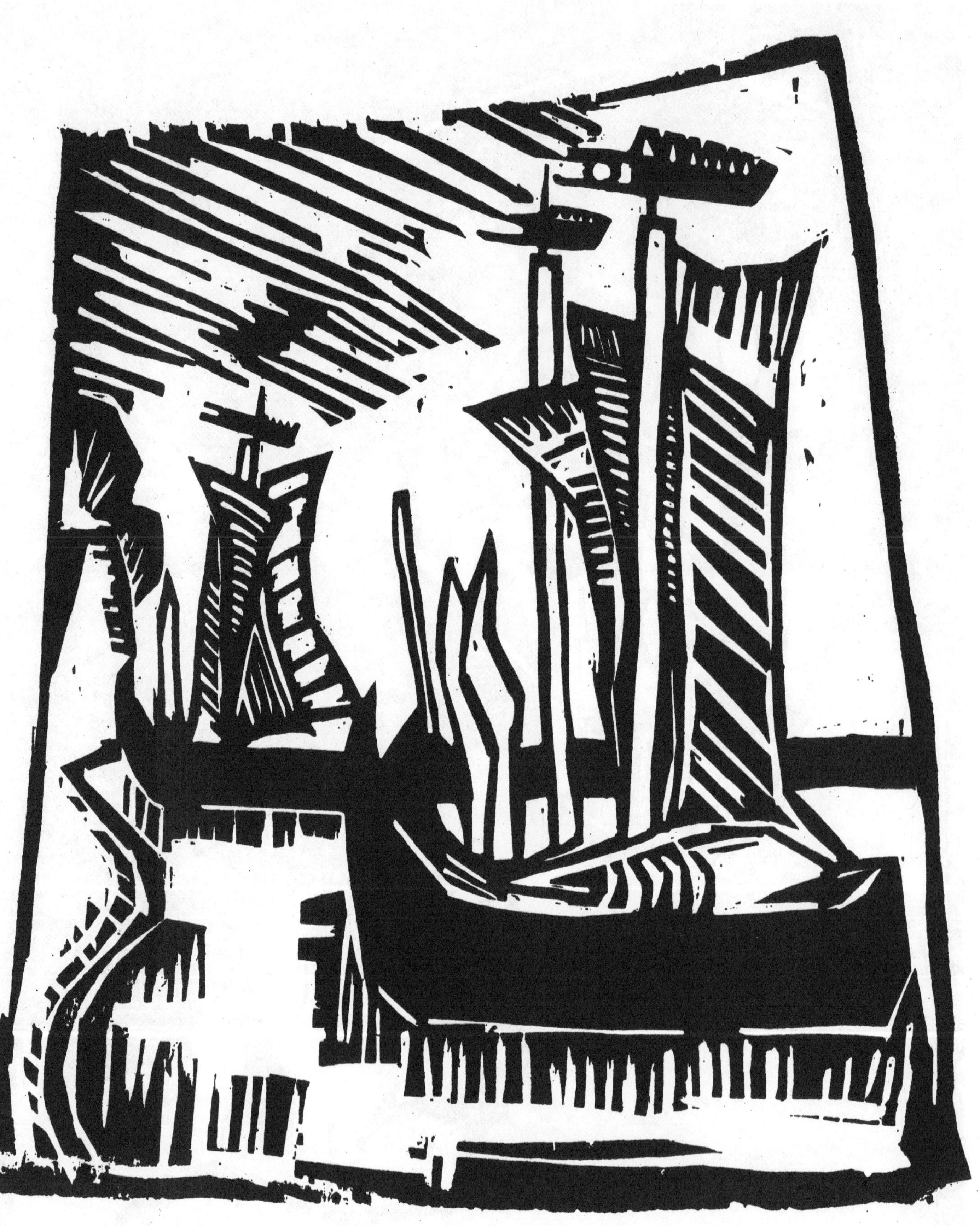

Karl Schmidt-Rottluff. *Fishing Boats*, 1913.

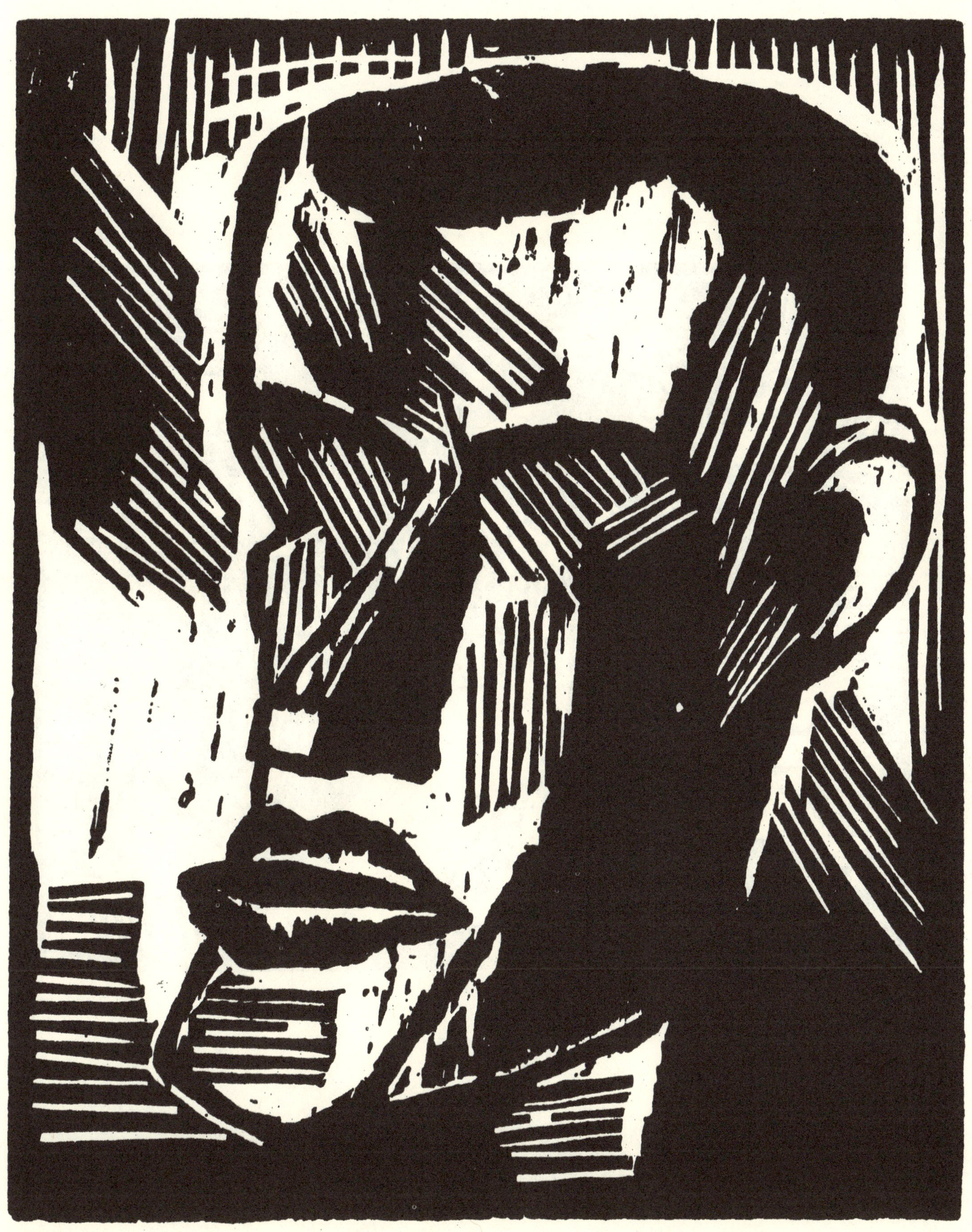

Karl Schmidt-Rottluff. *Self-portrait*, 1914.

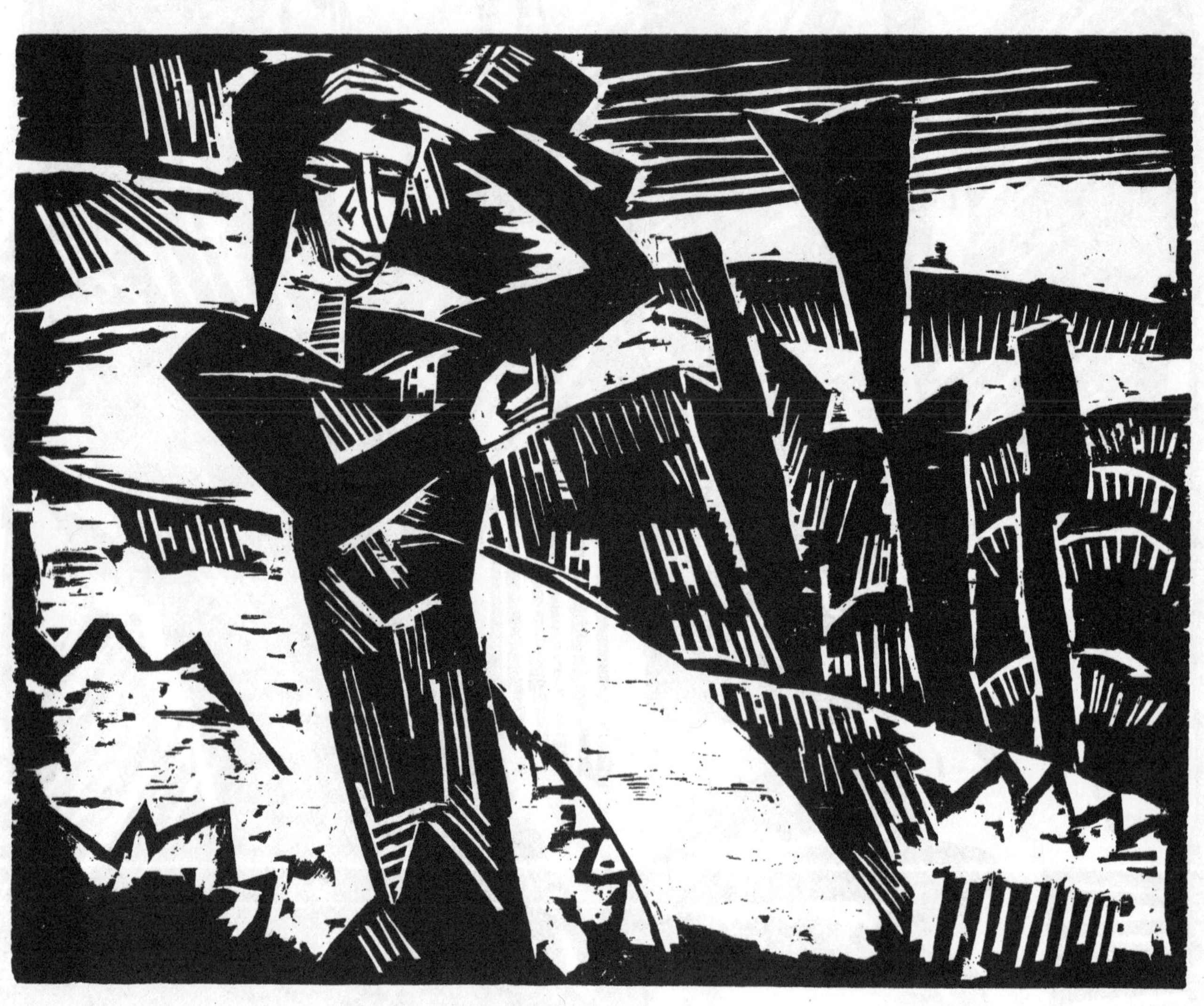

Karl Schmidt-Rottluff. *Woman in the Dunes*, 1914.

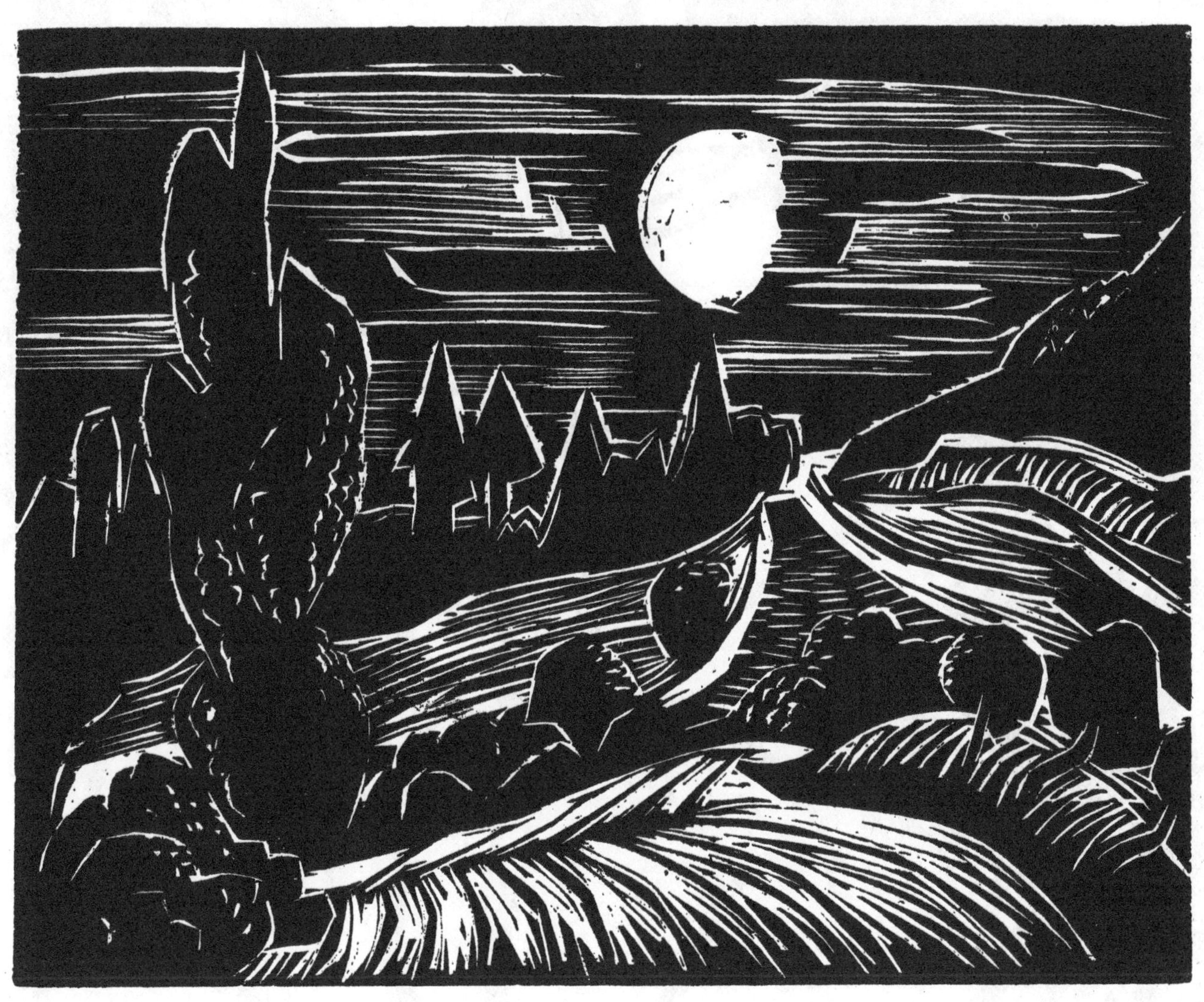

Karl Schmidt-Rottluff. *Moonlight*, 1924.

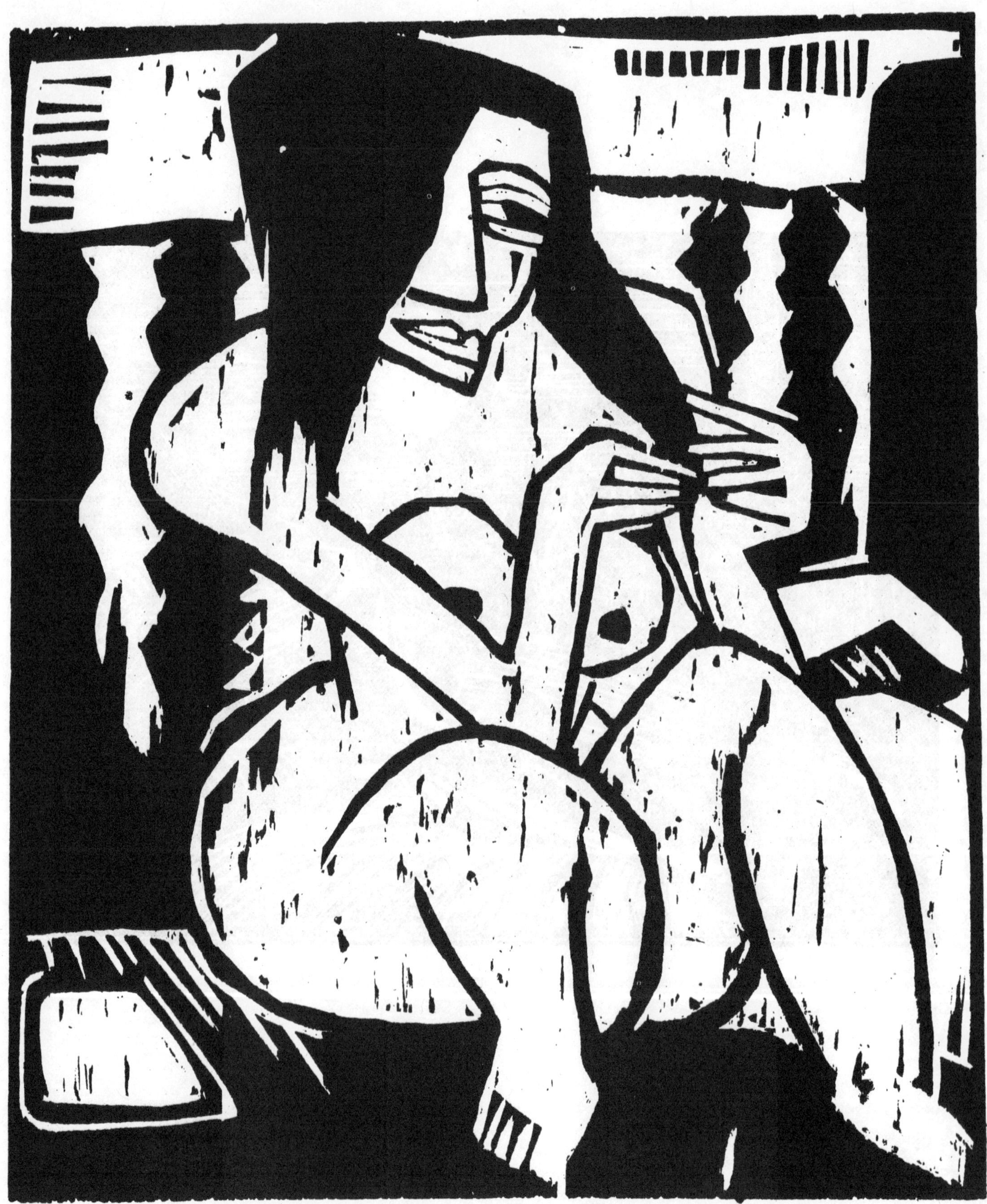

Karl Schmidt-Rottluff. *Reclining Model*, 1911.

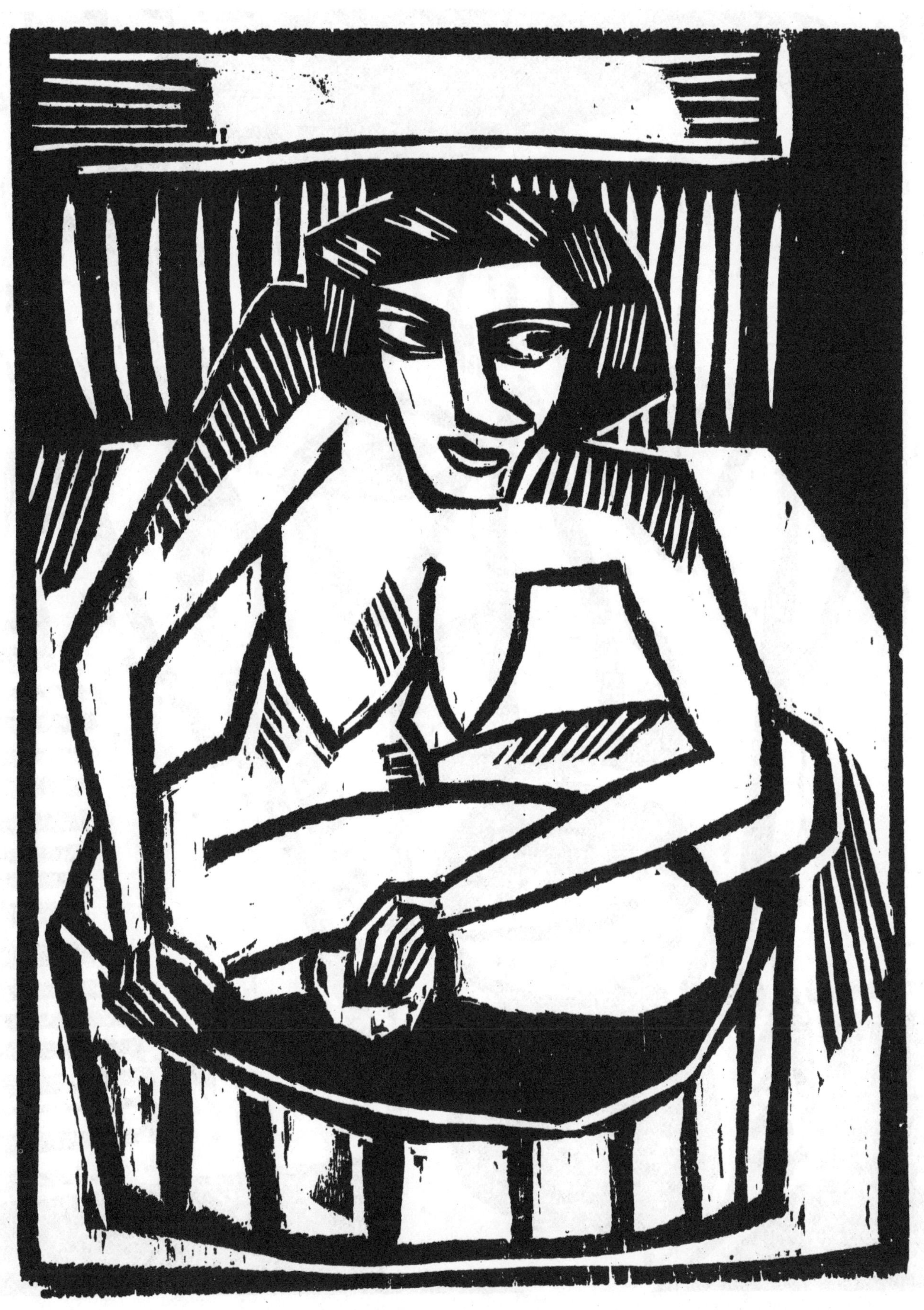

Karl Schmidt-Rottluff. Untitled, 1915.

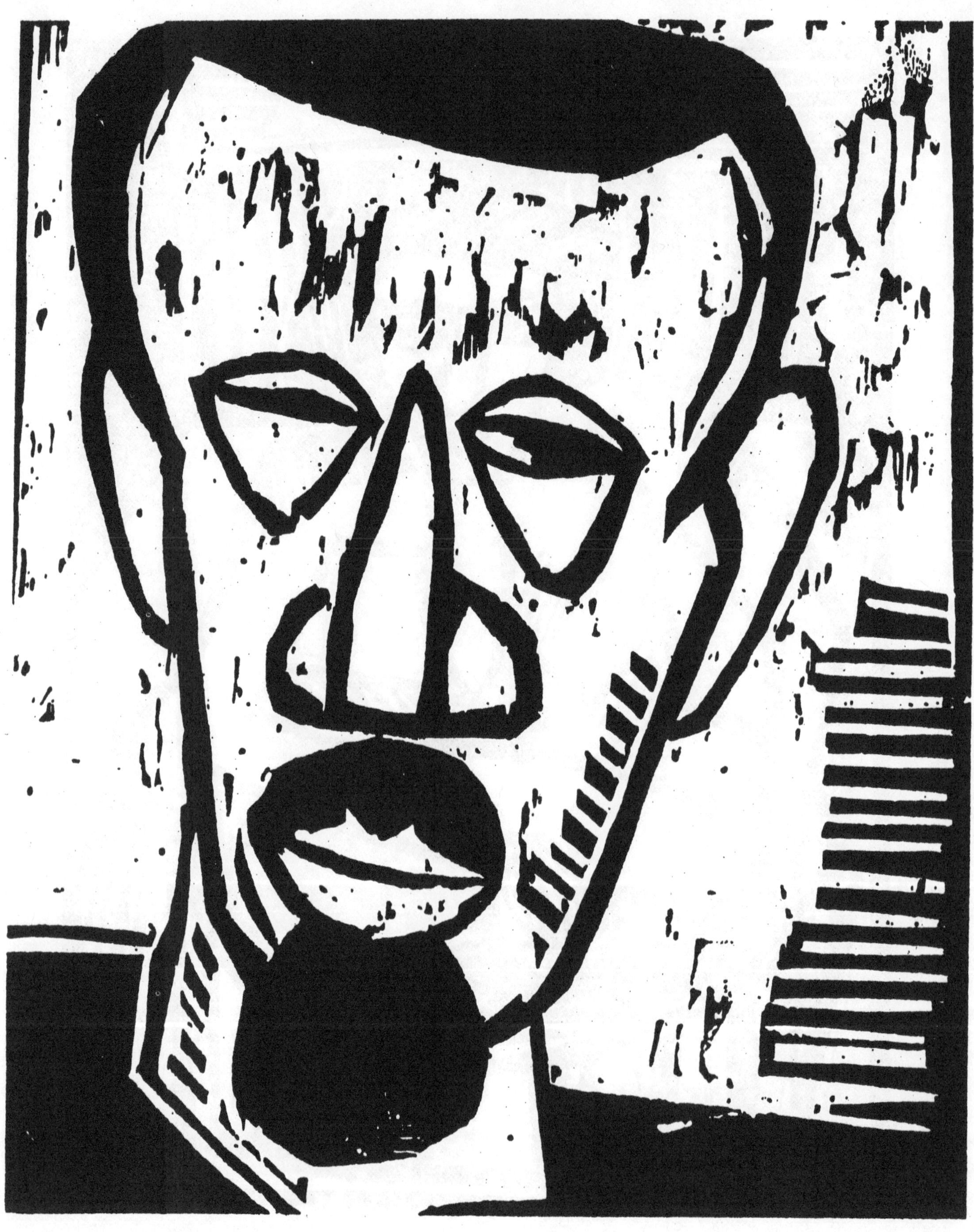

Karl Schmidt-Rottluff. *Self-portrait*, 1917.

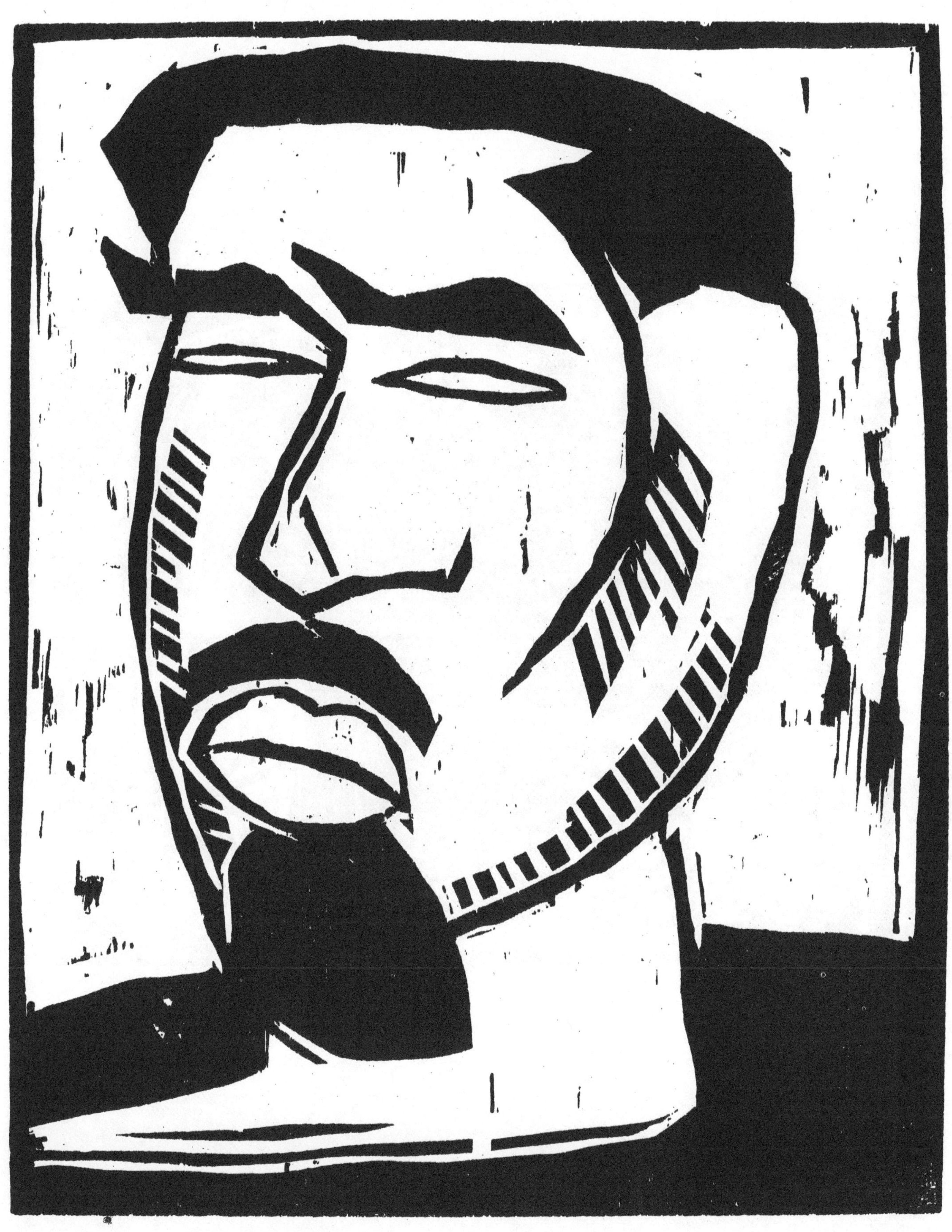

Karl Schmidt-Rottluff. *Self-portrait*, 1914.

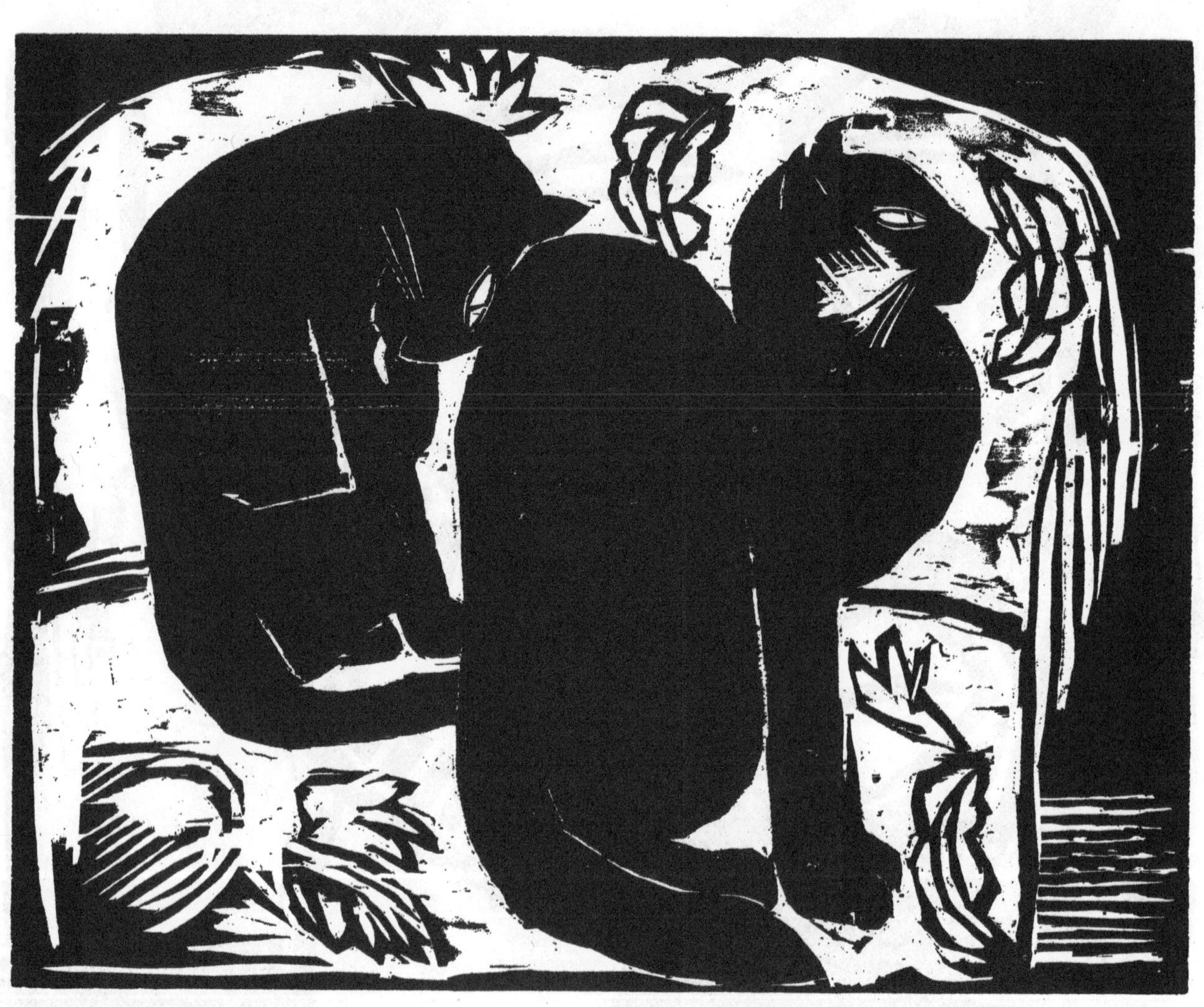

Karl Schmidt-Rottluff. *Cats*, 1914.

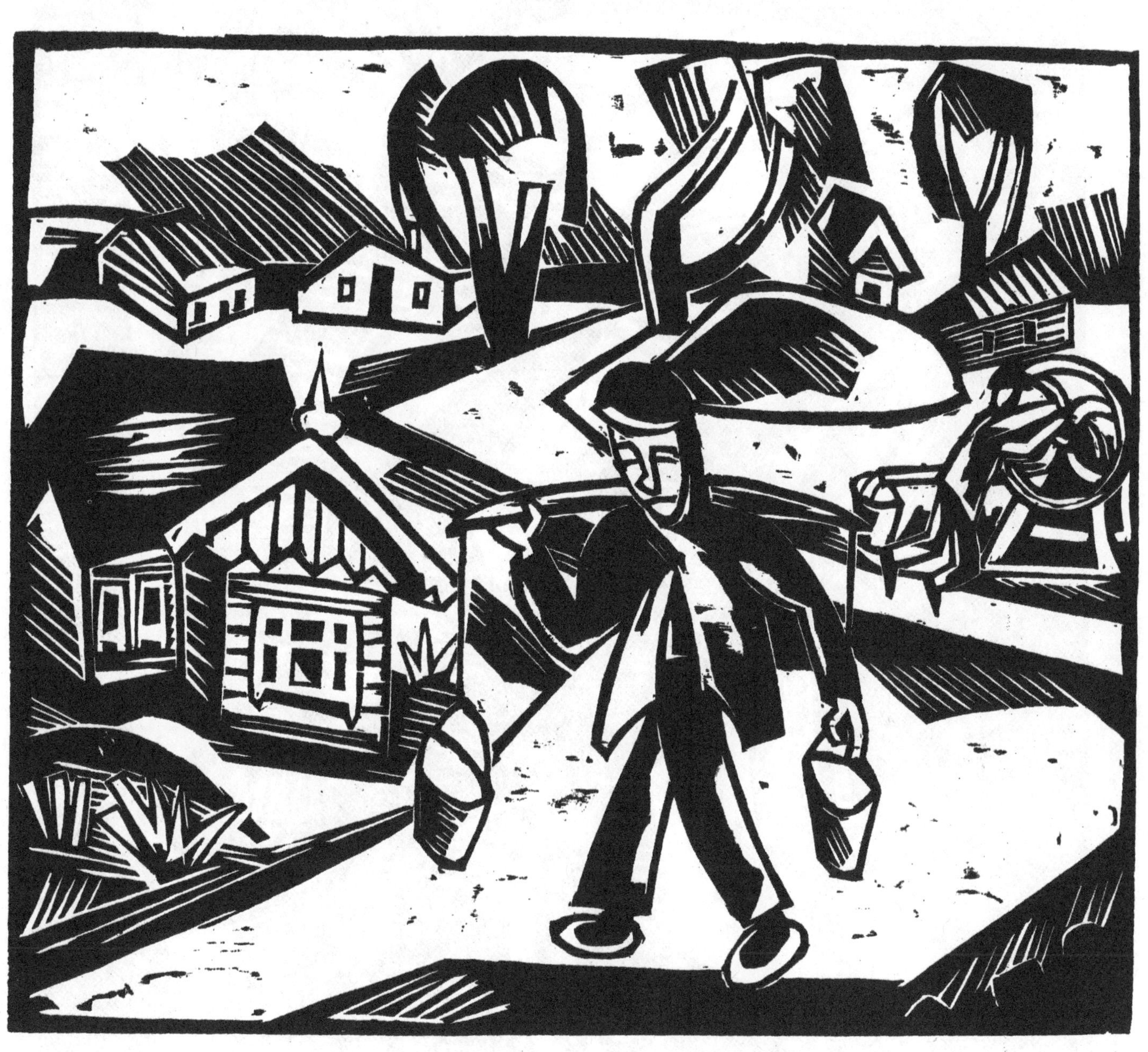

Karl Schmidt-Rottluff. *Russian Landscape with Water-carrier*, 1919.

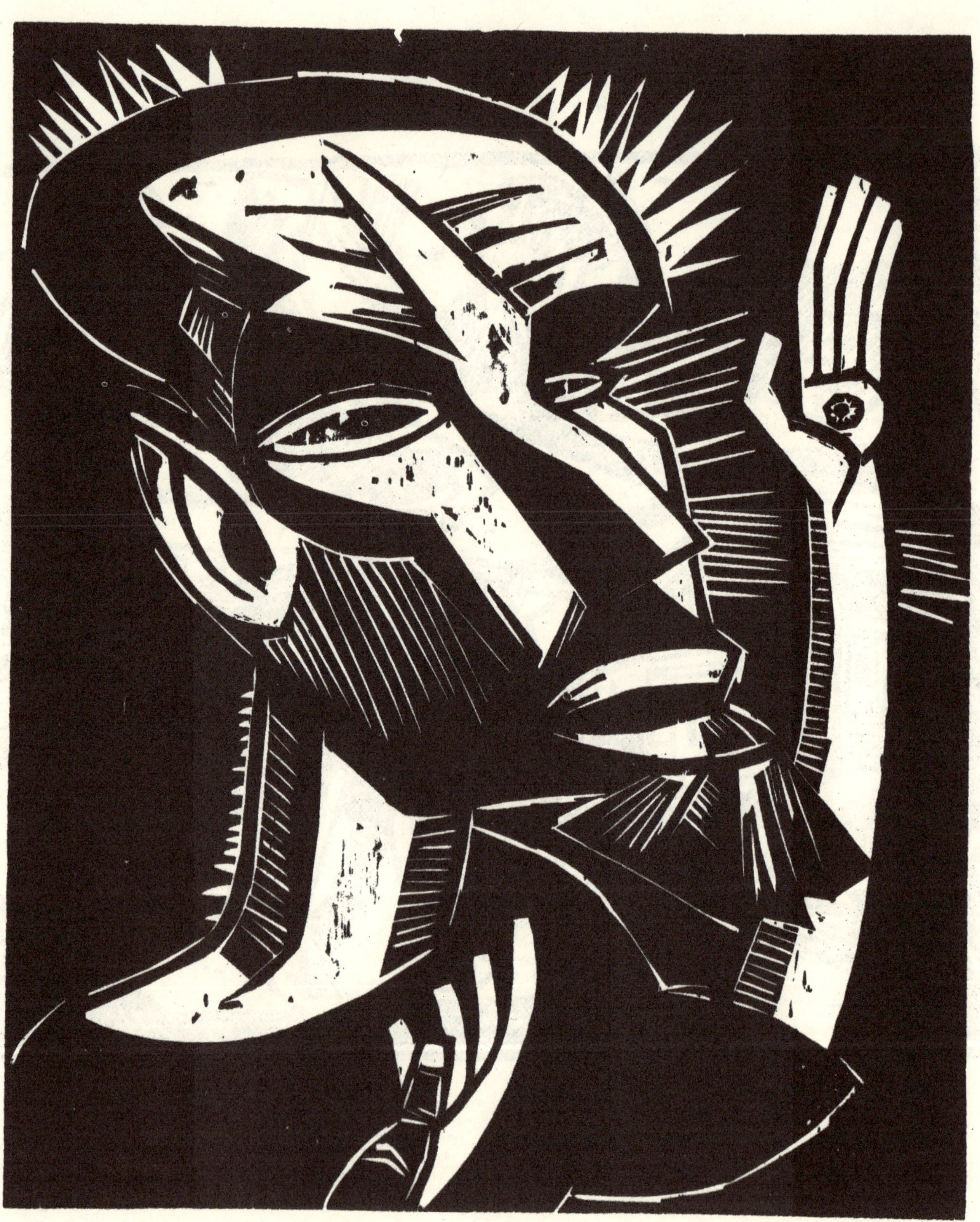

Karl Schmidt-Rottluff. *Saint Francis*, 1919.

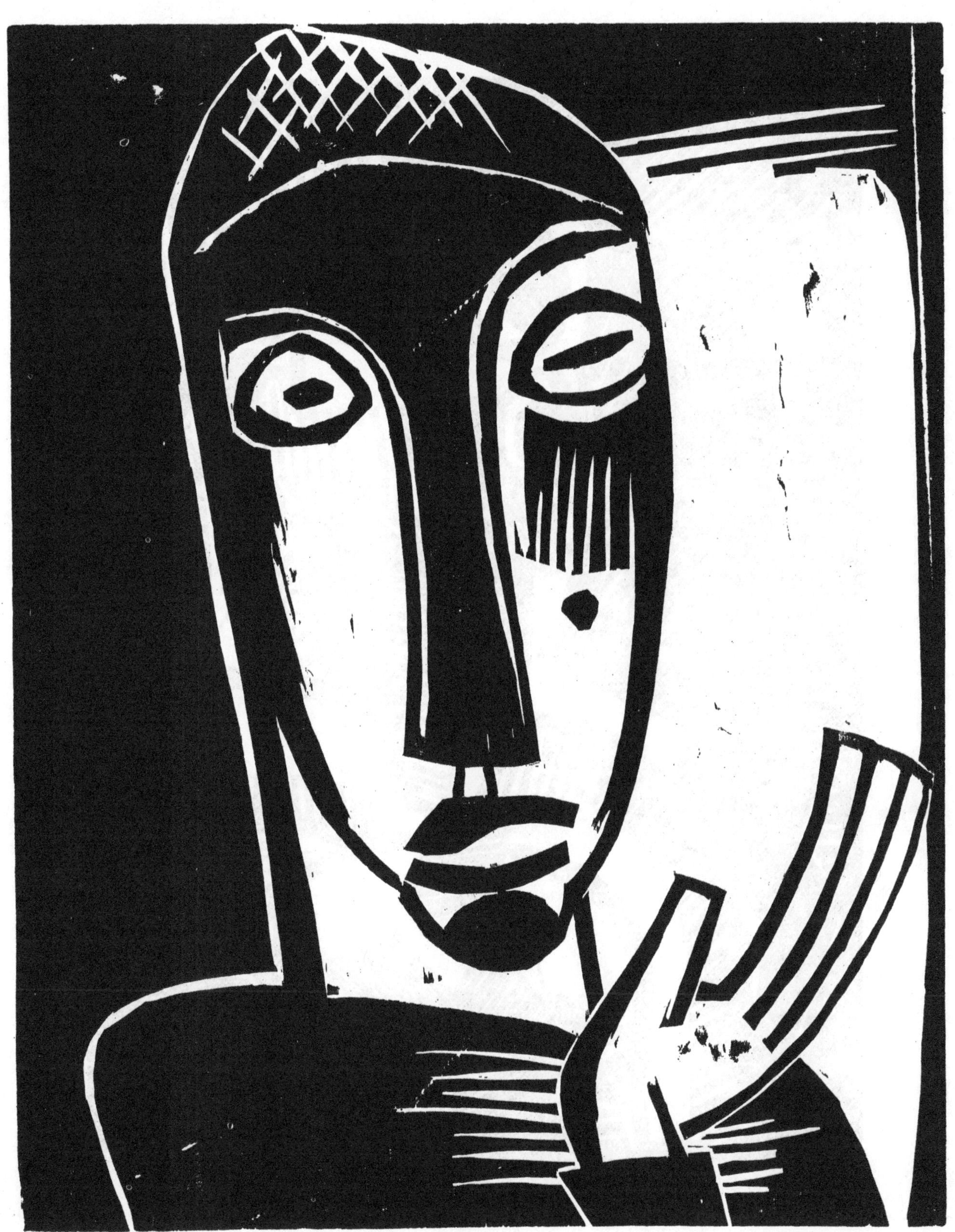

Karl Schmidt-Rottluff. *Prophetess*, 1919.

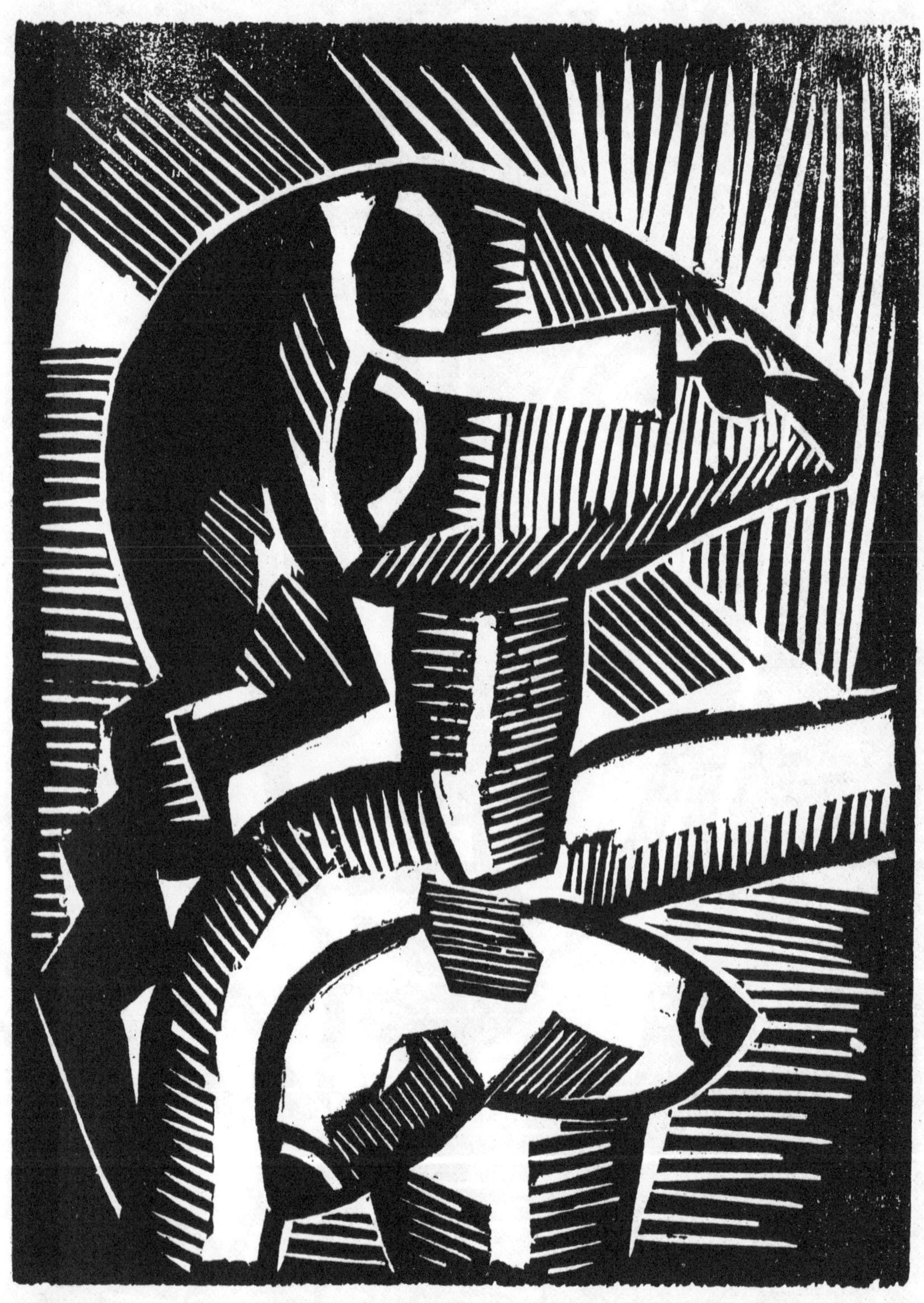

Karl Schmidt-Rottluff. Untitled, 1918.

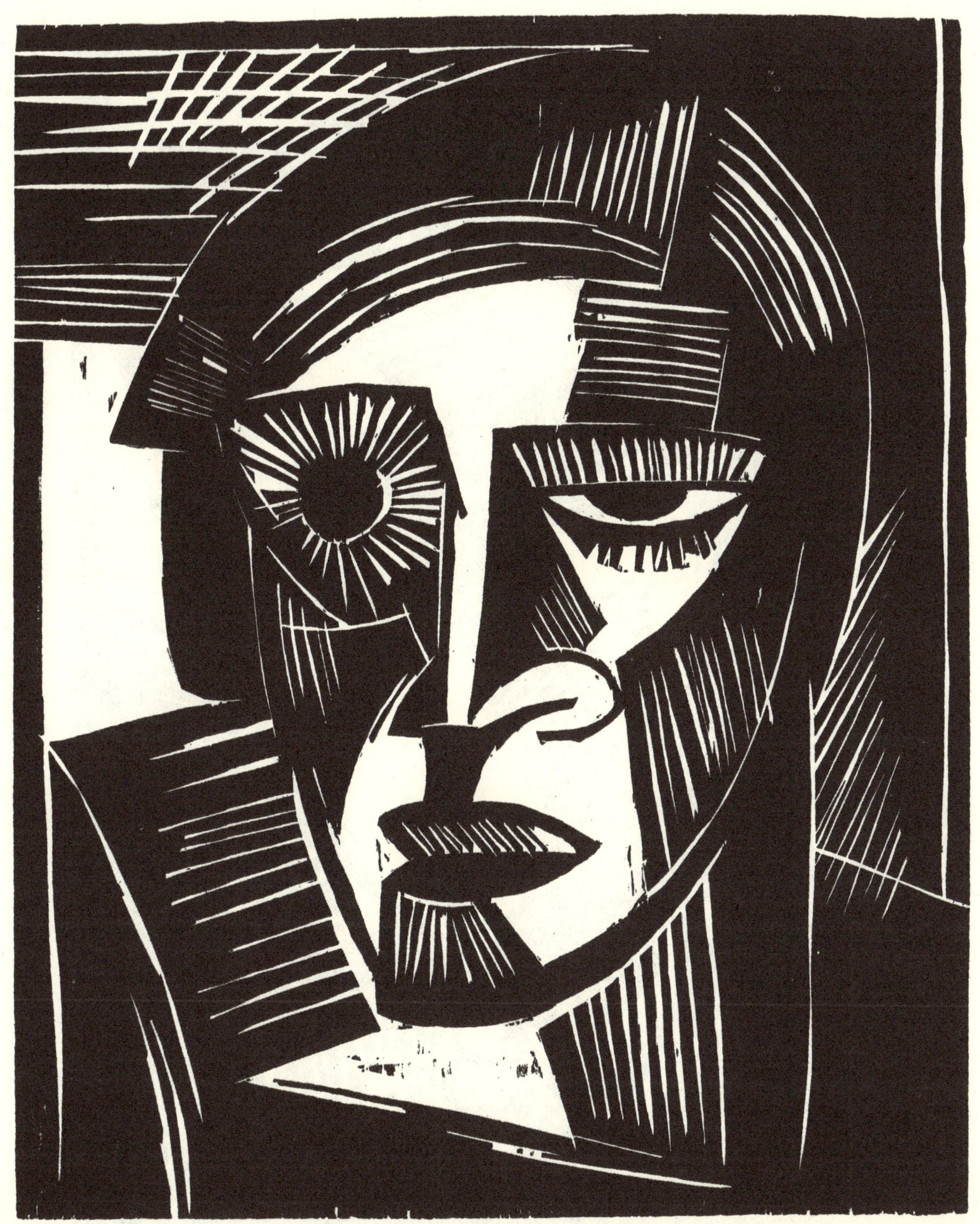

Karl Schmidt-Rottluff. *Head of a Woman*, 1919.

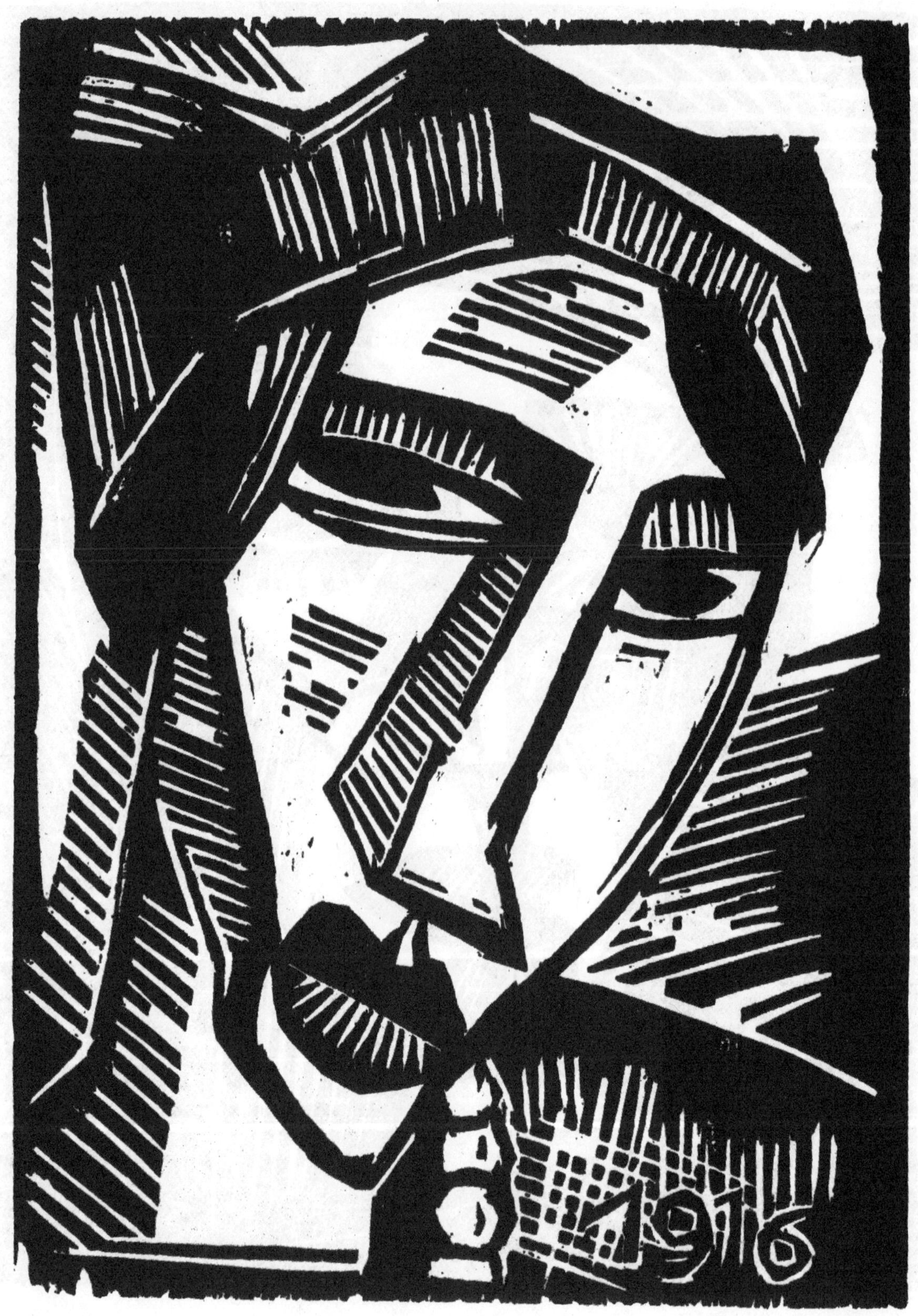

Karl Schmidt-Rottluff. *Head of a Woman*, 1916.

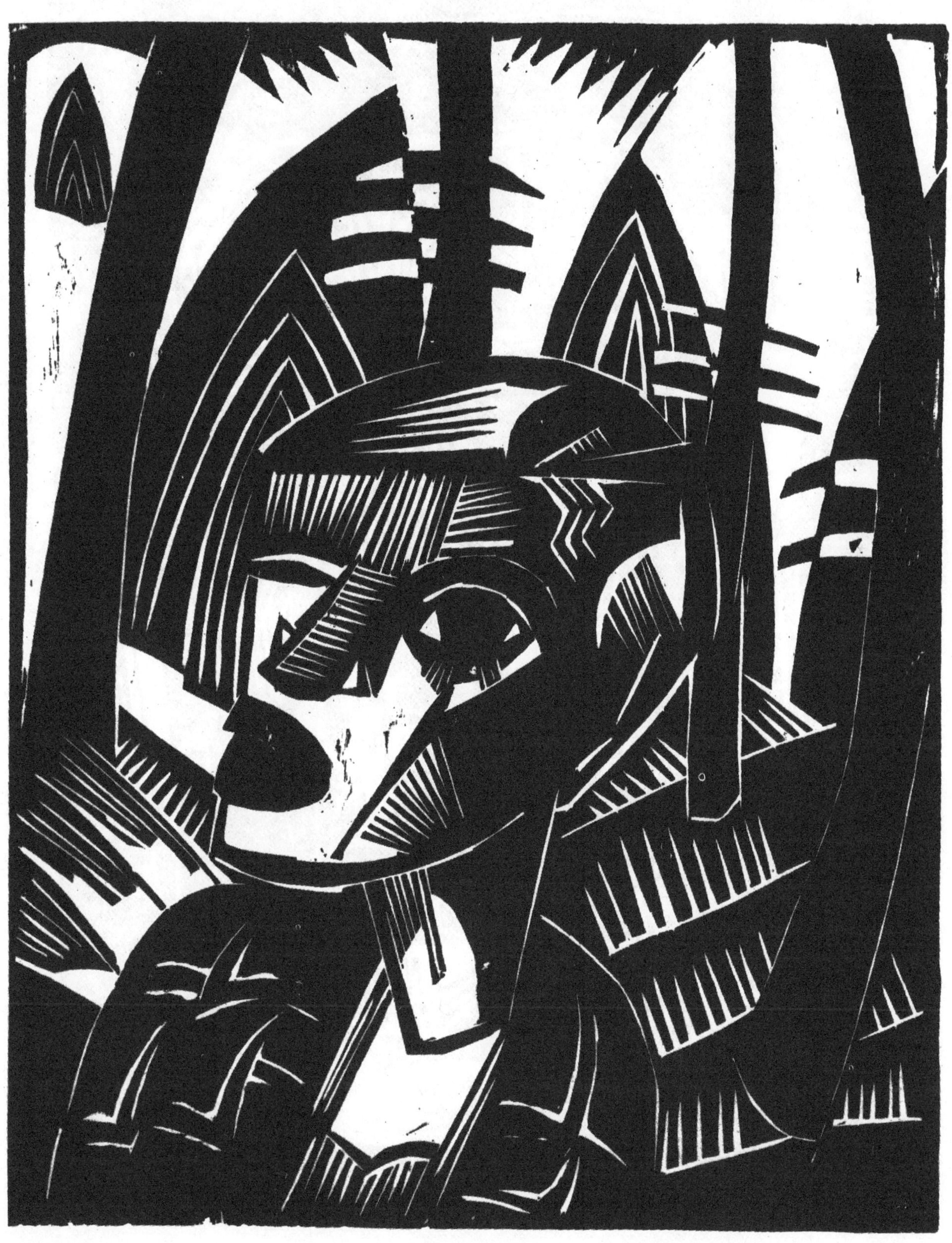

Karl Schmidt-Rottluff. *Woman in a Forest*, 1919.

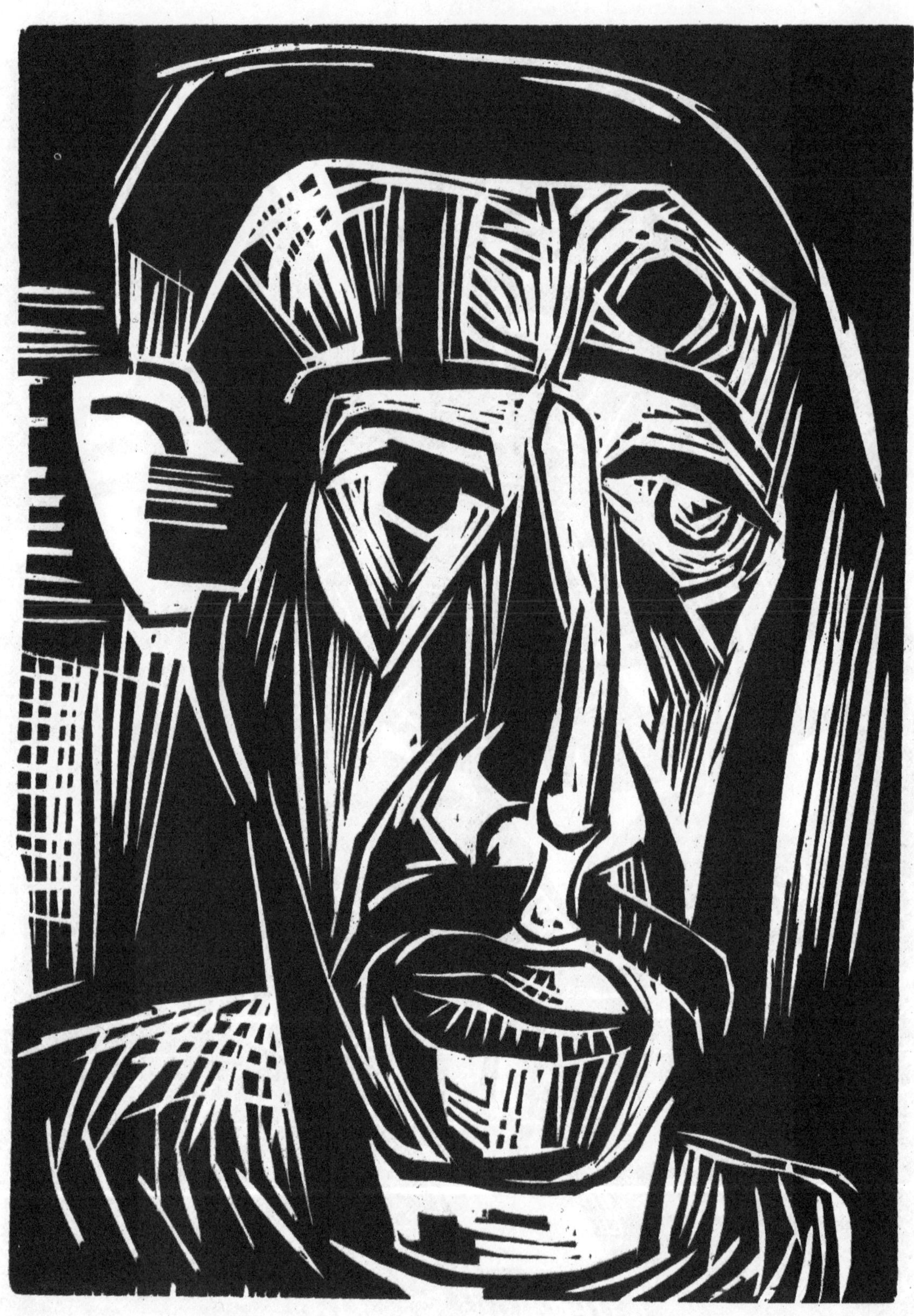

Karl Schmidt-Rottluff. *Head of a Man*, 1922.

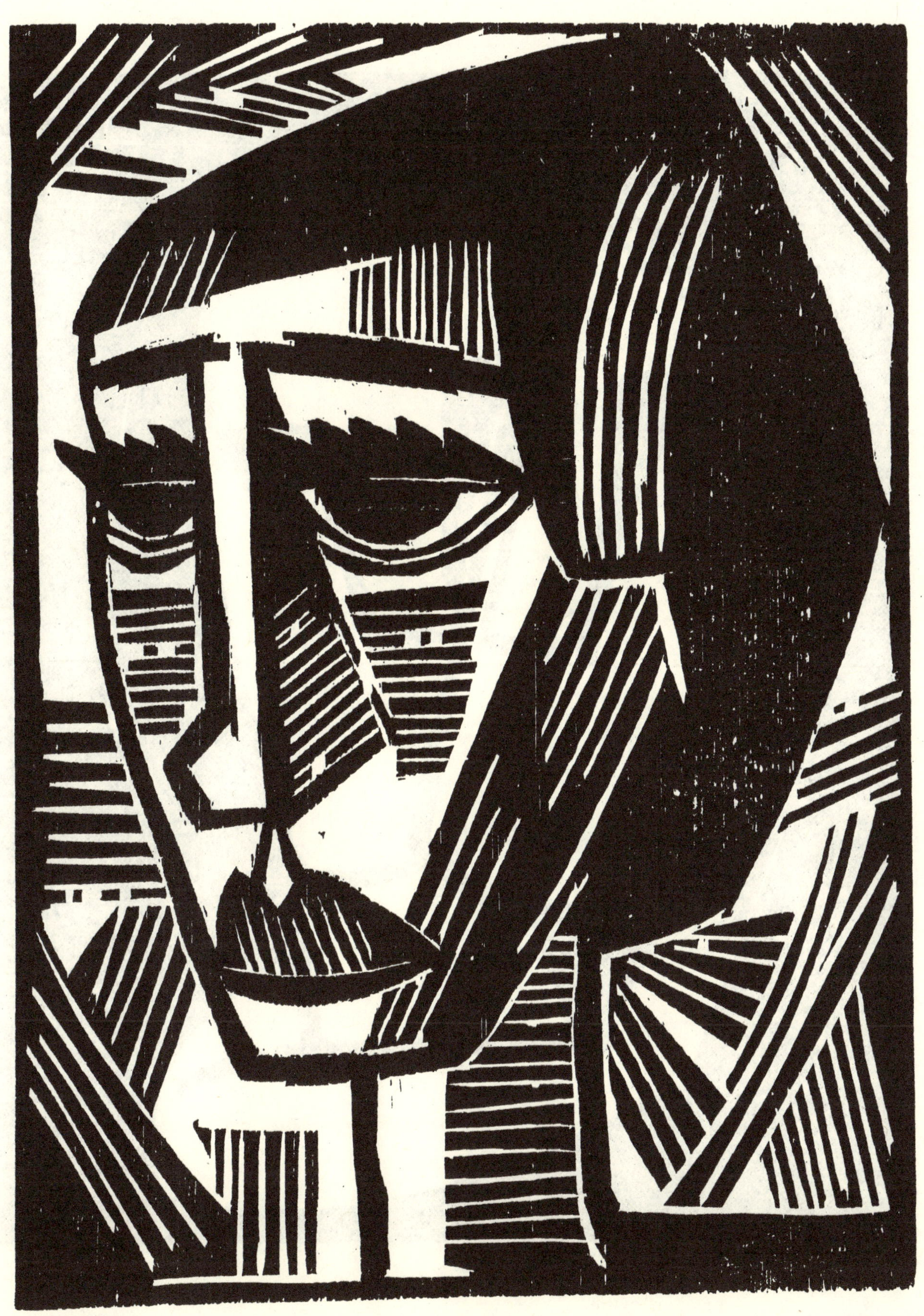

Karl Schmidt-Rottluff. Untitled, 1915.

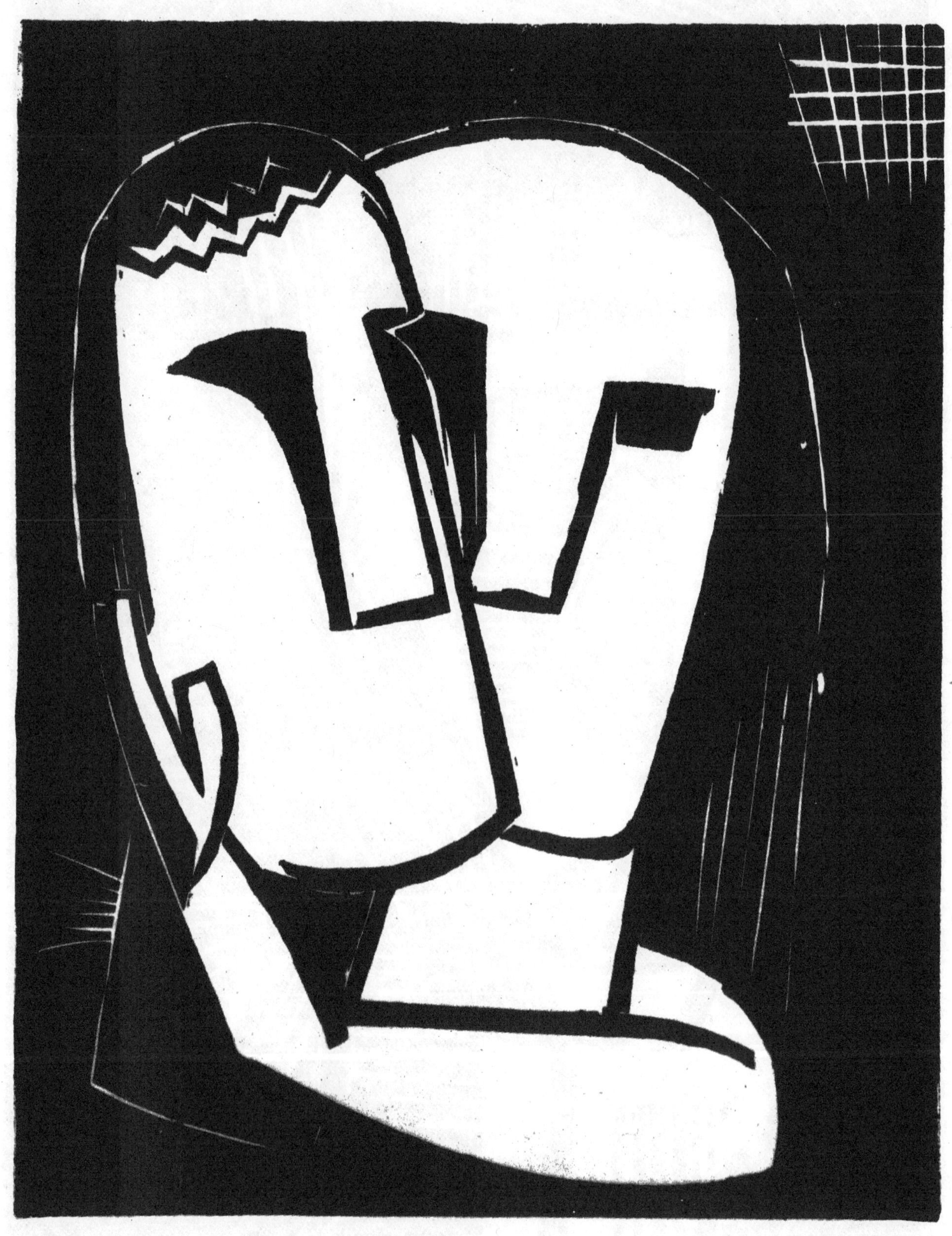

Karl Schmidt-Rottluff. *Lovers*, 1920.

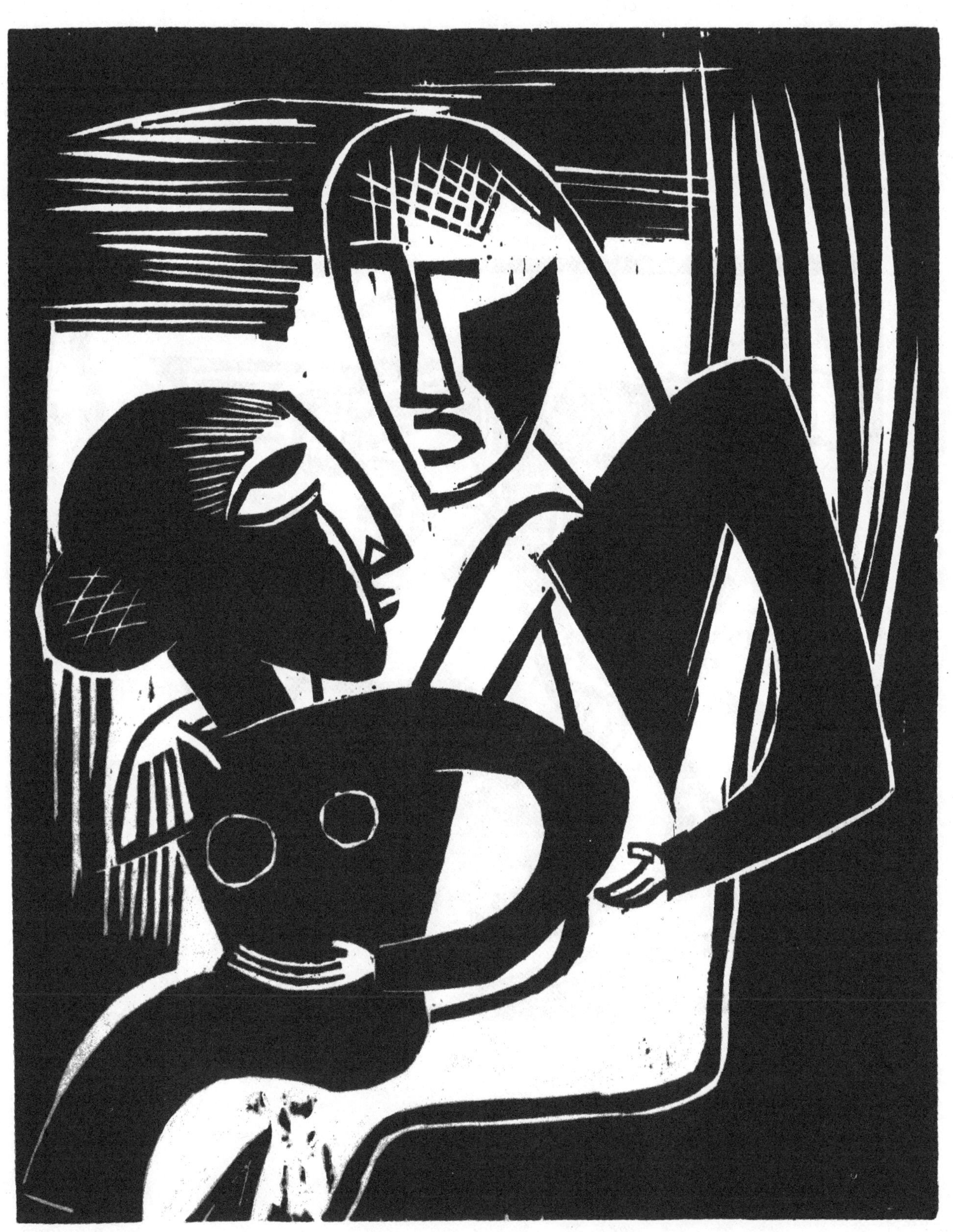

Karl Schmidt-Rottluff. *Man and Maid*, 1919.

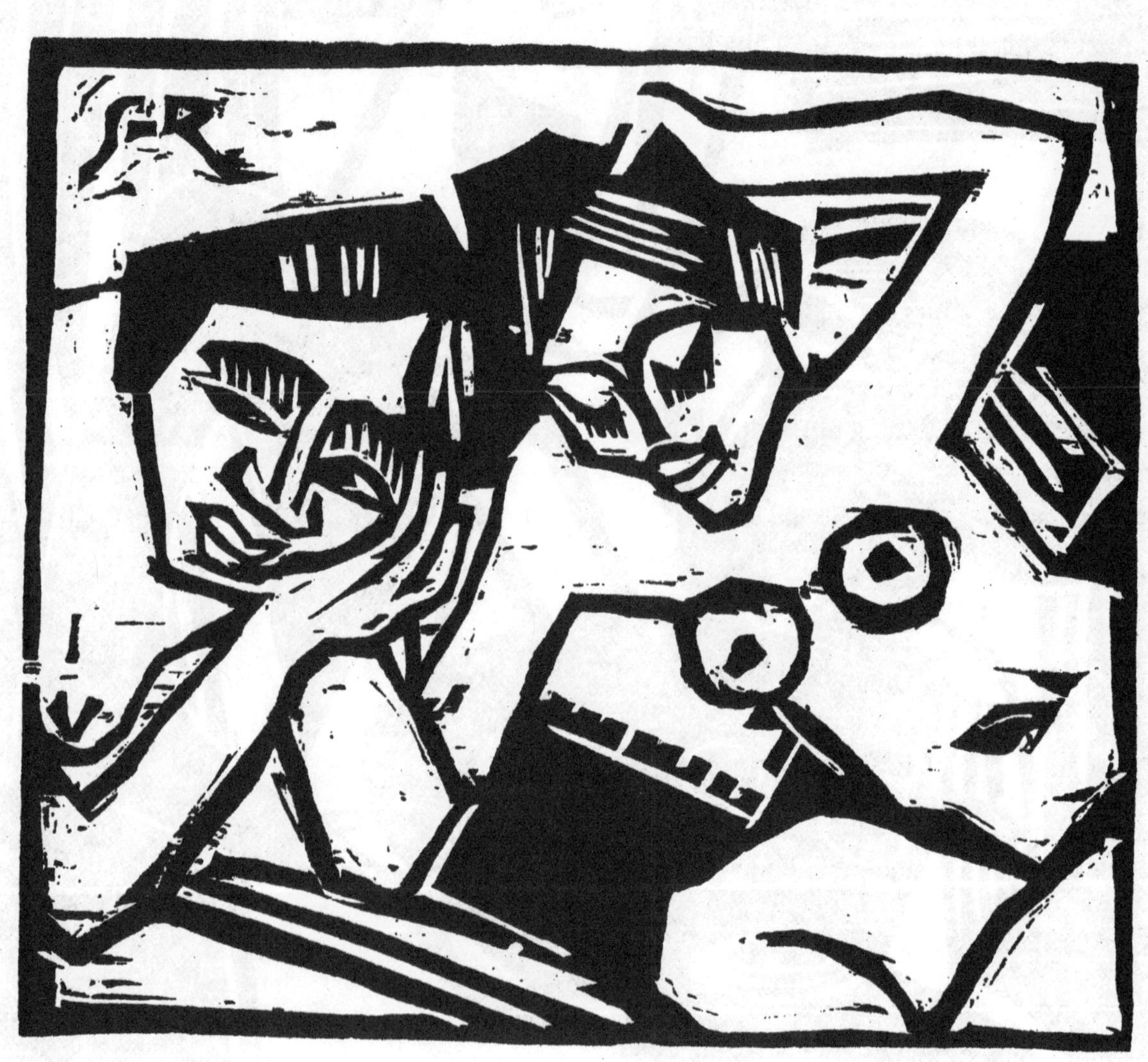

Karl Schmidt-Rottluff. Untitled, 1914.

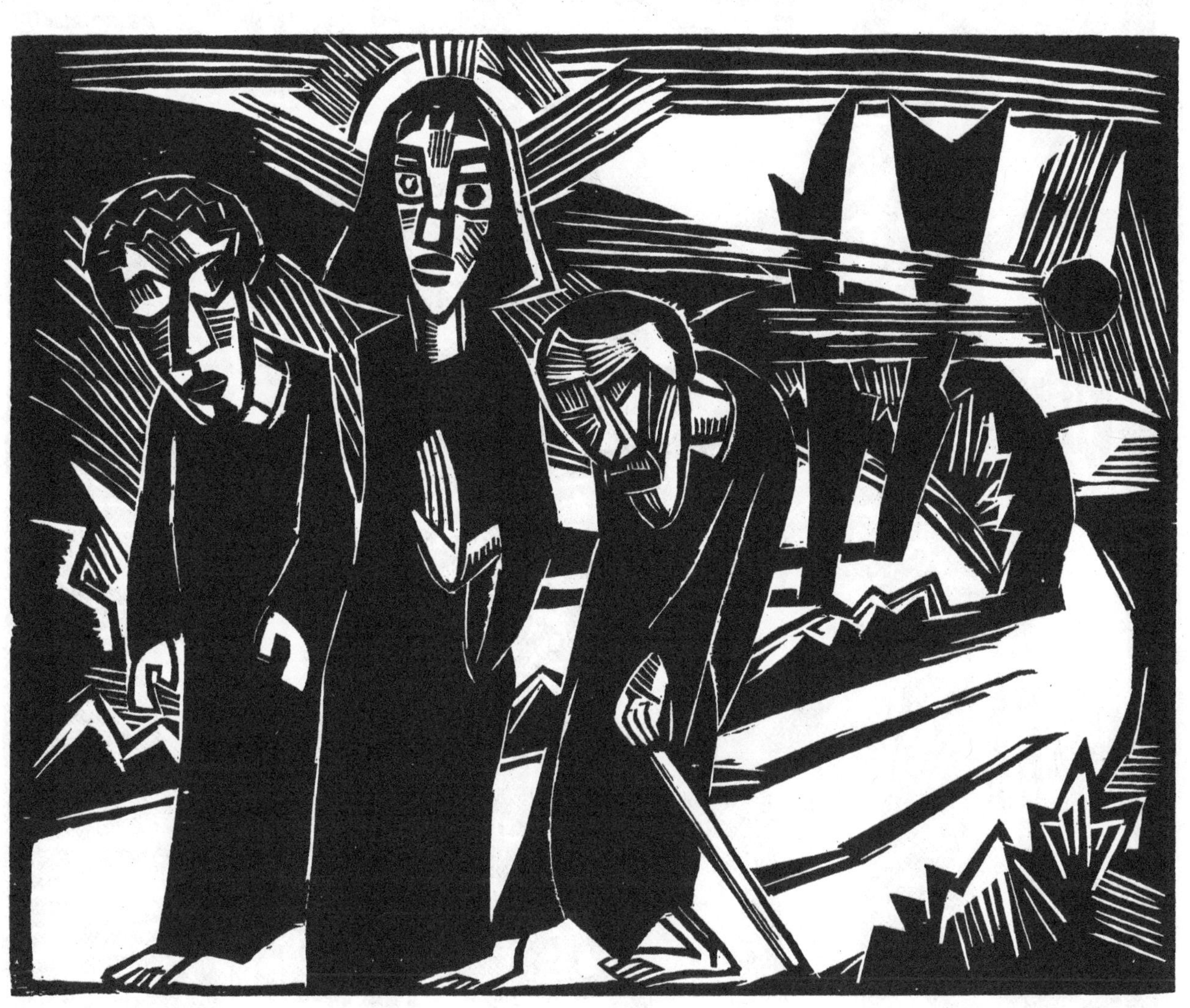

Karl Schmidt-Rottluff. *Way to Emmaus*, 1918.

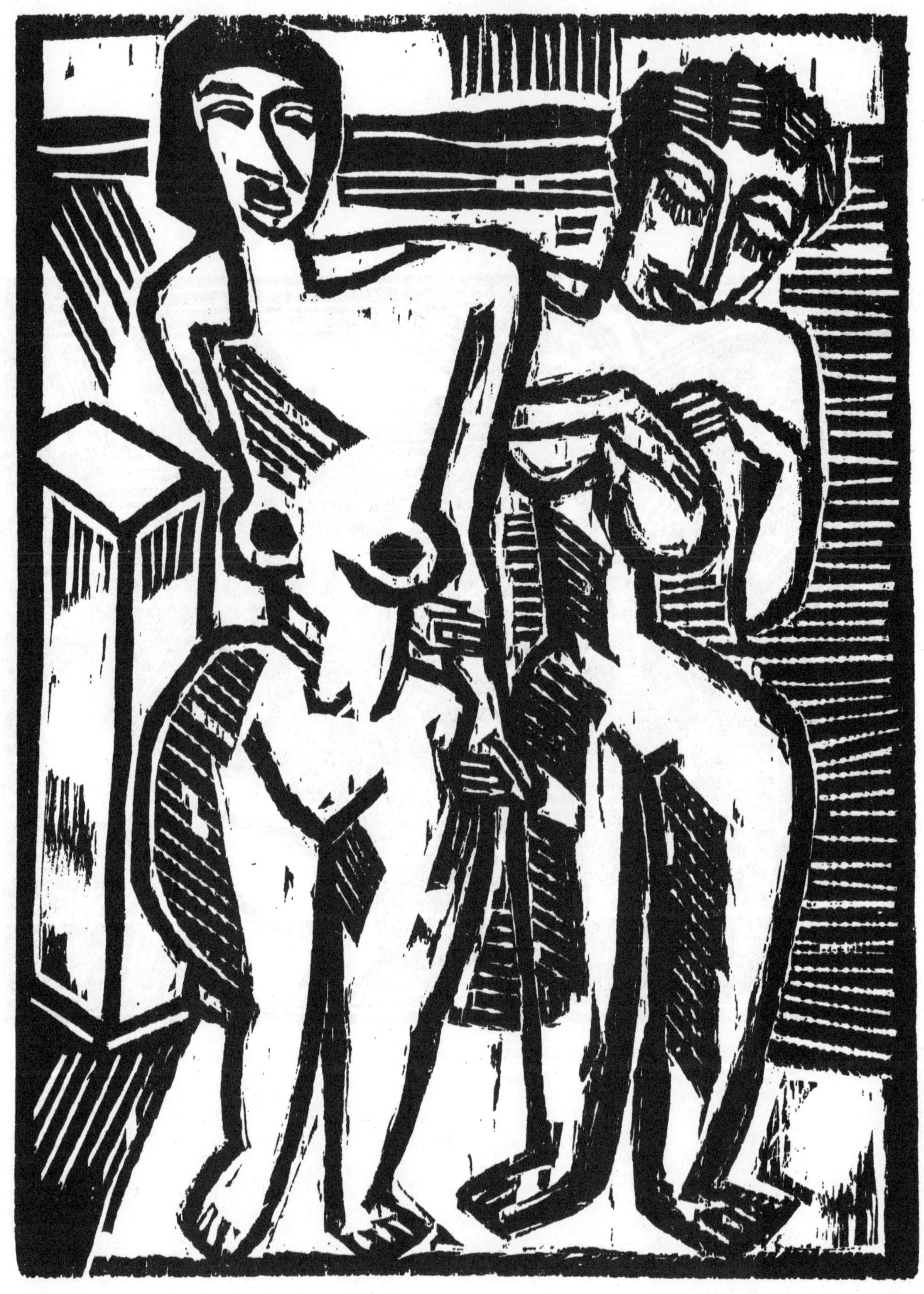

Karl Schmidt-Rottluff. Untitled, 1915.

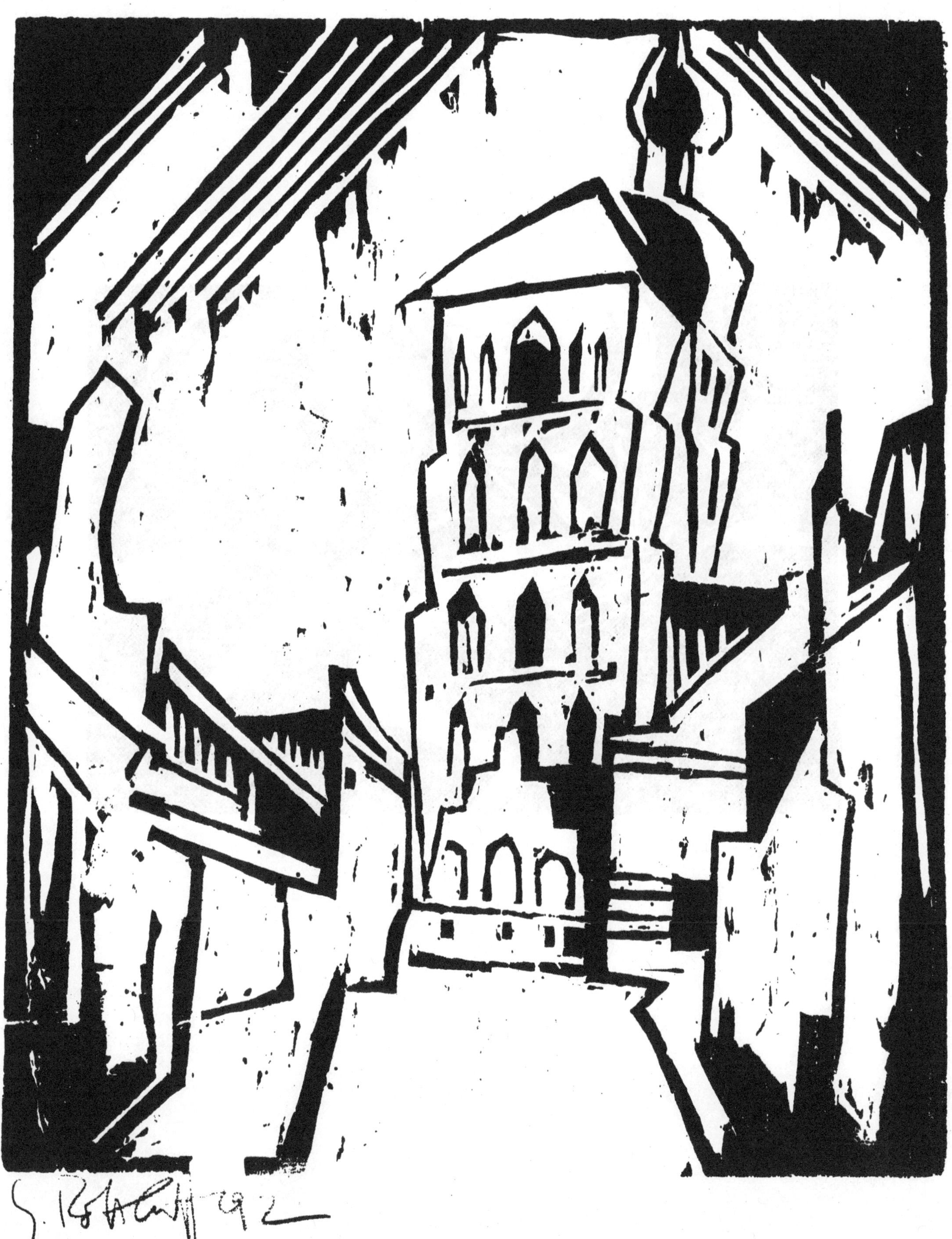

Karl Schmidt-Rottluff. *Towers of Stralsund*, 1912.

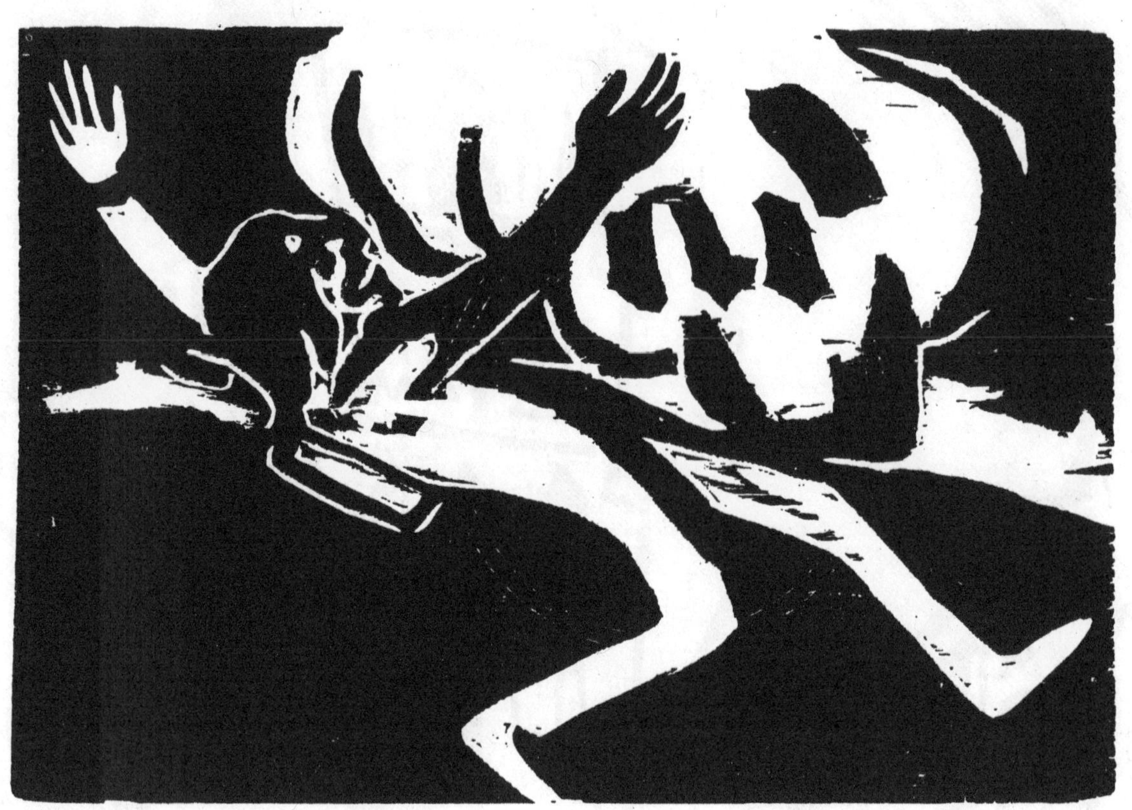

Arthur Segal. *Exploding Grenade*, 1915.

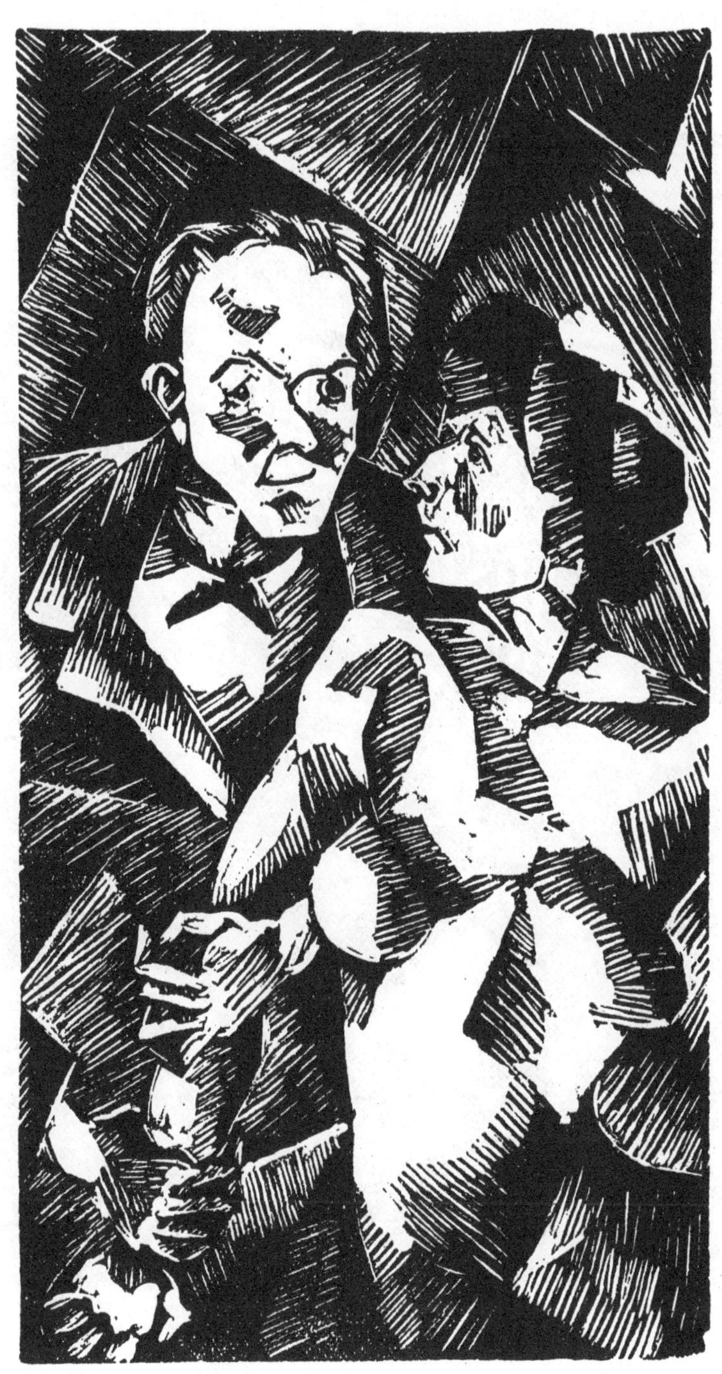

Marcel Słodki. Untitled, 1915.

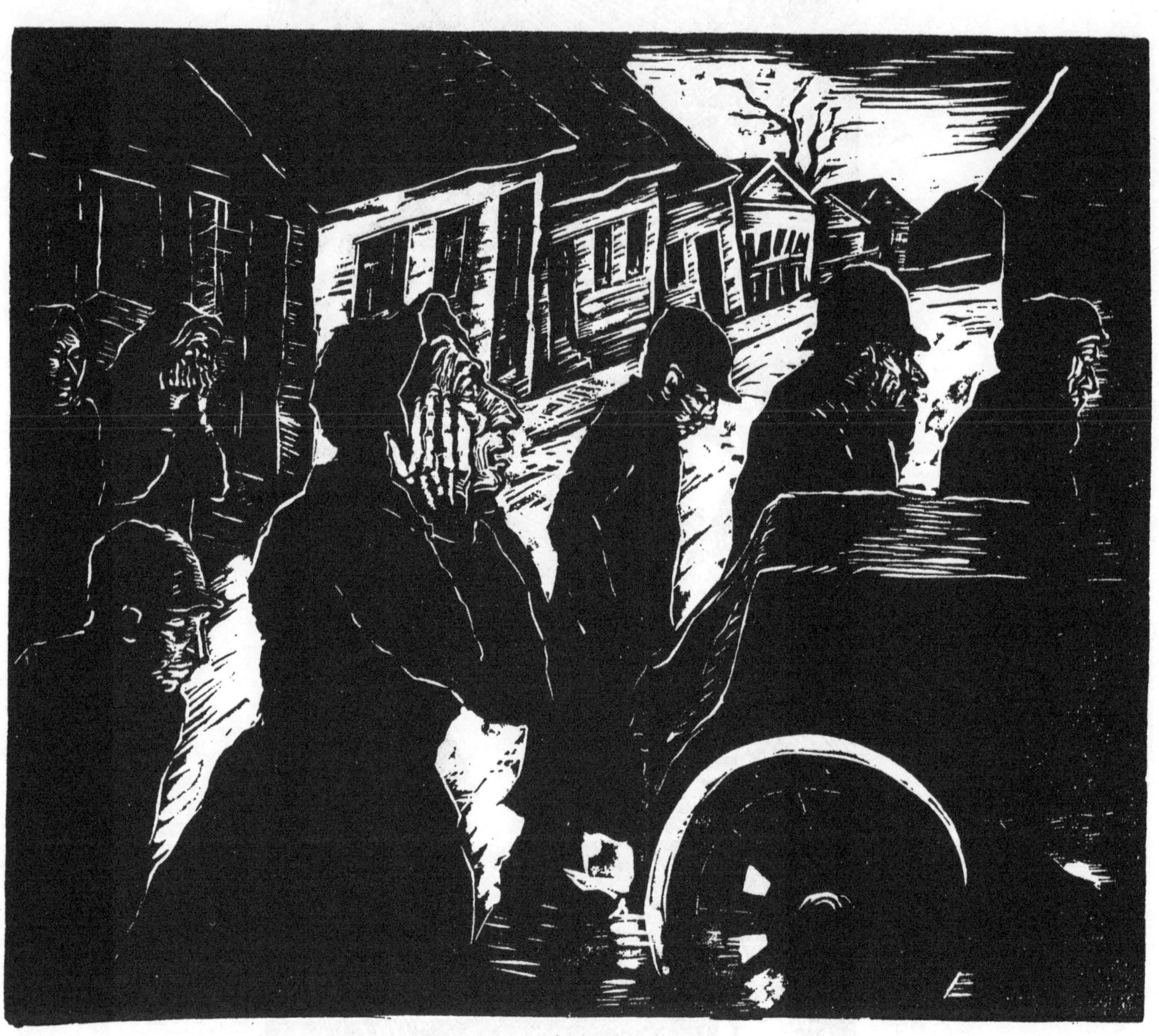

Jakob Steinhardt. *The Funeral*, 1922.

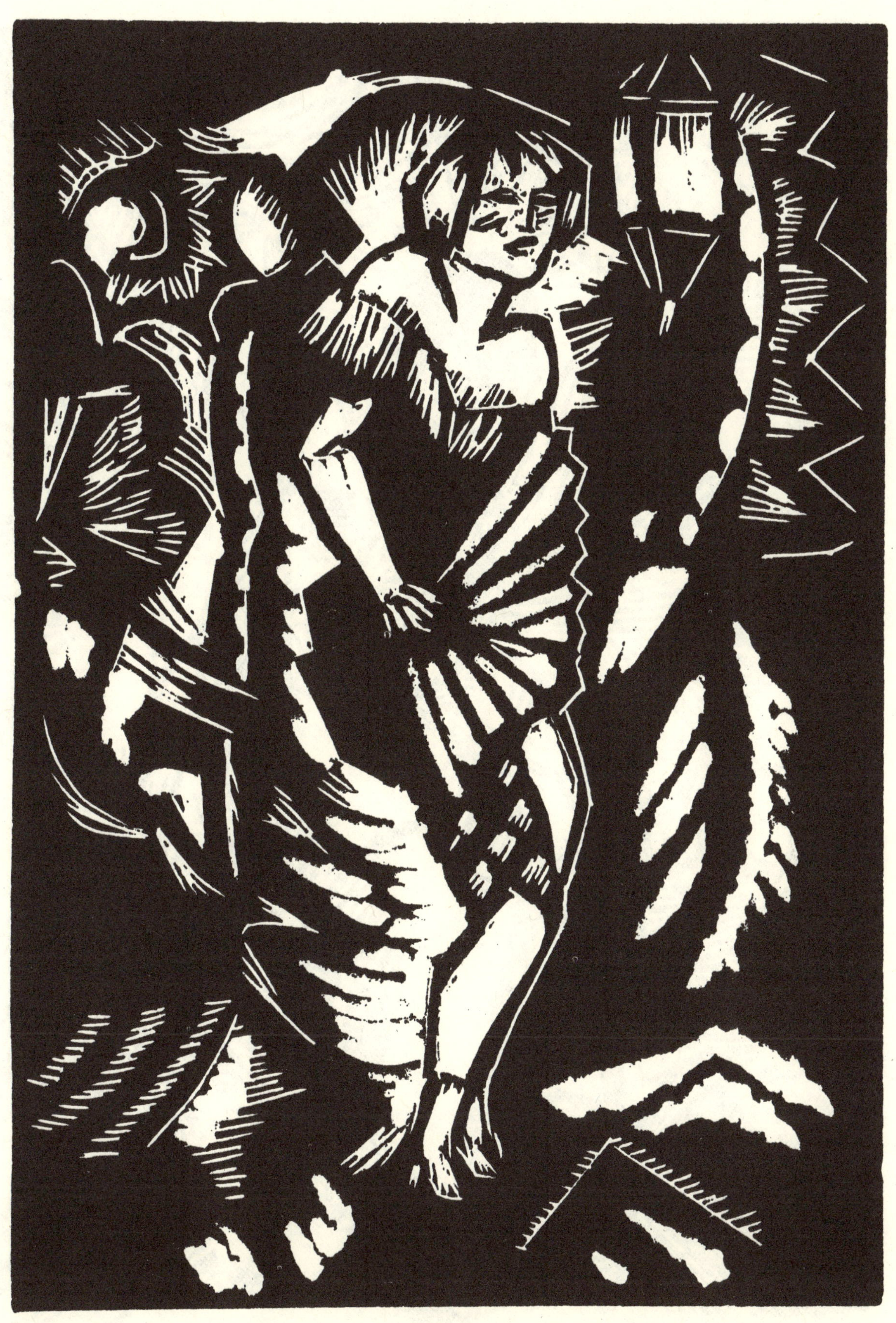

Georg Tappert. *Chansonette*, 1914.

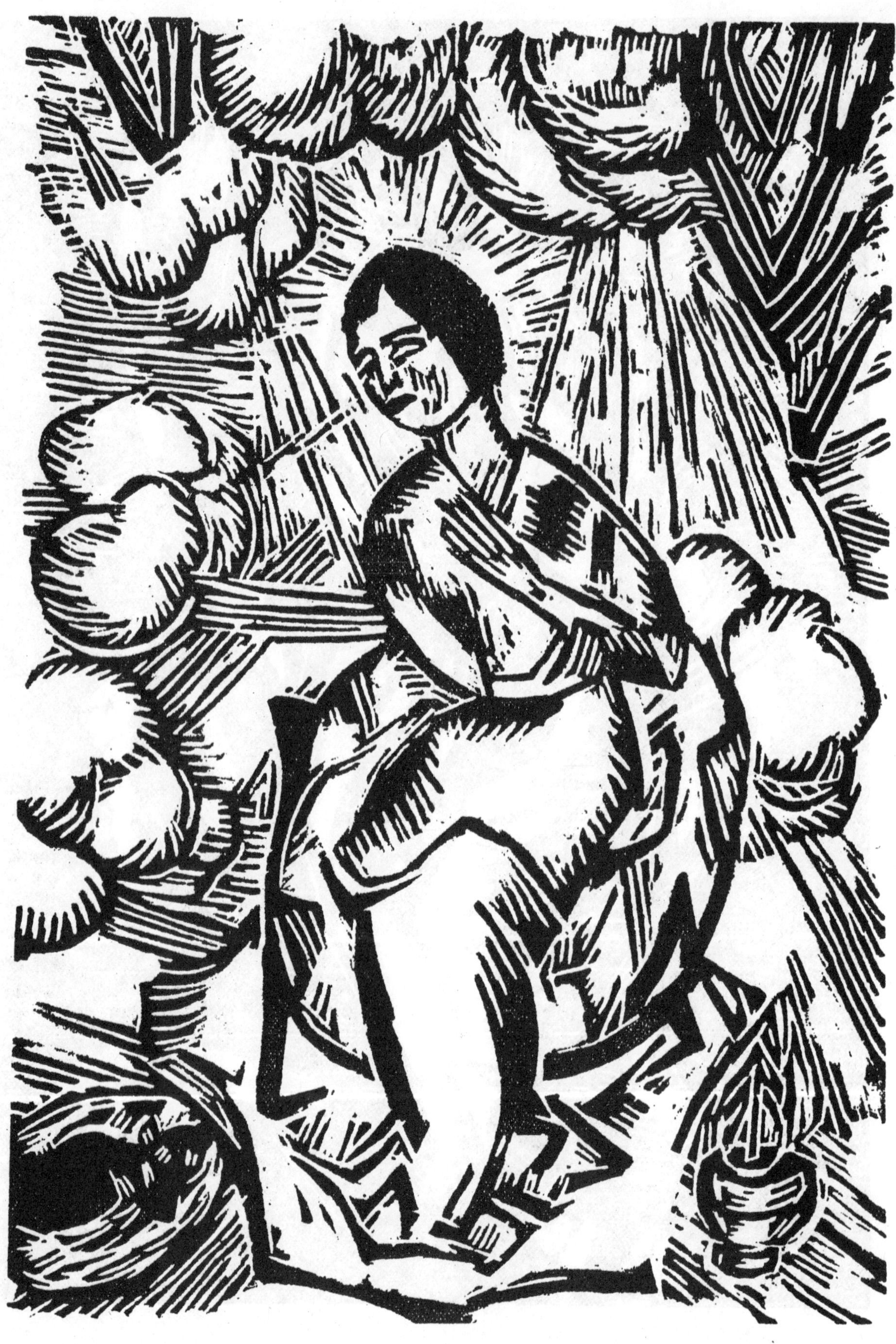

Georg Tappert. Untitled, 1916.

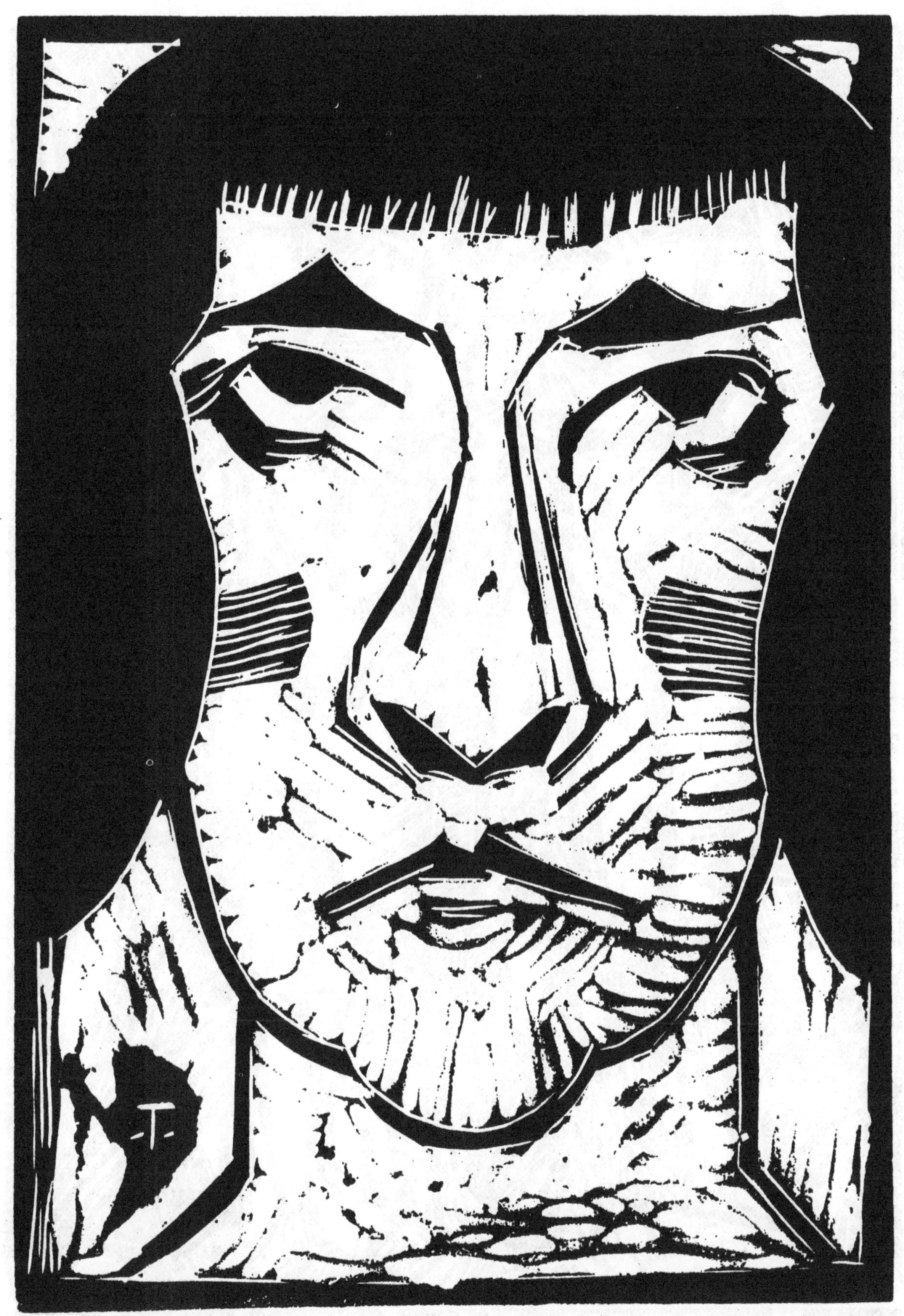

Georg Tappert. *Silence*, 1914.

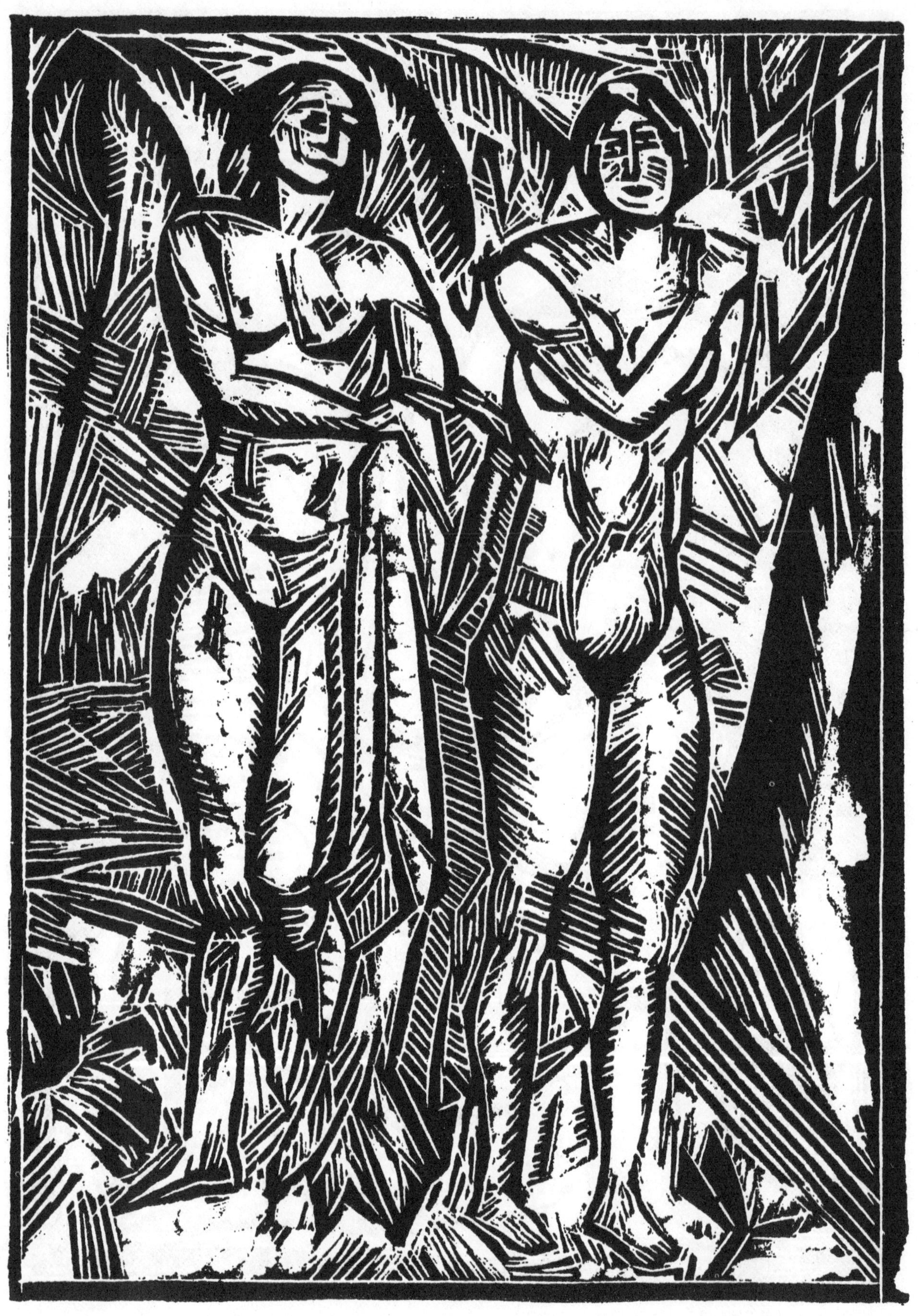

Georg Tappert. Untitled, 1916.

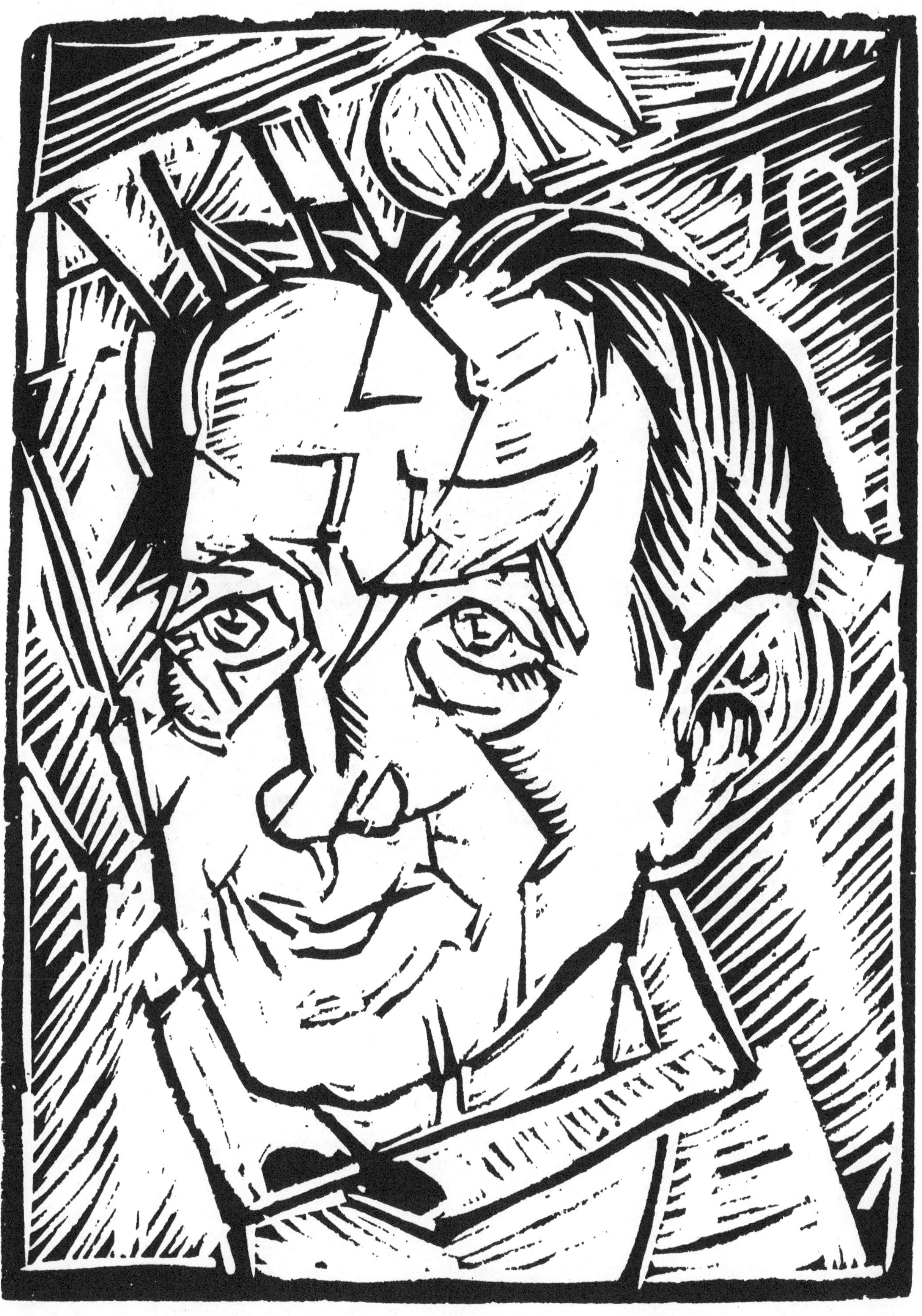

Georg Tappert. *Franz Pfemfert* [founder of *Die Aktion*, 1879–1954], 1921.

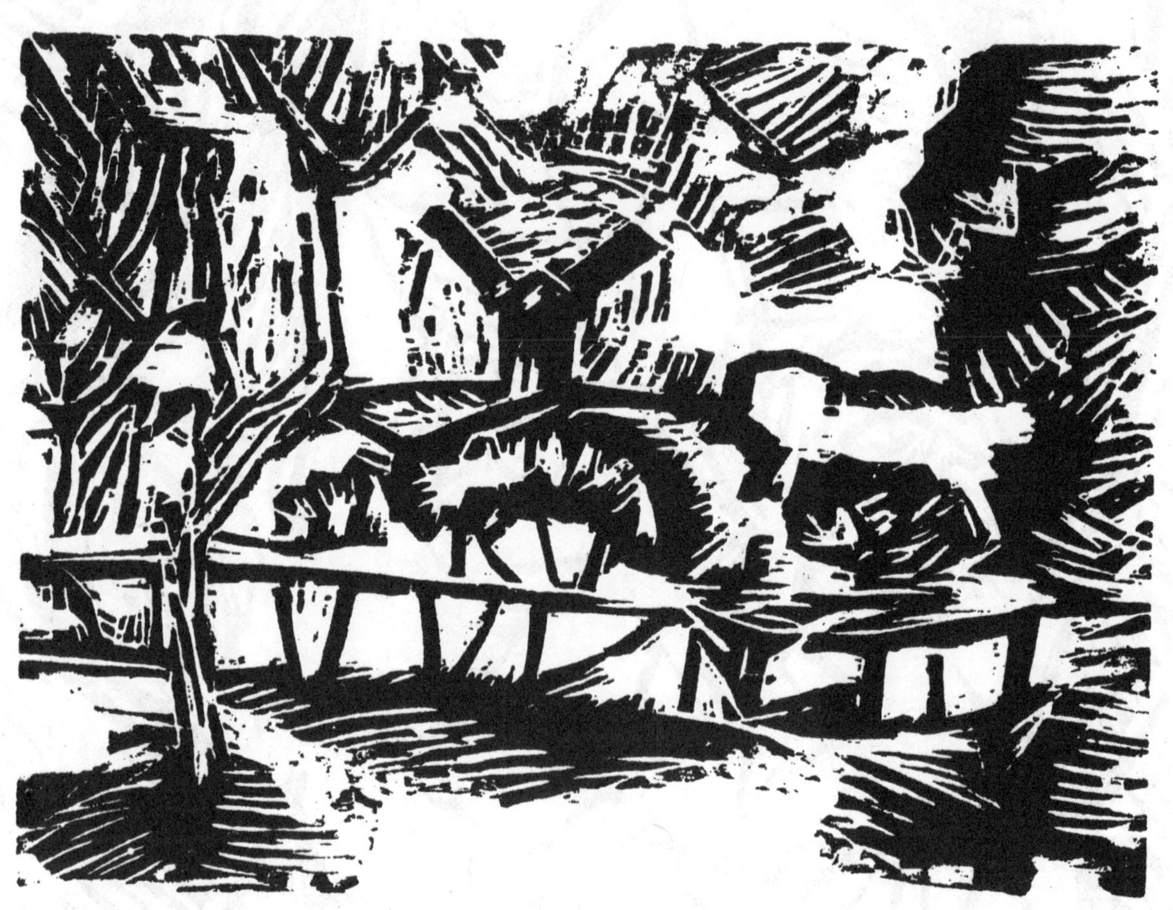

Georg Tappert, *Landscape*, 1917.

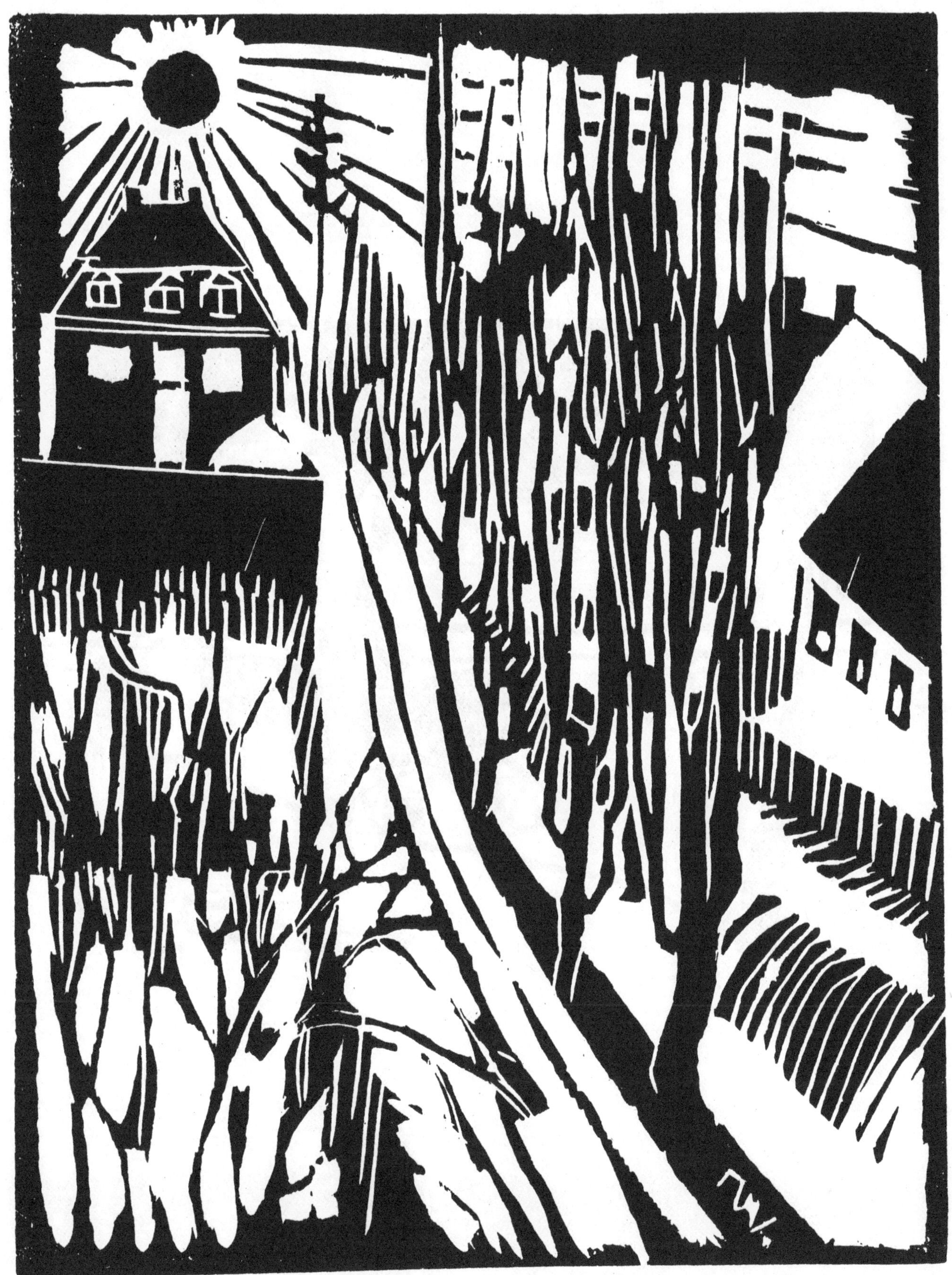

Ines Wetzel. Untitled, 1917.

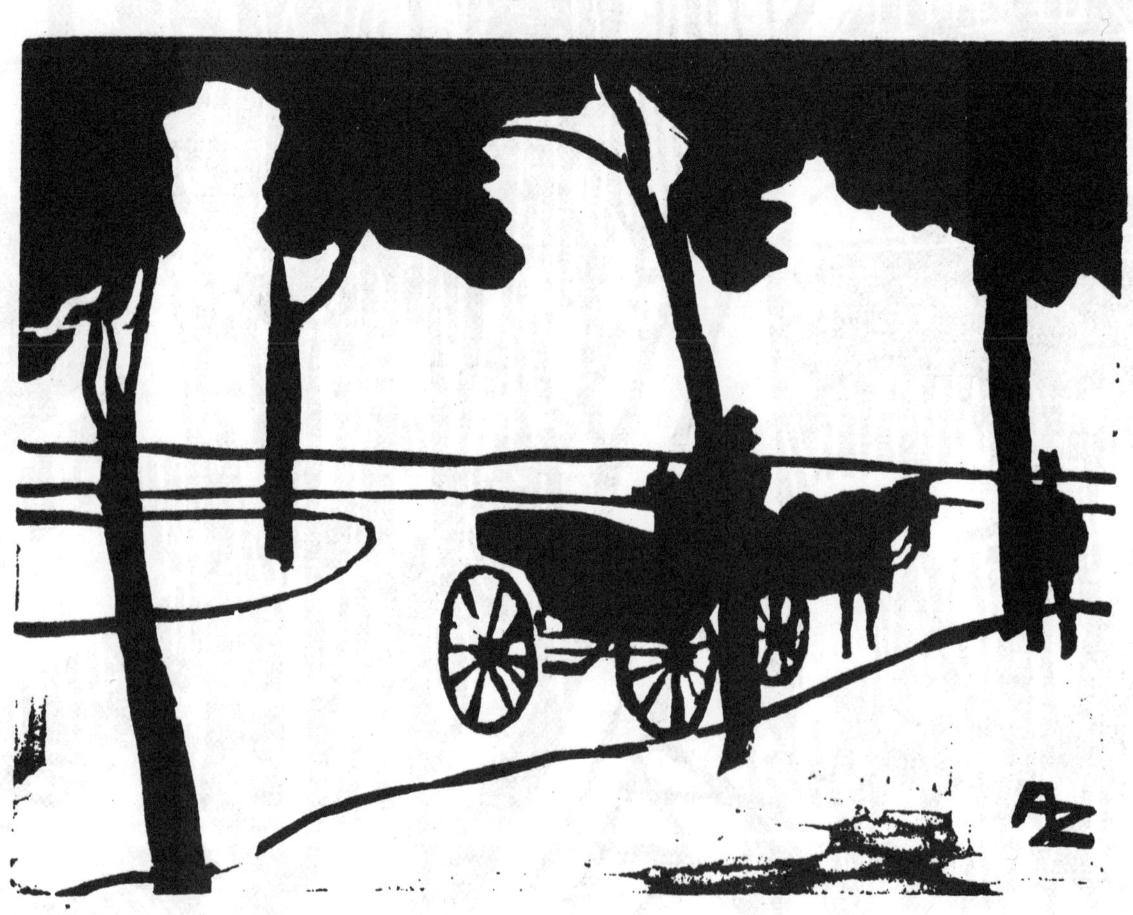

Auguste von Zitzewitz. Untitled, 1917.

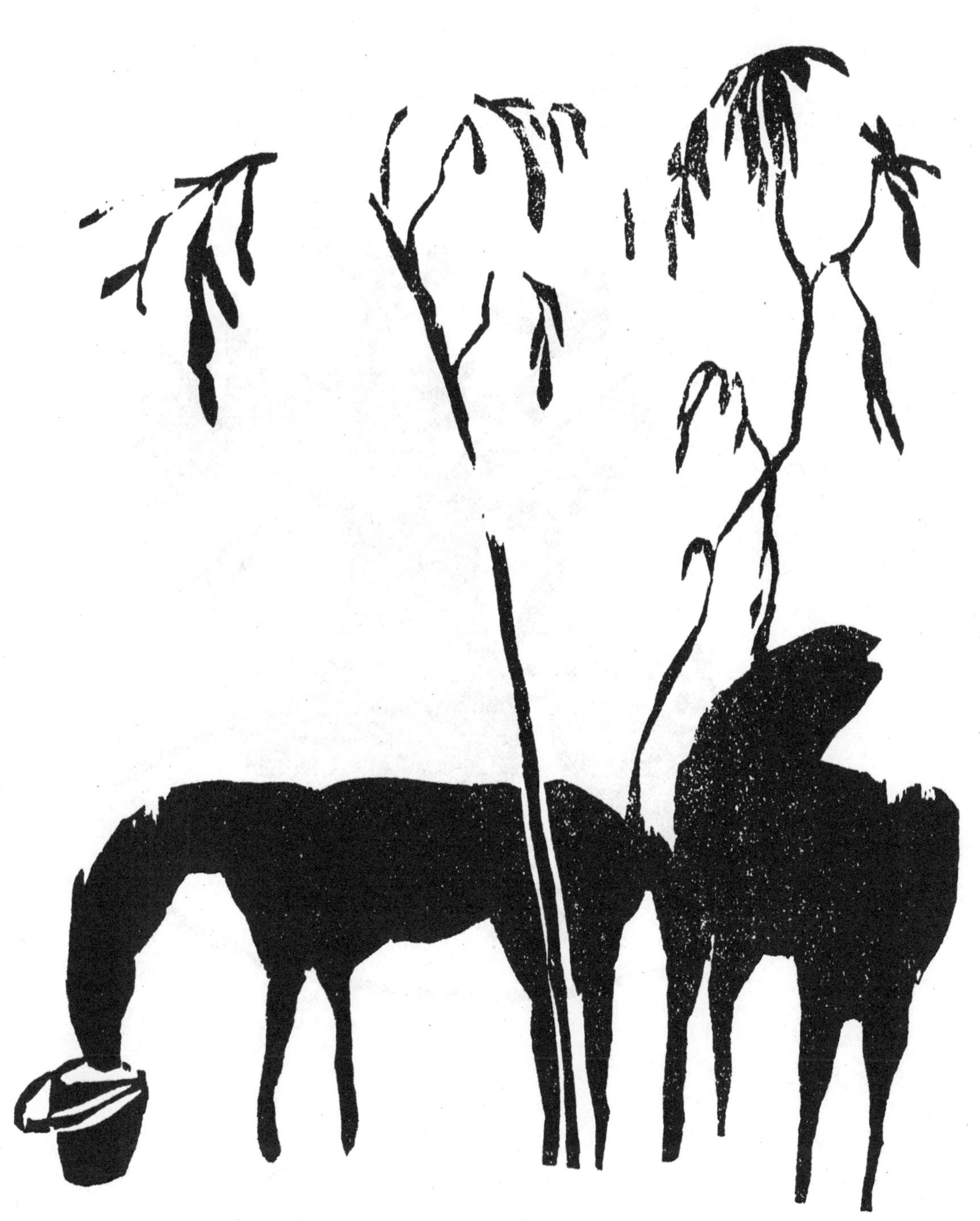

Auguste von Zitzewitz. *Horses*, 1918.

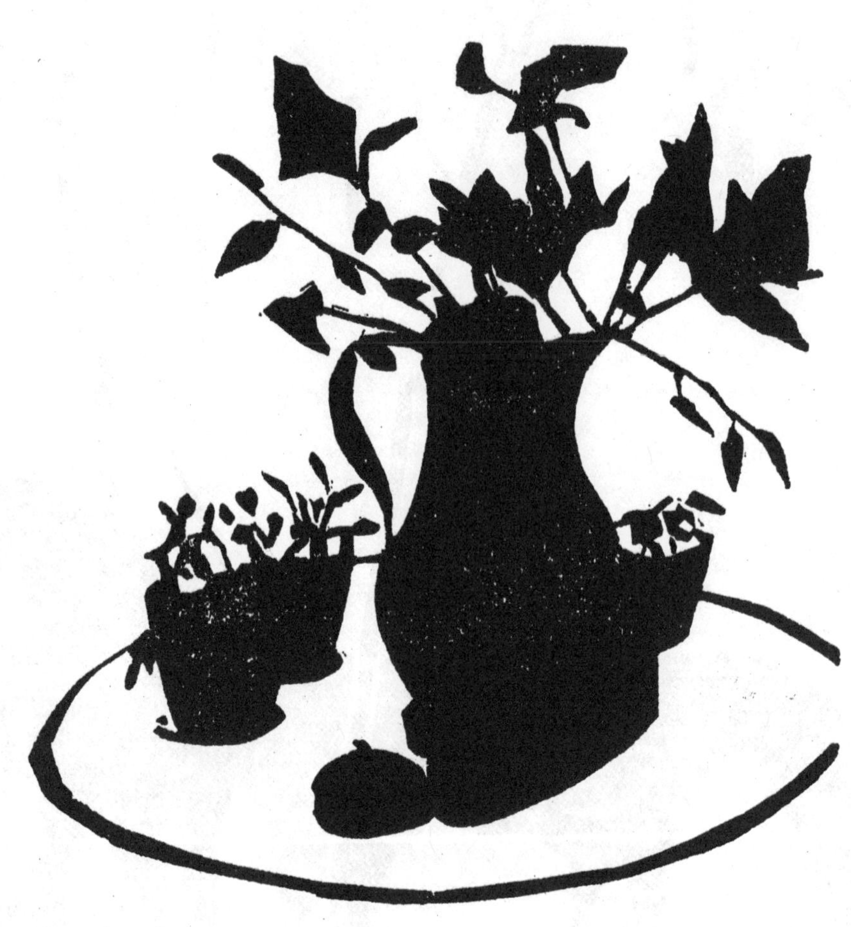

Auguste von Zitzewitz. *Still Life*, 1918.

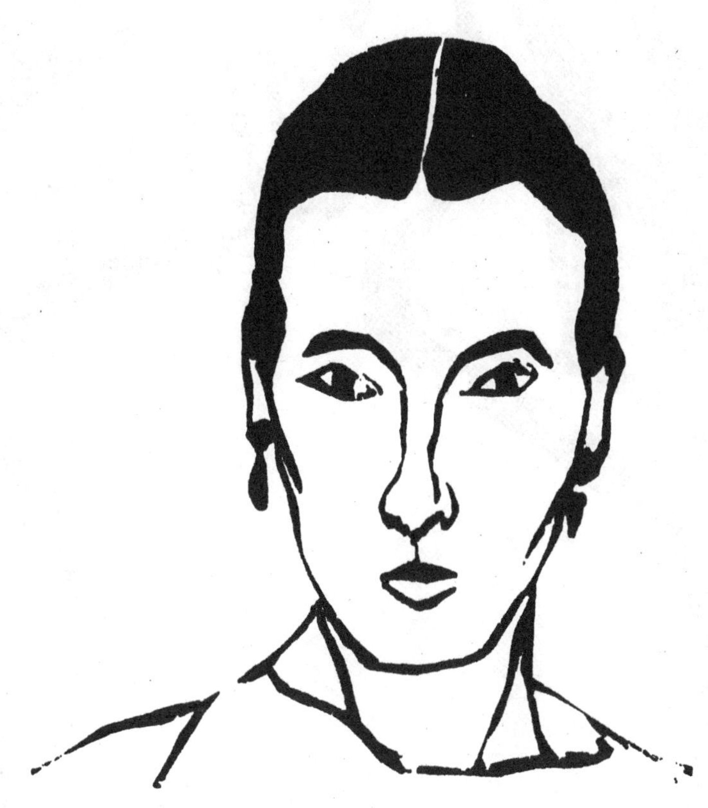

Auguste von Zitzewitz. *Self-Portrait*, 1918.

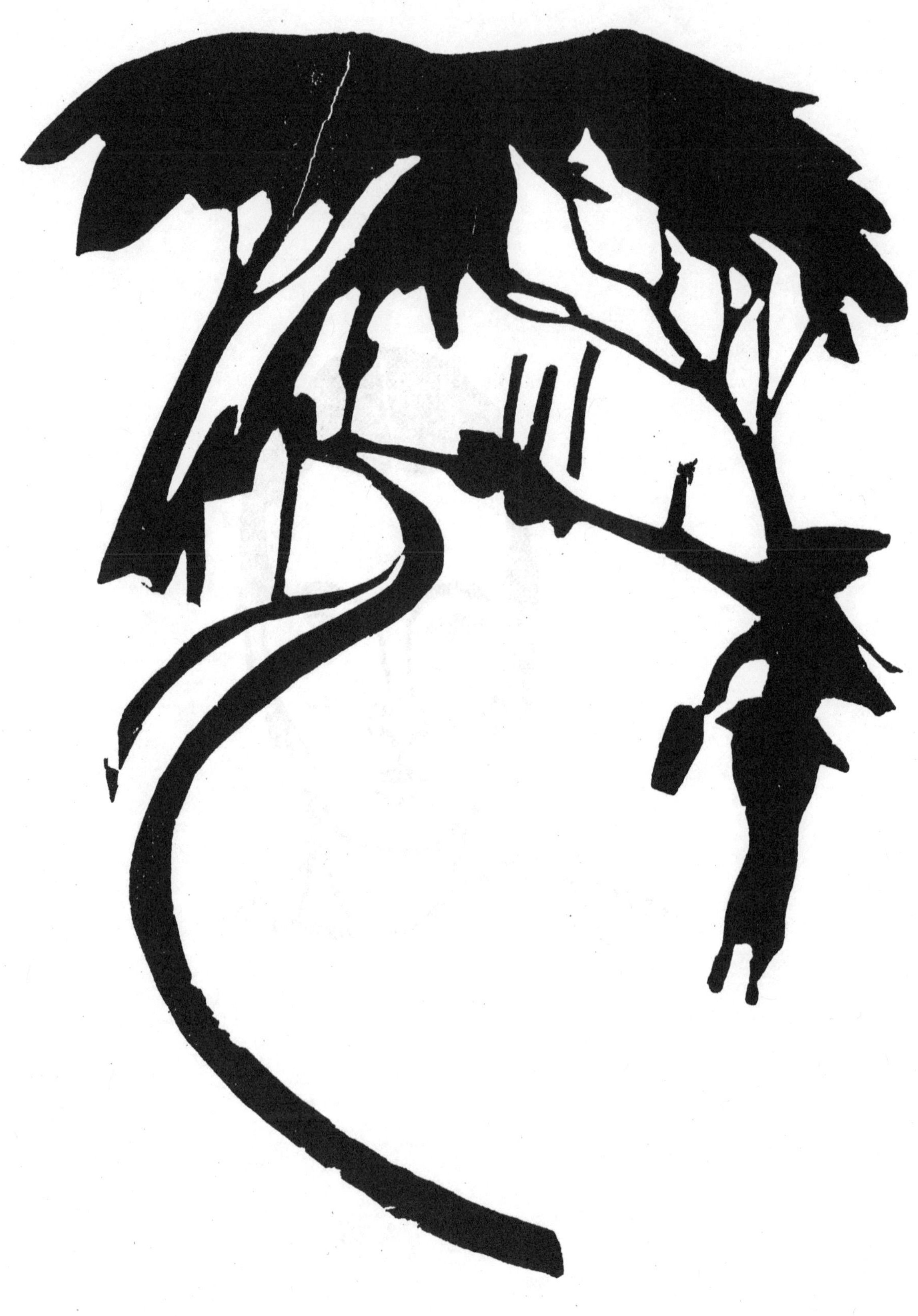

Auguste von Zitzewitz. *Street Scene*, 1918.

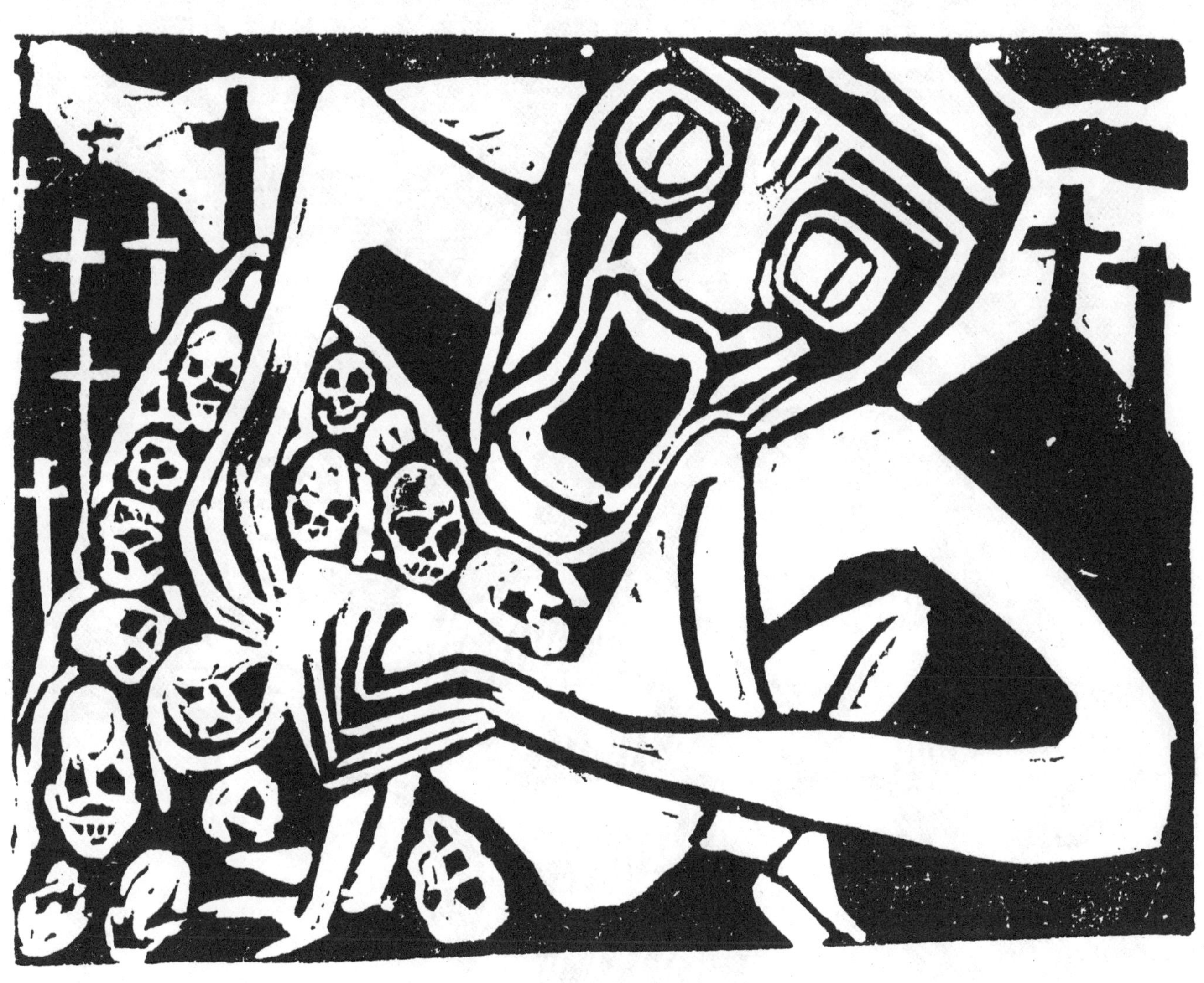

Anonymous. *Capitalism*, 1918.

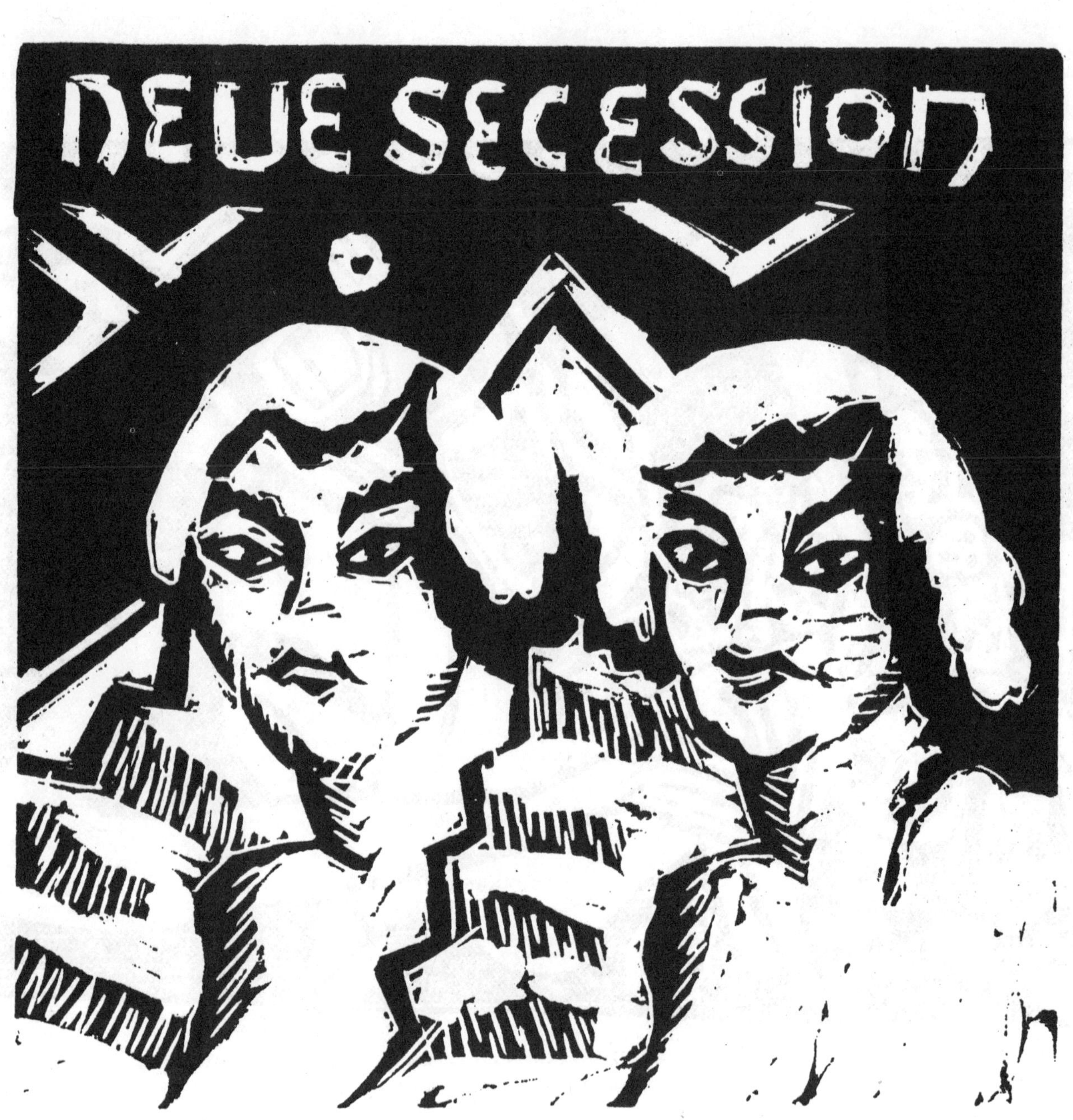

Anonymous. *Neue Secession*, 1914.